Human Tra

Human Trafficking

The Complexities of Exploitation

edited by
Margaret Malloch and Paul Rigby

EDINBURGH
University Press

Edinburgh University Press Ltd
The Tun – Holyrood Road
12 (2f) Jackson's Entry
Edinburgh EH8 8PJ
www.euppublishing.com

First published in hardback by Edinburgh University Press 2016

Typeset in 11/13 Sabon by
Servis Filmsetting Ltd, Stockport, Cheshire,
and printed and bound in Great Britain by
CPI Group (UK) Ltd, Croydon CR0 4YY

A CIP record for this book is available from the British Library

ISBN 978 1 4744 0112 8 (hardback)
ISBN 978 1 4744 2838 5 (paperback)
ISBN 978 1 4744 0113 5 (webready PDF)
ISBN 978 1 4744 0502 7 (epub)

Contents

Acknowledgements

Thanks to the Scottish Universities Insight Institute for funding our 2012–13 programme, 'Human Trafficking: Conceptualising Definitions, Responses and "What Needs to be Done"', in particular, to Ann Logie, Nicola Allen and Charlie Woods. Beth Smith did an excellent job of chairing the programme, and we appreciate her input and that of WithScotland. We would like to thank the participants at the three programme events for their contributions, and for the discussions and debates that followed. We are very grateful to the young people at the NSPCC (Child Trafficking Advice Centre) for allowing us to use their design for the front cover of this book. Thanks to Jenny Daly and Michelle Houston at Edinburgh University Press for their support in taking the book forward to publication, and to the anonymous reviewers who provided helpful advice and suggestions at the outset.

Contributors

Stefano Bonino is a lecturer in the Department of Social Sciences at the University of Northumbria.

Hazel Cameron is a Lecturer in the School of International Relations and the current Director of the Centre for Peace and Conflict Studies, University of St Andrews.

Claire Cody is a Research Fellow in youth participation and European knowledge exchange at the University of Bedfordshire.

Sharon Doherty is a Clinical Psychologist working with the Trafficking Awareness Raising Alliance (TARA) in Glasgow Community Safety Services.

Philip Ishola is an independent child protection, human trafficking and human rights consultant.

Jim Laird works for Inverclyde Council in Scotland and was previously with Migrant Help working across the United Kingdom with trafficking victims.

Margaret Malloch is a Reader in Criminology with the Scottish Centre for Crime and Justice Research, based at the University of Stirling.

Rachel Morley is a Clinical Psychologist in the Compass service with NHS Glasgow and Greater Clyde.

Bill Munro is a Lecturer in Criminology at the University of Stirling.

Sheila Murie is a Senior Officer in the child protection team in Glasgow City Council, Social Work department.

Liz Owens is a Senior Officer in the child protection team in Glasgow City Council, Social Work department.

Paul Rigby is a Lecturer in Social Work at the University of Stirling.

Kiril Sharapov is Senior Lecturer in Sociology at the University of Bedfordshire and an affiliate researcher at the Centre for Policy Studies, Central European University, Budapest, Hungary.

Kirsty Thomson is Head of the Women and Young Persons' Department of the Legal Services Agency in Glasgow. She is a member of various advisory, operational and working groups, and is currently developing a Scottish Women's Rights Centre with key partner agencies.

Jackie Turner works as an independent consultant in the fields of violence against women and human trafficking.

Adam Weiss is the Legal Director of the European Roma Rights Centre, Budapest, and before that was the Legal Director of the Advice on Individual Rights in Europe (AIRE) Centre, London.

No paradox of contemporary politics is filled with more poignant irony than the discrepancy between the efforts of well-meaning idealists who stubbornly insist on regarding as 'inalienable' those human rights, which are enjoyed only by citizens of the most prosperous and civilized countries, and the situations of the rightless themselves. Their situation has deteriorated just as stubbornly, until the internment camp – prior to the Second World War the exception rather than the rule for the stateless – has become the routine solution for the problem of domicile of the 'displaced persons'.

Hannah Arendt 1986: 279

It should be evident by now that the exercise of civil rights by those who don't have them presupposes the withdrawal of civil rights from those who prevent their exercise, and that liberation of the Damned of the Earth presupposes suppression not only of their old but also of their new masters.

Herbert Marcuse 1965: 124

1 Contexts and Complexities

Margaret Malloch and Paul Rigby

Human Trafficking: The Complexities of Exploitation is a collaborative endeavour by practitioners and academics working in the field of 'human trafficking'; a term that does little to convey the myriad acts that underpin the forced movement, exploitation and enslavement of men, women and children across the world. Specifically, the book sets out to locate this trade in human lives within a wider context of exploitative practices and to focus attention on the issues facing victims and survivors.

Trafficking in human beings is a worldwide phenomenon with increasing recognition that an urgent and effective response is required. However, despite legislative developments and the introduction of national and international interventions, responses to victims and perpetrators have been limited in effect. Aspirations to prioritise a human rights model within a wider discourse of 'vulnerable people' on the move are frequently overtaken by law enforcement and border control priorities.

As we finalised this edited book in spring 2015, international news reports provided images and commentary on the numerous people believed to have drowned in the Mediterranean on route from Libya. The deaths of unquantifiable numbers of men, women and children were clearly a significant concern to the United Nations, European Union (EU) and individual nation states, yet the identified causes and proposed solutions were contested and disputed. Save the Children estimated that around 400 people, many of them unaccompanied children, died on 13 April 2015 after their boat capsized 24 hours after leaving the Libyan coastline heading for Italy (*EU Observer*, 15 April 2015). Around 800 migrants were estimated to have drowned over the following days (*EU Observer*, 20 April 2015). The International Organisation for Migration (IOM) (2014) estimate that up to 3,072 people died in the Mediterranean in 2014, a significant increase from the estimated 700 deaths in 2013. The death toll for 2015 marks an upward trajectory, with over 1,500 deaths estimated in its first four months. Amidst almost universal calls for action, the conflation of terminology used to describe these events has become apparent and disturbing. Political attention to the need to rescue passengers on these unseaworthy craft, initially referred to as 'migrants', was soon accompanied by calls for action against 'smugglers' (some of whom, it was claimed, had locked hundreds of people inside the hold of boats with no way of escape).

While debates surrounding the expansion of search and rescue missions were ongoing, the concerns of some national governments were focused upon the potential influx of people if deterrence was not in place. This can be set within a context where the Italian coast-guard and other boats rescued around 13,000 people from the sea within a seven-day period in April 2015.

While most EU states agreed that action was required, many also expressed a reluctance to accommodate incoming migrants, and this was evident as attention focused increasingly on sea surveillance, while plans to disperse asylum seekers and refugees remained muted. Amidst these concerns, the term 'human trafficking' made an appearance, as some EU representatives highlighted increased measures to fight human trafficking and counter-terrorism. As this focus shifted, so too did the interchangeable language and 'smugglers' was a term that transformed into 'traffickers', legitimating declarations to 'identify, capture and destroy' migrant vessels 'before they are used by traffickers' (Nielsen 2015: 3). A joint meeting took place between EU interior and foreign ministers to discuss potential action across the EU, amongst which were calls to 'capture and destroy vessels used by smugglers' (*EU Observer* 21 April 2015). Notably, other proposals in this hastily collated ten-point plan included options to reinforce joint operations in the Mediterranean; increase collaboration between European bodies (Europol, Frontex, EASO and Eurojust) aimed at smuggler operations; and that Member States should ensure fingerprinting of 'all migrants' (Peers 2015).

This desperate situation highlights concerns about large-scale migration, which feed into already existing concerns about unsecured borders and threats to national security and economies. While humanitarian work has been evident at the ground level, the dominant response among political forums has appeared to prioritise border security rather than humanitarian interventions, such as the creation of a safe passage for asylum seekers fleeing states in conflict.

The interchangeable language used, the diverse solutions posited and the highly politicised context that surrounds the way in which these complexities impact upon the depiction, representation and responses to 'victims' is the focal point for this edited book.

Human Trafficking: The Complexities of Exploitation provides contributions from academics and practitioners which examine the competing discourses surrounding human trafficking as exploitation, and explores the impact of this phenomenon in the United Kingdom and globally. Our focus on responses to victims and survivors of human trafficking at a national and international level provides an opportunity to compare and contrast the local with the global in terms of impact and response.

In 2000, the United Nations defined trafficking in human beings in the Convention against Transnational Organized Crime, which was supplemented by a Protocol to Prevent, Suppress and Punish Trafficking in Persons, Especially Women and Children (the Palermo Protocol/the Trafficking Protocol). Article 3(a) of that protocol defines trafficking in persons as:

> the recruitment, transportation, transfer, harboring or receipt of persons, by means of the threat or use of force or other forms of coercion, of abduction, of fraud, of deception, of the abuse of power or of a position of vulnerability or of the giving or receiving of payments or benefits to achieve the consent of a person having control over another person, for the purposes of exploitation.

The key aspects of this definition include movement, harbouring, receipt and exploitation, although the latter is never fully defined and movement is the aspect usually referred to. It refers to 'at a minimum, the exploitation of the prostitution of others or other forms of sexual exploitation, forced labour or services, slavery or practices similar to slavery, servitude or the removal of organs'. The two other protocols to the UN Convention relate to smuggling of migrants and trafficking in firearms, and all three were developed to strengthen border controls and improve police cooperation. Although encouraging the protection of victims, actual obligations are minimal and protection provisions are weak.

The Council of Europe Convention on Action against Trafficking in Human Beings 2005 provides a series of measures to protect and promote the rights of victims. The Convention applies to both national and transnational trafficking, whether related to organised crime or not.[1] The Convention also acts as an international instrument for defining a 'victim' of trafficking in human beings; where other international instruments left it to individual states to define victimhood and accordingly, entitlement to protection and assistance (Secretariat of the Committee on Equal Opportunities 2009).

In 2011, the UK Government opted-in to the EU Directive on Human Trafficking (EU Directive) adopted by the European Parliament in 2010. The EU Directive takes a victim-centred approach, including a gender perspective, to direct action in areas such as criminal law provisions, prosecution of offenders, victims' support and victims' rights in criminal proceedings, prevention and monitoring of the implementation of these actions by national rapporteurs or equivalent mechanisms.

Victim support includes national mechanisms for early identification and assistance to victims, based on cooperation between law enforcement and civil society organisations; providing victims with shelter, medical and psychological assistance, information and interpretation services. A victim must be treated as such as soon as there is an indication that she/he has been trafficked, with assistance in place before, during and after criminal proceedings.

The European Court of Human Rights has also ruled that trafficking in human beings falls within the scope of Article 4 of the European Convention for the Protection of Human Rights and Fundamental Freedoms, and that, accordingly, 'States have a positive obligation to put in place an appropriate legal and administrative framework against trafficking, to take measures to protect victims and to investigate acts of trafficking, including through effective cooperation with other States concerned on criminal matters.' This now means that trafficking in human beings can be combated as a violation of the European Convention on Human Rights.

It is widely acknowledged that official figures on reported victims of human trafficking are significant underestimates. Statistics for forced or bonded labour, domestic servitude and commercial sexual exploitation are varied, with the *Global Slavery Index* suggesting that worldwide, 35.8 million people are enslaved (Walk Free Foundation 2015). Many victims of human trafficking will never come to the attention of services or the authorities; the number referred to National Referral Mechanisms (NRM), a central plank of UK and European policy on trafficking and a mechanism intended to support the identification of victims, is small. Reasons for this vary, but include victim reluctance to be referred due to fear of authorities, and concerns that they may be detained or deported (OSCE/ODIHR 2004).

Trafficking for the purpose of commercial sexual exploitation has been given prominence in the media, leading to claims that other forms of trafficking (for forced labour and domestic servitude) are often overlooked (Kelly 2005; Goodey 2008; Equality and Human Rights Commission 2013). Law enforcement agencies tend to have substantial expertise in identifying 'vice' crimes such as sexual exploitation and, indeed, police officers are perhaps less likely to recognise other forms of exploitation, notably labour exploitation and domestic servitude without access to relevant information and training. In respect of child trafficking, there are concerns that the specific vulnerabilities of children are sometimes lost amidst a focus on adults (Rigby 2011; Rigby *et al.* 2012). The challenges of working with children, in a system largely developed to respond to adults, is a further complicating issue within the wider context of providing effective services to victims.

Internationally, there is ongoing recognition of the limitations of research on trafficking and the challenges in estimating prevalence (Kangaspunta 2003; Segrave *et al.* 2009). Accurate estimates are doubtless impossible to achieve. Methodologies for data collection are inconsistent between agencies and across regions. Additionally, internal trafficking is often excluded from the statistical data, while human smuggling is at times included (UNODC 2006: 120). The result is that anti-trafficking non-governmental organisations (NGOs), as well as the numerous documents from national and international bodies which report estimates of the size and scale of the trafficking problem, are inconsistent. Yet all agencies working in this area agree that the problem of human trafficking is increasing (see also Home Affairs Committee 2009; Equality and Human Rights Commission 2011, 2013).

Identification is necessary for a variety of reasons, but crucially as a mechanism for directing victims to services, notably healthcare, support and accommodation, and access to legal advice. Practitioners find that trafficking victims do not always and immediately identify themselves as such; they are often unfamiliar with the terminology and may define their experiences in ways that are not immediately recognisable to untrained officials (Haynes 2007). Evidence suggests that unless victims fit into stereotypical roles of 'victimhood' as defined by law enforcement officials, they may not be identified as trafficking victims and may be labelled as criminals and further victimised (Haynes 2007; Srikantiah 2007: Hoyle *et al.* 2011). While not identifying an individual could compromise their safety and access to support, it can also mean that unidentified victims of human trafficking with irregular immigration status may be detained, criminalised and deported without consideration of the risks they face, particularly that of re-trafficking (Home Affairs Select Committee 2009). The psychological as well as physical coercion involved in the trafficking experience can problematise 'active agency', thus obscuring representations of the 'ideal victim' (Srikantiah 2007), while immigrant victims in particular 'remain in the shadows of our communities' (Haynes 2007: 366).

In practice, across Europe, provisions and practice vary and the extent to which responses have been implemented is variable. Each Member State in the EU is responsible for establishing its own mechanisms for implementing the Convention and Council Directive decisions, and, in many cases, anti-trafficking frameworks at the national level still lack explicit anti-trafficking laws, or instruments for enacting protective measures. Lack of funding across states can also prohibit the provision of necessary resources to protect victims or their families, and in practice any one of a multitude of national ministries and agencies may be responsible for enacting the policies set forth by the European Council. While Europe-wide institutions such as Europol have functioned effectively to improve investigation and prosecution efforts, no similar institution currently exists to assist with protection efforts. This has resulted in many of the protection activities falling to the various national- and local-level NGOs to implement. Despite the identification of a number of areas of good practice, concerns have been expressed that states overly rely on poorly resourced NGOs. Attempts to provide individualised support through NGOs has also been criticised where, in the absence of greater government funding, the NGO community is too constrained in terms of their financial and geographical coverage to sufficiently serve or protect the country's victims. The emphasis on law enforcement has also been noted more generally at the expense of victims' rights (ATMG 2010, 2013). Similarly, the close association between decision-making concerning claims for asylum and identification of victimisation from human trafficking have led to issues around irregular migration status being prominent among organisations who work to support individuals seeking support.

As contributions to this book highlight, legislation can be limited in its impact in this area in terms of both objectives and implementation. Arising from efforts to control organised crime, the ability of legal directives to protect individuals is open to challenge, and remains inextricably linked to the ways in which definitions of victimisation are depicted and enforced. These limitations highlight the difficulties of expecting legislation to impact on the wider social, political and economic contexts of poverty, inequality and greed. Importantly, attempts to bring about significant social change can bring legal reformers into conflict with vested (political and economic) interests; and efforts required to challenge exploitation, where the consequences of such exploitation benefit powerful groups, can be substantial and overwhelming. Indeed, trafficking in its various manifestations is upheld by both 'criminal' and 'legitimate' business interests; with overlaps between semi-legal and criminal economies (Ruggiero 1997, 2013; Office of the Special Representative 2014).

Trafficking is a form of abuse and exploitation that requires contextualisation within a continuum of restriction and economic exploitation experienced by some groups of migrants (O'Connell Davidson 2010). Focusing on trafficking as a 'local' issue ignores its globalised nature. Similarly, viewing the victimisation and exploitation that is a feature of trafficking as discrete, time-limited events also obscures the processual and ongoing nature of victimisation. Stanley and McCulloch (2013: 8) note the shift from historical slavery to fit the demands of contemporary economies, noting that 'the progressive eradication of the slave trade from the eighteenth century and an end to formal racial discrimination have been replaced by new forms of economic, political and social control and servitude'. Indeed, as O'Connell Davidson points out, separating 'trafficking' from other violations of human and labour rights can serve as a 'discourse of depoliticisation' (2010: 245) that legitimates and produces the division of people into categories of 'deserving' and 'undeserving' (see also Malloch and Stanley 2005).

Human trafficking occurs in a highly politicised arena with a flimsy evidence base on which to institute good practice and fragmented responses to this complex issue. Piecemeal and partial state responses to the globalised nature of exploitation has undermined and hindered critical dialogue and theoretical analysis of its wider meaning and consequences. While NGOs have consistently attempted to recognise human trafficking and exploitation as a violation of human rights, and to emphasise the support and protection of victims, this has been hindered by the wider attention to strategies and systems. State enforcement of law is often enacted by passing the responsibility for protecting and supporting victims/survivors to NGOs, in practice prioritising short-term responses. This is characterised by shifts away from movements aimed at achieving social change towards 'projects', often serving to depoliticise the anti-trafficking movement. Competition for funding is subsequently underscored by the disparity between projects that have short-term welfarist objectives, and those that have long-term politically informed goals. For many involved in developing responses within 'projects', it is often difficult to stand back far enough to see the bigger picture. Neither has there been a comprehensive conceptual and theoretical analysis of the social and economic developments and conditions that perpetuate exploitation through trafficking. The overlaps between trafficking, smuggling and irregular migration, although specified in law, are relatively difficult to determine in practice, as recent events in the Mediterranean Sea evidence. The depiction of trafficked 'slaves' is often juxtaposed against the need to control 'ordinary' economic migrants; problematic when migrants may also experience various and significant forms of exploitation.

Human Trafficking: The Complexities of Exploitation developed from a programme of three symposia funded by the Scottish Universities Insight Institute (SUII), based in Glasgow in 2012–13. The Institute provided facilities and funding with the specific objective of bringing together academics, practitioners and policymakers to create a space (in place and time) to support an opportunity to look afresh at a specific topic and, in doing so, to improve practice and understanding.

The discussions and debates that took place challenged the definitions of human trafficking currently in use. Despite international policy and directives, the frames that define human trafficking are largely drawn from attempts to counter organised international crime (originally trafficking of drugs, arms and people), so definitions are limited by this context. There was shared agreement of the need to prioritise human rights (and see ATMG 2010, 2013), yet acknowledgement of the need to account for the 'porous' distinctions between human trafficking, smuggling and migration which require a critical examination of processes of criminalisation and criminal justice responses. Accounting for wider contexts of exploitation also creates challenges for law enforcement, statutory agencies and NGOs, and has consequences in terms of funding and the potential development of services.

It was recognised that responses to victims are often partial, sometimes due to service provision, but often as a result of the prioritisation of a particular kind of victim, reinforced by the media and NGOs working in the area; creating a problematic distinction between trafficking and the wider political and economic context of exploitation.

Human Trafficking: The Complexities of Exploitation is based on the SUII programme and includes contributions from attendees at the conference, as well as several others that were commissioned specifically to develop this work further. The title of the book is indicative of the challenges we faced throughout the programme in our attempts to agree on definitions, the nature of the issue and how best to respond. There were areas of agreement between the programme participants, but also disagreement as to the cause, nature and potential solutions of the problem of human trafficking. Practitioners and policymakers were often limited by their focus on the immediacy of victim needs and the priority of interventions, which were often short-term; while academics had the opportunity to consider the issues from a theoretical perspective, which enabled a more outward-looking analysis that swept the horizon for the causes and conditions within which exploitation could fester. Our focus was continually drawn towards the broader context of exploitation, and the ways in which avoiding or ignoring this context resulted in limited and partial accounts of human trafficking and the structural underpinnings that contextualise the trade in people on a global scale; in essence, depoliticising injustice.

This book aims to highlight these complexities, challenging simplistic and simplified definitions and responses. In doing so, it highlights the need for more nuanced awareness of the complex issues that constitute the ongoing exploitation of men, women and children across the globe, illustrating the need to expose the intrinsic operations of political economies both in terms of 'legal' and 'illegal' forms of exploitation. Contributors to this book consider the systemic nature of exploitation within political and economic systems, exposing this as it is manifested through internal and interstate trafficking, and calling for a wider commitment to tackle human rights abuses, inequalities and exploitation.

By examining the complex nature of human trafficking and the challenges of conceptualising it in terms of exploitation discourses, the book considers the appropriateness of current responses to victims/survivors, and will examine attempts to provide 'holistic' and 'effective' intervention. Within this analysis, the challenges that the wider sociopolitical sphere imposes on survivor care will be examined. Our opening contributor, Kiril Sharapov, explores the 'evidential data deficit' surrounding trafficking and presents outcomes of public opinion surveys in Ukraine, Hungary and Britain that examine the extent to which knowledge about human trafficking is integrated into the actions of 'consumer-citizens'. Drawing on agnotology, biopolitics and socially organised denial, Sharapov considers how ignorance and denial occur in response to social circumstances and remain related to political economy. His chapter contributes to debates on the link between public knowledge and public policies, and highlights how individual and public knowing (and not-knowing) about human trafficking are biopolitical features of neoliberal governmentalities.

The collective contributions from practitioners working with victims of trafficking and academics conducting research and developing theory in this area provides an important opportunity to challenge some of the 'taken for granted' assumptions about what human trafficking is and how best to respond. The direct involvement and views of practitioners allows the reader to consider the complex legal and practical circumstances that surround individuals as victim-survivors and professionals as practitioner-responders, with the broader conceptual issues. The extent to which anti-trafficking legislation can be truly effective is debatable, and contributors to this book highlight the aspirations and limitations of the law in the context of European and state legislation. The complicated nature of the European legal system in this area, which includes both Council of Europe and EU legal instruments, has resulted in some confusion as to the implementation of anti-trafficking policy and legislation across the United Kingdom. European law is frequently mediated through the UK legal system, especially in relation to asylum and immigration issues. Responsibility for ensuring compliance with the different legal instruments – particularly in respect of victim services – further complicates legislative implementation. European legal instruments can often appear 'woolly' as they are frequently products of intergovernmental compromise. Case law is often relied upon to clarify definitions and examples in different jurisdictions. Consequently, the use of legislation to inform practice guidelines and procedures can lead to unclear processes in practice, especially when concepts of 'appropriate' or 'minimum' levels of subsistence are not clearly defined. Adam Weiss focuses upon the complexities of implementing international law into domestic legislation. His focus is on the particular difficulties associated with the adoption of EU human trafficking law and conventions into domestic contexts, with examples where this has been achieved or is progressing. The chapter considers how European law may apply to victim protection, while acknowledging the challenges and difficulties of achieving this in practice.

Kirsty Thomson outlines the legal rights and responsibilities that relate to both adult and child victims of human trafficking using the legal landscape in Scotland as a case study to consider the implementation of these rights and responsibilities. Her chapter examines the rights and responsibilities of public authorities in the United Kingdom in relation to human trafficking and victim support, and the systems for identification and protection in place within the United Kingdom. She considers the impact of these largely policy-based interventions. The chapter also expands on Weiss' input to locate legal practice in Scotland, exploring the implications of devolved government in Scotland and the interplay with the reserved matter of immigration, as Scotland attempts to implement international, European and UK law.

There has been much debate about the shortcomings of the child protection system in responding to victims of trafficking. Paul Rigby and Philip Ishola examine the development of a child-centred response, drawing on the implementation and monitoring of the NRM for children across the United Kingdom, and a programme of response and evaluation developed in Glasgow. Arguing that rather than a central mechanism allied closely with immigration, the existing child protection systems and agencies are best placed to identify, protect and rehabilitate children, Rigby and Ishola illustrate the importance of placing the needs of children as central to processes of identifying child victims of human trafficking, thus increasing the likelihood of positive outcomes for children and young people.

Practitioners have an important contribution to make to the development of both practice and policy, and provide a front-line perspective to the support and recovery of victims of human trafficking. Jim Laird argues that there is a measure of agreement on the most important needs of victims of human trafficking, particularly in the immediate and short term, and for comprehensive and coordinated services. His chapter, based on experience of dealing with over 200 victims of human trafficking and involvement in a number of 'operations', looks at the interventions employed over the last few years across the United Kingdom. Laird focuses, in the main, on law enforcement agencies, but also considers the experience of other agencies, including support organisations. Examining models of good practice, and giving specific examples of interventions that have been less than successful, he outlines where promising actions have been hindered by poor strategic coordination and considers how things can be improved in future.

Sheila Murie and Liz Owens, Glasgow social workers, provide their account of a response to child trafficking that emerged from pertinent questions asked ten years ago. They describe the developments and challenges in attempting to locate responses to child victims firmly in a well-established child protection system to provide appropriate holistic support to vulnerable children. Murie and Owens focus on the frustrations of promoting a child-centred response where prioritisation is immigration and criminal justice focused. A well-developed and respected model of practice in Glasgow appears to have been overtaken by political imperatives.

Sharon Doherty and Rachel Morley outline the multiple traumas and human rights violations experienced by victims of human trafficking. The combination of multiple traumas, multiple losses and little or no access to any of the protective factors that might buffer the effects of trauma causes cumulative harm to victims, and can lead to serious mental health difficulties. Doherty and Morley focus on what is known about promoting and supporting the psychological recovery of the victims of human trafficking, and explore principles of trauma-informed good practice for all agencies working with trafficking victims. They highlight expert guidance and outcome studies indicating which psychological therapies are useful when working with victims of complex trauma of all ages, and at different stages in their recovery, and draw on practice-based evidence to detail practical and helpful responses to the challenges of working in this area.

The academic contributions add an additional dimension to the views and experiences of practitioners through exploration of the wider social, political and economic context within which individuals, organisations and nation states are located. Understandings that focus only on practical interventions can result in the broader structural determinants that influence the displacement and exploitation of individuals being ignored. Similarly, theoretical accounts that omit an understanding of the practical, individualised impediments that characterise this area are themselves partial.

Claire Cody examines the difficulties of monitoring and evaluating support programmes for young survivors of exploitation and trafficking. Drawing on the findings from a survey of professionals involved in support programmes in twenty-one countries, she presents findings from a consultation process involving eighty-nine young survivors of exploitation and trafficking living in seven countries; a process that gave young people a chance to share their own stories of change and identify aspects of the reintegration process that they felt were important. Their responses provide guidance on what should be measured and assessed in order to determine whether reintegration has been 'successful'. Cody concludes by making a number of recommendations to improve monitoring and evaluation in this area. These include developing common, yet contextualised, tools across the sector and using sensitive and appropriate participatory techniques with survivors to understand what 'successful reintegration' looks like in the eyes of young survivors.

Stefano Bonino examines the experiences of forced marriage in British Pakistani communities and explores forced marriage in relation to human trafficking. This practice is addressed as a complex patriarchal cultural practice, which takes on a transnational dimension with the settlement and development of Pakistani communities within the United Kingdom. Locating this practice within the context of human trafficking indicates that sexual and domestic exploitation, economic disadvantage and gender inequality is influenced by more than simply 'culture', while exploring the limitations of legislation in the context of cultural issues.

Margaret Malloch examines the presumption against the prosecution of victims who commit crimes as a direct result of their victimisation, noting the increasing international evidence that victims of trafficking continue to be detained or imprisoned in state institutions following 'liberation' from traffickers. Her chapter considers the social, political and economic depiction of 'deserving' and 'undeserving' victims, and the political basis for the criminalisation of certain victims of human trafficking. The ambiguity of 'justice' in this context is considered; where the exploitation of victims clearly contravenes any concept of 'justice', yet nation states still attempt to differentiate 'genuine' situations of enforced criminality. The broader questions that this raises in terms of appropriate responses to victims of human trafficking, and the limitations of effective survivor care, are considered.

Jackie Turner draws attention to transnational mobility and formations of patriarchy in the cross-border trafficking of women for sexual exploitation. Her chapter draws on the findings of an empirical study, conducted between January 2009 and May 2010, and based on an examination of selected Crown Prosecution Service completed trafficking cases in England and Wales between 2004 and 2008. Turner examines the ways in which the collapse of the former Soviet Union, towards the end of the last century, has produced economic and social asymmetries which form part of the 'fertile field' (Kelly 2005) or conditions conducive to sex trafficking, underpinned by the rise of a 'militant patriarchy' (Connell 2009) in Russia and parts of the former Eastern bloc. She argues that the reconfiguration of borders in Europe has fuelled changes in rates and patterns of migration, which have seen the creation of new diasporic connectivities and the emergence of different transnational formations. Increasingly, in a globalised world, transnational mobility is key to the modus operandi of cross-border sex traffickers, while distant and local formations of patriarchy intersect in the racialised prostitution industries in which women are held in 'conditions of confinement' (O'Connell Davidson 1998) and exploited.

Hazel Cameron examines an under-analysed area of civil warfare: the relationship between conflict around the globe and organised criminality, which results in the trafficking of human beings from conflict and post-conflict environments. Human trafficking is a crisis of global proportions to human security and a key development issue. Her chapter explores the scourge of human trafficking at the intersection of war and global profiteering to illuminate the socioeconomic and political context of the trafficking of persons and to locate human trafficking in a theoretical framework of global political and economic development. Cameron gives particular attention to the role of neoliberal assumptions in exacerbating the vulnerability of women and children in the post-conflict management phase and challenges neoliberal approaches to 'peace-making'.

Bill Munro's chapter situates human trafficking as a paradigm of the market economy. Many of the most dynamic markets in the world deal with illicit goods and substances – arms, drugs, ivory – as well as human beings (prostitution, pornography, forced labour, work in unsafe labour environments). While, on the one hand, laws prohibit the distribution of these commodities, on the other hand, the state effectively abrogates the enforcement of other laws in relation to the illegal market and often unwittingly creates the very conditions that facilitate the emergence of such markets. Munro argues that organised crime and the services that it provides, including that of the trafficking in human beings, can be understood as a response to a particular institutional demand by the nascent market economy. His chapter examines the business of human trafficking and explores the emergence of different models in relation to their historical and spatial contexts.

Human Trafficking: The Complexities of Exploitation provides a compendium of comment and analysis from across policy, practice and academia. While each of the chapters offer a different focus and emphasis, the multidimensional layering is intentional, to challenge the reader to consider the many facets of a trade that politicians and the media often report through a reductionist lens, usually linked to immigration and asylum. While there are no simple solutions or conclusions to this complex reality, Malloch and Rigby provide some pointers to future developments in a final postscript.

The book brings together micro and macro understandings of people trafficking and, in doing so, highlights the need to start to make nuanced connections and explore deeper understandings; to challenge the exploitation of individuals as a problem resulting from individual vulnerabilities. Instead, the book locates the features and processes of exploitation as a global phenomenon underpinned by relations of power, dominance and greed; historical vices that continue into the twenty-first century and perpetuate the ongoing exploitation and abuse of people.

Note

1. Thus, the Convention differs from the Trafficking Protocol which applies to certain offences of a transnational nature and involves organised criminal groups.

References

Anti-Trafficking Monitoring Group (ATMG) (2010), *Wrong Kind of Victim*, London: ATMG.
Anti-Trafficking Monitoring Group (ATMG) (2013), *In the Dock: Examining the UK's Criminal Justice Response to Trafficking*, London: ATMG.

Arendt, H. (1986), *The Origins of Totalitarianism*, London: Andre Deutsch.

Connell, R. W. (2009), *Short Introduction – Gender*, Cambridge: Polity Press.

Equality and Human Rights Commission (2011), *Inquiry into Human Trafficking in Scotland*, Glasgow: Equality and Human Rights Commission.

Equality and Human Rights Commission (2013), *Inquiry into Human Trafficking in Scotland: Follow-on Report*, Glasgow: Equality and Human Rights Commission.

Goodey, L. (2008), 'Human trafficking', *Criminology and Criminal Justice*, 8(4): 421–42.

Haynes, D. (2007), '(Not) found chained to a bed in a brothel: conceptual, legal, and procedural failures to fulfil the promise of the Trafficking Victims Protection Act', *Georgetown Immigration Law Journal*, 21: 337.

Home Affairs Select Committee (2009), *The Trade in Human Beings: Human Trafficking in the UK*, Sixth Report, Session 2008–9, London: Home Affairs Committee Publications.

Hoyle, C., M. Bosworth and M. Dempsey (2011), 'Labelling the victims of sex trafficking', *Social and Legal Studies*, 20(3): 313–29.

International Organisation for Migration (IOM) (2014), *Fatal Journeys: Tracking Lives Lost during Migration*, Geneva: IOM.

Kangaspunta, K. (2003), 'Mapping the inhuman trade', *Focus on Crime and Society*, 3(1/2): 81–103.

Kelly, L. (2005), 'You can find anything you want', *International Migration*, 43(1/2): 236–65.

Malloch, M. and E. Stanley (2005), 'The detention of asylum seekers in the UK: representing risk, managing the dangerous', *Punishment and Society*, 7(1): 53–71.

Nielsen, N. (2014), 'EU to target migrant smugglers', *EU Observer*, 24 April, available at: https://euobserver.com/justice/128447, last accessed 27 April 2015.

O'Connell Davidson, J. (1998), *Prostitution, Power and Freedom*, Cambridge: Polity Press.

O'Connell Davidson, J. (2010), 'New slavery, old binaries: human trafficking and the borders of "freedom"', *Global Networks*, 10(2): 244–61.

Office of the Special Representative and Co-ordinator for Combating Trafficking in Human Beings (2014), *Ending Exploitation*, Vienna: Organization for Security and Co-operation in Europe.

OSCE/ODIHR (2004), *National Referral Mechanisms: Joining Efforts to Protect the Rights of Trafficked Persons, A Practical Handbook*, Poland: OSCE/ODIHR.

Peers, S. (2015), 'The EU response to migrant deaths: protection and prevention – or policy laundering?', *EU Law Analysis*, available at: http://eulawanalysis.blogspot.be, last accessed 27 April 2015.

Rigby, P. (2011), Separated and trafficked children: the challenges for child protection professionals', *Child Abuse Review*, 20(5): 324–40.

Rigby, P., M. Malloch and N. Hamilton-Smith (2012), *Child Trafficking and Care Provision: Towards Better Survivor Care*, London: Love 146.

Ruggiero, V. (1997), 'Trafficking in human beings: slaves in contemporary Europe', *International Journal of the Sociology of Law*, 25: 231–44.

Ruggiero, V. (2013), *The Crimes of the Economy: A Criminological Analysis of Economic Thought*, London: Routledge.

Secretariat of the Committee on Equal Opportunities for Women and Men (2009), *Handbook for Parliamentarians*, Strasbourg: Parliamentary Assembly of the Council of Europe.

Segrave M., S. Milivojevic and S. Pickering (2009), *Sex Trafficking: International Context and Response*, Cullompton: Willan Publishing.

Srikantiah, J. (2007), 'Perfect victims and real survivors', *Boston University Law Review*, 87: 157–211.

Stanley, E. and J. McCulloch (eds) (2013), *State Crime and Resistance*, London: Routledge.

United Nations Office on Drugs and Crime (UNODC) (2006), *Toolkit to Combat Trafficking in Persons*, New York: United Nations.

Walk Free Foundation (2015), *2014 Global Slavery Index*, available at: http://www.globalslaveryindex.org, last accessed 26 May 2015.

2   Productive Ignorance: Assessing Public Understanding of Human Trafficking in Ukraine, Hungary and Great Britain

Kiril Sharapov

Introduction

The failure of a public response in the 'western world'[1] to the presence of unfree labour[2] in the global economy, including exploitation[3] of sexual, physical and emotional labour trafficked across and within national borders, has become a significant socioeconomic and cultural quandary. Recent policy and media discussions emphasise the lack of information as a limiting factor in the public's non-response to the increasing evidence of 'modern slaves'[4] indentured in 'our' factories, on 'our' farms, begging in 'our' streets, and of products of forced labour increasingly available on 'our' supermarket shelves. The notion that 'if people only knew they would act differently' – that is, consume differently, question companies and suppliers of 'unethically' produced consumer goods and services, and recognise and report victims – underlies the majority of recent anti-trafficking awareness campaigns.

In 2011, the UK Government suggested that although 'many members of the public already care deeply about the plight of trafficking victims', 'awareness and vigilance' should be raised in 'particular communities' (UK Government 2011: 8). In 2014, it launched a 'Modern Slavery is Closer than You Think' awareness campaign (UK Government 2014a) to explain 'the nature of modern slavery' and to encourage reporting by members of the public. The focus of this campaign appears to be on 'concerned' citizens, who may not be sufficiently aware of the 'signs of slavery' and therefore may not be able to recognise and report potential cases of trafficking, or who may become 'enslaved' themselves. Such co-production of threat, fear and awareness by the UK Government has increasingly become one of its biopolitical tools of 'managing' migration. Tyler (2010), for example, highlights the government's capacity to control and fashion populations by marking out and failing specific groups against the background of a continually re-enacted myth of threatened national belonging and community cohesion. The evidence base used by the UK Government in making overstated claims on the extent of public awareness of trafficking appears to be as thin as the evidence base relied upon by many national governments in Europe in formulating their anti-trafficking responses. As the anti-trafficking 'community'[5] prepares to mark the fifteenth anniversary of the Palermo Protocol (United Nations 2000) in December 2015, the lack of robust research and data continues to be one of the barriers in planning for, implementing and monitoring the implementation of numerous anti-trafficking initiatives. The evidential data deficit includes not only the often lamented lack of statistics in relation to victims of trafficking, but also areas in which quantitative assessments can be made, including, for example, anti-trafficking funding allocations,[6] or the extent of public understanding and awareness of human trafficking. In addition, very little sociological work has been undertaken so far to interrogate how 'consumer-citizens'[7] (Bauman 1998; White 1999) experience and come to terms with some of the media messages that highlight the links between 'living well for less',[8] on the one hand, and the hardships and poverty of people in other parts of the world and, increasingly, of the immigrant 'Other' – trafficked, smuggled and exploited in our own backyard.

This chapter addresses some of these knowledge gaps by offering an overview of the outcomes of representative public opinion surveys in Ukraine, Hungary and Great Britain. The surveys took place between December 2013 and February 2014 as part of the 'Understanding Public Knowledge and Attitudes towards Trafficking in Human Beings' project.[9]

The discussion that follows provides an insight into how people make sense of the disturbing information regarding human trafficking and its victims, and tells a story of awareness co-existing with apathy and acts of knowing and unknowing. It suggests that although the majority of survey respondents were aware of human trafficking and its exploitative contexts, they failed to integrate this knowledge into their everyday life of 'consumer-citizens'. In considering the survey outcomes within the context of specific policy and media representations of human trafficking in these case study countries, the chapter draws on the three theoretical frameworks: agnotology, to highlight the process of cultural production of ignorance (Proctor and Schiebinger 2008); biopolitics, to highlight the role of neoliberal governmentality in the dissemination of risk and responsibility (Nadesan 2008); and socially organised denial (Norgaard 2011), to highlight how ignorance and denial on a collective level occur in response to social circumstances and remain related to political economy.

By focusing on the national case studies, three broad objectives are achieved. The chapter addresses the existing deficit of comparative empirical data on public knowledge and understanding of human trafficking. It makes a contribution to the ongoing scholarly debates on the link between public knowledge and public policies. Finally, it highlights how individual and public knowing and unknowing of human trafficking are biopolitical in their nature and remain embedded within the context of neoliberal governmentalities – the arts of governments, linking individuals to social and economic relations of power (Foucault 1979; Nadesan 2008).

Human trafficking as a very specific issue of concern

Over the last decade, human trafficking has become an established policy concern for governments in all European countries, a domain of ideological rivalry and competition for limited anti-trafficking funding among the growing number of non-governmental organisations (NGOs) and anti-trafficking 'professionals' (Agustin 2007; Goodey 2008), a rich fare for the scandal-hungry media (Small 2012), and an almost limitless field of enquiry for researchers attempting to theorise human trafficking and assess its magnitude. European Union (EU) policymakers identified trafficking as an issue of concern in 1989 with the adoption of the Resolution on the Exploitation of Prostitution and the Traffic in Human Beings (European Parliament 1989). By 2015, the 1989 priority of preventing prostitution as a key anti-trafficking measure had expanded in its scope and scale into a separate legal, policy and institutional domain. A dedicated anti-trafficking unit was set up within the European Commission's Directorate General for Home Affairs. The EU Anti-Trafficking Directive (European Parliament 2011) and the EU Strategy towards the Eradication of Trafficking in Human Beings (European Commission 2012) were adopted to set out legal and policy frameworks for EU-wide anti-trafficking activities. Among other priorities, both documents emphasise the importance of information and awareness-raising campaigns, with the Strategy taking a step further by suggesting that 'little has been done to systematically evaluate the impact of such prevention programmes in terms of their achieving their objectives, such as changes in behaviour and

attitudes, thus reducing the likelihood of trafficking in human beings'
(*ibid.*: priority B, action 3). Overall, however, the EU response has
been criticised for approaching trafficking as an issue of organised
crime and illegal border crossing, for overlooking the rights and
protection of victims, and for its failure to address the issues of
demand for cheap labour, goods and services, and exploitative sex
(McRedmond and Wylie 2010: 8).

Despite the policy prominence given to the issue of data collection
in the EU and the subsequent publication of the two Eurostat reports
on human trafficking in Europe (Eurostat 2013, 2014), little remains
known about the true scale of trafficking into and within Europe,
and, overall, about the scale of labour exploitation in European
economies, including exploitation of people trafficked across EU
borders, of people who crossed borders 'voluntarily' as clandestine
migrants or were smuggled, and of the EEA citizens freely moving
across Europe in search of employment.

According to the 2012 International Labour Office's (ILO) global
estimate of forced labour, there were 1.5 million forced labourers in
the developed economies and European Union[10] (ILO 2012) gener-
ating almost US$ 47 billion in profits annually (about US$34,800
per victim) (ILO 2014: 14). Also, little is known about public
understanding of human trafficking, public awareness of labour
exploitation, and public attitudes towards these phenomena. In her
2009 study of public opinion on human trafficking in Russia, Mary
Buckley, for example, noted: 'What is missing from this accumulat-
ing multivariate picture [of trafficking] is ... the extent of people's
knowledge about its scale and of what the process entails, and views
on what action, if any, should be taken' (Buckley 2009). This lack
of statistics did not, however, prevent policymakers and lawmakers from locating trafficking, understood as an issue of crime and
immigration control, at the centre of their anti-trafficking strategies. In the absence of any reliable benchmarks against which the
success of such anti-trafficking interventions could be measured,
individualised stories of rescue, salvation and punishment shifted the
overall anti-trafficking focus towards the realm of heightened border
surveillance, security anxiety, moral harm (O'Brien *et al.* 2013)
and the individualisation of risk and responsibility. The biopolitical
setting up of new zones of racialised and gendered exclusion remains
equated in policy and anti-trafficking discourse with the eradication of prostitution, 'illegal' immigration and the 'heinous' crime of
trafficking. A new moral vocabulary of vilifying the dehumanised,
threatening and 'illegal' 'Other', whilst pitying powerless, duped,
'fallen' and, therefore, deserving 'genuine' victims serves the purpose
of removing these increasingly securitised concerns from both the

economic domain of neoliberal accumulation and from the moral domain of concerned 'consumer-citizens'.

One of the key ontological and epistemological assumptions underlying such policy, legal and media misrepresentations of trafficking is that as a phenomenon of crime, irregular(ised) migration and prostitution, trafficking can be fully understood and therefore eradicated. This chapter, however, suggests that human trafficking must be approached as epiphenomenal, or linked, to a series of wider socioeconomic and political processes at work. Understanding human trafficking as a relation of biopolitical power within the context of political economy, locates it at the intersection of uneven development, state-sanctioned capital–labour imbalances, and 'axes of inequality such as gender, race and class' (Strauss and Fudge 2013: 19), which 'produce, and institutionalise, new forms and relations of unfree labour' (*ibid.*)

Within this context, it is possible to conceive of human trafficking as lying outside the reductive and ahistorical migration–crime and 'modern slavery' paradigms, and located on the continuums of (neoliberal) mobility, labour and individual agency. However, any deviations from the established policy dyads of legal–illegal migration, forced–voluntary labour or individual freedom–enslavement are thwarted by the power of new biopolitical and disciplinary apparatuses to organise and structure problem spaces in which both direct and indirect state surveillance and control can be exercised to 'manage' security risks. The normativity of passive victimhood, evil criminality, 'concerned' individual and corporate citizenship, and 'protective' statehood is enacted and reaffirmed without any fundamental alteration to the operations of neoliberal governmentality that produces such risks in the first place. The following five elements of the established anti-trafficking framework encompass both the 'formal' arena of laws, regulations and policies that have framed neoliberal governments' responses to human trafficking, but also the operation of informal 'norms and mores, expectations and ideals that shape particular practices of thought, speech and action' (FitzGerald 2012):

1. The international legal anti-trafficking framework includes legal instruments and policies emanating from the UN, ILO and, where applicable, the Council of Europe and the EU; they become operationalised, over time, at the national level.
2. International law enforcement and border protection agencies, including Interpol and, at the European level, Europol and Frontex. In addition, the Organization for Security and Co-operation in Europe (OSCE) has been undertaking a range of anti-trafficking initiatives in cooperation with its member states.

3. National legal frameworks and anti-trafficking policies developed, implemented and enforced by national lawmakers, governments and criminal justice systems. Anti-trafficking work is usually delegated to national law enforcement and immigration/border control agencies, and, in some cases, departments with responsibilities to provide social services to victims of trafficking or groups identified as vulnerable and at risk of trafficking.
4. A broad range of NGOs, including academic and policy think tanks, organisations working with victims of trafficking, and various interest groups, including religious organisations, trade unions, consumer groups, anti-trafficking experts.
5. National media and, recently, the entertainment sector, with celebrity 'expert-advocates' (Haynes 2014; Steele and Shores 2014), news articles, documentaries, films, theatrical plays, music videos, poetry and fiction dedicated to highlighting the plight of 'modern slaves', often offering little or no insights into the complexity of structural issues that underlie human trafficking.

Within the crime–immigration–victimhood–rescue frame of understanding human trafficking, the above five elements are normally located on the positive end of the disciplinary and normalising continuum of anti-trafficking interventions. Productive of knowledge, statuses and subjectivities, such regimes allow 'genuine' victims of trafficking, in need of identification, assistance and protection, to assume a neutral position. Criminals and criminal groups, deemed to bear most, if not full, responsibility for the crime of trafficking and exploitation of victims, are positioned on its negative side. However, two other major constituents – businesses and members of the general public – remain, to a large extent, excluded from national anti-trafficking policies and agendas. The only exceptions are tightly PR-controlled corporate performances at the corporate social responsibility 'theatres of virtue' (Rajak 2011) and a more recent 'business and human rights' agenda (Deva 2013); awareness-raising initiatives designed to induce pity towards victims and indignation towards criminals, increase reporting of trafficking as crime and to prevent groups of population deemed as 'vulnerable' from 'enslavement' and exploitation; and recent campaigns focusing on 'ethical consumption' and individualising responsibility for unfree labour by shifting the blame onto individual consumers. Figure 2.1 outlines the contours of such a regime.

The establishment of these regimes of control, risk management, and of gendered, racialised and spatial distribution of people across most, if not all, EU Member States and its neighbours, gives what Kapur describes as an 'outward sense of progress of something being

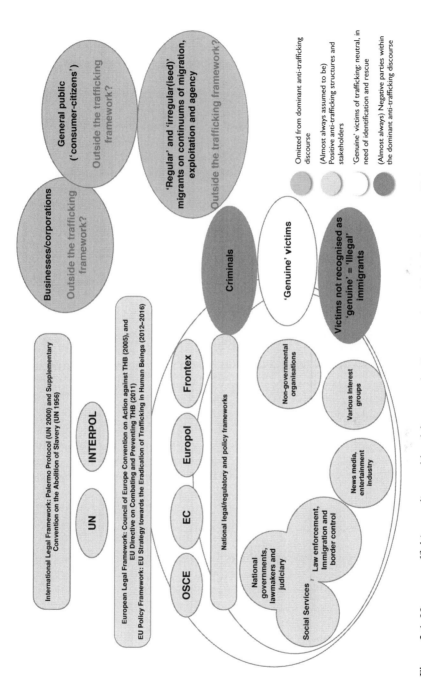

Figure 2.1 Human trafficking: policy and legal frameworks (in countries with defined anti-trafficking agendas)

International Legal Framework: Palermo Protocol (UN 2000) and Supplementary Convention on the Abolition of Slavery (UN 1956)

UN

INTERPOL

European Legal Framework: Council of Europe Convention on Action against THB (2005), and EU Directive on Combating and Preventing THB (2011)
EU Policy Framework: EU Strategy towards the Eradication of Trafficking in Human Beings (2012–2016)

OSCE

EC

Europol

Frontex

National legal/regulatory and policy frameworks

National governments, lawmakers and judiciary

Law enforcement, immigration and border control

Social Services

Non-governmental organisations

News media, entertainment industry

Various interest groups

Criminals

'Genuine' victims

Victims not recognised as 'genuine' = 'illegal' immigrants

Businesses/corporations

Outside the trafficking framework?

General public ('consumer-citizens')

Outside the trafficking framework?

'Regular' and 'irregular(ised)' migrants on continuums of migration, exploitation and agency

Outside the trafficking framework?

Omitted from dominant anti-trafficking discourse

(Almost always assumed to be) Positive anti-trafficking structures and stakeholders

'Genuine' victims of trafficking: neutral, in need of identification and rescue

(Almost always) Negative parties within the dominant anti-trafficking discourse

done, of a social justice being pursued in the name of the human rights of these have-nots' (2005: 26). However, promises of progress and emancipation, and the seeming international unity in fighting the *crime of trafficking* remain, Kapur argues, myopic, exclusive and informed by a series of new global panics as a form of biopolitical government of populations: a panic about the survival of the nation; a moral panic feeding the anti-sex work agenda; and a cultural panic treating the 'Other' as cultural contaminant disrupting a nation's social and cultural fabric (*ibid.*: 26). The policing of physical borders and the production of racialised and gendered subjectivities as part of the anti-immigration and anti-trafficking discourses attracted an increasing volume of scholarly discussions of anti-trafficking measures as a biopolitical tool of governing at a distance. They urge that the state, the market and the population should be approached as being constituted and entwined within the globalised contexts of neoliberal accumulation and wealth existing alongside growing poverty (Eisenstein 2010), socioeconomic and cultural displacement, and pockets of 'neoliberal abandonment' (Povinelli 2011).

Governmentality, ignorance and public opinion

The concept of governmentality is useful in understanding human trafficking as a playing field on which 'expert authorities, explanations, and technologies are organised in relation to particular kinds of action/policy orientations, problem-solution frameworks, subjectivities and activities' (Nadesan 2008: 1). It also helps to reveal how some individuals are privileged as autonomous and self-regulating agents (concerned and aware 'consumer-citizens'), whilst others are marginalised, disciplined or subordinated as invisible (non-citizens exploited to make 'living well for less' possible), or as dangerous and in need of 'normalisation' (criminals, victims, 'illegal' immigrants). The biopolitics of human trafficking, citizenship, immigration and, increasingly, consumption must be considered in terms of its capacity to serve the interest of neoliberal capital accumulation by maximising the utility of the subordinated, disciplined and marginalised 'Others' for market capitalisation. From this perspective, neoliberal market logic and technologies present human trafficking as a particular biopolitical problematic and as an opportunity: for the state to embed a repressive apparatus of policing, disciplining and normalising into the everyday life of citizens and non-citizens alike; for the market to ensure the continuous circulation of capital without limit and without attending to the new forms of inclusion and exclusion produced in the process; and for an array of private actors to self-regulate in becoming expert, aware and concerned consumer-citizens or consumer-activists. At the same time, the very same technologies of governance continue to shape governmental approaches to representing and addressing the problematic of human trafficking through shifting technologies and strategies of power. One of these technologies is the making and unmaking of ignorance through 'myriad of forms of inherent (or avoidable) selectivity', theorised by Proctor and Schiebinger (2008: vii) in their study of 'knowledge that could have been but wasn't, or should be but isn't' (*ibid.*).

In recent years, more sustained and critical scholarly efforts have uncovered and challenged the way in which subjectivities of victimhood, rescue and suffering have been embedded into the dominant narrative of trafficking as a problem of crime, immigration, victimhood and selective rescue (Ardau 2004; Berman 2010; FitzGerald 2010). Less attention, however, has been devoted to appraising how dominant anti-trafficking discourses have been invisibilising those non-trafficked but exploited, and those aware of exploitative labour but unconcerned about it not only at the level of political, legal and media developments, but also at the level of public imagination. The condition of 'knowing and not knowing', in which individuals have certain knowledge but fail to integrate this knowledge into their sense of immediate reality, has been described by Norgaard (2011) as 'socially organised denial', which can be understood only within the context of 'both social norms shaping interpersonal interaction and the broader political economic context' (Norgaard 2011: 7). Within 'a new society of control governed by market-defined risks and opportunities' (Nadesan 2008: 211), the co-production of deliberately engineered ignorance about the root causes of trafficking by state–capital entanglements, and of public non-response to human trafficking organised through cultural practices of everyday life by aware but unconcerned citizens results in a specific neoliberal problem–solution frame in which privileged people reproduce existing power relations as they enact denial in their everyday life. As Norgaard notes:

> More people are made superfluous and marginal: the deskilled, unskilled and sinking poor; the old, who no longer work; the young who cannot find work; the massive shifting populations of migrants, asylum seekers and refugees. The 'solution' to these problems now physically reproduces the conditions of denial. The strategy is exclusion and segregation: enclaves of losers and redundant populations, living in the modern version of ghettos, remote enough to become 'out of sight, out of mind,' separated from enclaves of winners, in their guarded shopping malls, gated communities and retirement villages. (2011: 220–1)

Having set up the background for the discussion of public under-standing of human trafficking as located within the context of ideo-logical and material constitutions of security threats co-existing with and co-dependent on the neoliberal promotion of empowerment through the 'market', this chapter reviews the outcomes of public opinion surveys in Ukraine, Hungary and Great Britain, including a synopsis of the research design. It discusses the public response as an outcome of biopolitical framing of human trafficking, which allows people to be aware of human trafficking, but to craft and maintain a sense of distance from it – an invisible yet facilitated and managed process of social production of ignorance and manufactured denial. The study discussed in this chapter was designed to collate previ-ously unavailable data on how much the general public knew about human trafficking, and to explore whether such knowledge received a degree of ethical, political and social traction in individual con-structions of relevance and irrelevance within the specific context of biopolitical governmentality of human trafficking discussed above. Three case study countries were selected to represent one of the traf-ficking 'routes' into Western Europe: Ukraine, represented within the dominant anti-trafficking discourse as a country of origin; Hungary, as predominantly a country of transit; and the United Kingdom, as a country of destination. Over recent years, however, the distinctions between countries of origin, transit and destination have become less representative of the actual complexity of movements of people trafficked within and outside Europe, with traditional countries of origin increasingly becoming both transit and destination countries. In addition, further evidence is emerging of trafficked people origi-nating from countries traditionally regarded as destination countries for human trafficking, including the United Kingdom (NCA 2014), and of the increasing incidence of internal trafficking (*ibid.*)

Survey research and survey methodology

Despite the well-known methodological issues surrounding survey research, including arguments around sampling, question ambigu-ity and a fundamental concern about the extent to which large-scale surveys provide a valid representation of public views, opinion polling remains the 'best methodology yet invented to investigate public opinion' (Stromback 2012: 1). The pro-survey consensus highlights the issues of feasibility and representativeness, and the capacity of properly designed and analysed surveys to deliver a 'highly representative picture of what citizens as a collectivity think' (Page 2002: 325). It is also accepted that having an understanding of public opinion as expressed by the outcomes of opinion polls is usually 'better for democracy than not having it. Good information is better than misinformation' (Taylor 2002: 316).

To minimise potential survey errors within the constraints of cost, time and ethics, Weisberg's 'survey research triangle' (Weisberg 2008) guided the development of the survey methodology to account for survey errors (including the issues of measurement, non-response, sampling and coverage), survey constraints (including costs, time and ethics), and survey effects (including question-related, mode and comparison effects). Three experienced market research companies were appointed to undertake face-to-face surveys of representative national samples as part of their Omnibus surveys. The Omnibus survey is a shared cost, multi-client approach to survey research carried out by market research companies on behalf of commissioning organisations. As a cost-effective and time-efficient way of interviewing representative population samples, Omnibus surveys are relied upon to explore both consumer opinion, and public opinion on social and political issues held by various population groups (see, for example, DEFRA 2010). Annex 1, below, provides further details on survey methodology for each of the national samples.

The first question was open-ended; it provided no prompts and asked respondents to describe what they thought human trafficking was. Having provided a response to the first question, all respondents were read out a prompt, which explained what human trafficking was. Respondents were asked to indicate their degree of agreement or disagreement with a series of statements on human trafficking using a five-point Likert scale (strongly agree, agree, disagree, strongly disagree, do not know). For ease of presentation and interpretation, agree and strongly agree responses were combined into a single 'agree' category, and disagree and strongly disagree responses were combined into a single 'disagree' category. The survey data were weighted using national-level weights supplied by survey providers. The original data sets are representative of national populations falling within three different age ranges: 15–59 in Ukraine; 18 and older in Hungary; and 16 and older in Great Britain. To enable a cross-national comparison between datasets, national samples were adjusted for age so that responses falling within the age range of 18–59 shared across the three samples could be compared. As a result, the final number of respondents for each sample decreased to 693 ($N = 693$) resulting in the increased margin of error of $\pm$ 3.72 at the standard 95 per cent confidence level. In the discussion of survey outcomes, references to the 'United Kingdom' are made when discussing legislation, policies and anti-trafficking activities enacted by the UK Government; references to 'Great Britain' are made when discussing survey results to reflect the fact that the survey sample covered England, Scotland and Wales and their associated islands, but did not include Northern Ireland.

Imagining human trafficking: the general public's views

For the majority of 'consumer-citizens' (White 1999: 57) in developed countries, human trafficking – understood within the context of the dominant policy, legal and media representations as a conflation of crime, illegality, immigration, victimhood, immorality and rescue – remains a phenomenon that, despite being a threat to their ontological sense of security ('It is closer than you think!', 'Criminals are targeting our borders!' governments tell them), remains ethereal – something that the majority will never come face-to-face with or experience directly in their everyday life. The very same majority is also unlikely to be direct targets of recent anti-trafficking policies apart from state-sponsored awareness campaigns and specific media reporting of trafficking designed to embed a specific understanding of trafficking into the public imagination based on a biopolitical distinction between (desirous) 'right' and (dangerous/threatening) 'bad' populations, between those deserving rescue and those requiring surveillance, segregation and disciplining. It is therefore important to assess the extent to which these specific policy and media interpretations of trafficking permeate and define how people think and feel about, and, ultimately, imagine human trafficking.

The first survey question sought to explore unprompted 'off the top of one's head' thoughts and ideas of what human trafficking was. The format of the survey did not allow for any in-depth discussion or guiding questions to be used; the analysis below provides an overview of what respondents associated human trafficking with and is based on full samples for each of the case study countries.

In Ukraine, public opinion can be described as a patchwork of different associations rather than a monolithic and easily identifiable public understanding of what human trafficking is. The most commonly reported associations included: slavery (26 per cent); buying and selling of people (23 per cent); unfree labour (21 per cent); abuse, violence, coercion and dependency (15 per cent); crime and illegality (15 per cent); and sexual exploitation and prostitution (15 per cent). In addition, the survey recorded a relatively high level of association with organ harvesting (9 per cent). Such distribution of opinions may reflect a complex anti-trafficking landscape in Ukraine influenced by a number of factors. First, a visible presence of national and international organisations undertaking anti-trafficking work in Ukraine and advocating their own vision of what human trafficking is and how it can be eradicated. In addition, the ongoing institutionalisation of the government anti-trafficking machinery at both regional and central levels has been guided by specific policy representations of trafficking informed by socioeconomic and political developments in Ukraine (see Sharapov 2014). Secondly, the impact of significant anti-trafficking funding distributed by the US Government in Ukraine (see Sharapov 2014: 10); and, thirdly, the sensationalised reporting of human trafficking by the Ukrainian news media, which reduces it to individualised stories of labour and sex 'slaves', and of innocent people having their organs harvested by ominous 'Black Doctors'. These developments have been taking place within the context of the deepening economic and political crises in the country, including the ongoing labour market re-structuring and its complex pattern of both external and internal labour migration, and, recently, the presence of nearly a million internally displaced people (as of February 2015) (UNHCR 2015) as a result of the conflict in the east of the country.

Only 10 per cent of Ukrainian respondents (aged 15–59) were unable to explain in their own words what they understood human trafficking to be in comparison with 22 per cent in Hungary (aged 18 and older) and 18 per cent in Great Britain (aged 16 and older). The comparative data for these three samples ($N = 693$, age 18–59) are 9 per cent in Ukraine, 19 per cent in Hungary, and 17 per cent in Great Britain.

In Hungary, similarly to Ukraine, the general public expressed a patchwork of associations and views on what they thought human trafficking was, including buying and selling of people (31 per cent of respondents), unfree labour (18 per cent), abuse, violence, coercion and dependency (16 per cent), movement of people (15 per cent), and sexual exploitation and prostitution (12 per cent). About 22 per cent of respondents were unable to explain what they understood human trafficking to be. These outcomes should be considered within the context of a specific policy representation of human trafficking in Hungary as a problem affecting mostly women trafficked for sexual exploitation and requiring assistance and care, in parallel with the law enforcement response to curb organised criminality. This representation appears to have little relevance to the everyday routines of 'ordinary' citizens in Hungary.

In Great Britain, public understanding of human trafficking reflected specific policy and media representations of trafficking as a matter of immigration, crime, slavery, prostitution and sexual exploitation (Sharapov 2014). More than a third of respondents (34 per cent) associated human trafficking with the movement of people, but did not mention immigration explicitly. The second most commonly mentioned association was 'sexual exploitation and prostitution' (19 per cent), which may reflect the initial policy and media framing of human trafficking as a problem of women trafficked into the United Kingdom for sexual exploitation. The identification of trafficking as 'slavery' (17 per cent) follows the reordering of the dominant policy discourse by the UK Government towards an ahistorical and reductive representation of human trafficking as 'modern-day slavery' (Dottridge 2014) mirrored by the sensationalist and individualised reporting of slave-holders and victim-slaves by the UK media. In addition, crime and illegality (16 per cent), unfree labour (14 per cent) and exploitation generally (11 per cent) were also associated with trafficking by the general public in Great Britain. About 18 per cent of respondents were unable to provide a definition of human trafficking.

The last two survey questions offered respondents a series of statements in relation to human trafficking and asked them to indicate their degree of agreement or disagreement on a five-point scale. The following majority viewpoint of human trafficking was recorded on the basis of respondents' answers even though there were significant differences between the national data sets:

> Anyone, including men, women and children, can be trafficked; however, the majority of victims of trafficking are women trafficked for sexual exploitation. Most victims come from poor countries and most of them are irregular immigrants looking for work. Human trafficking is a problem in respondents' countries but, as a problem, it does not affect them directly. Respondents do not normally think if goods or services they purchase were produced with the involvement of forced labour. However, they are prepared to pay 10 per cent more to ensure that goods and services are produced without labour exploitation and to boycott companies that rely on exploited labour. The majority of respondents agree that organised criminals bear the main responsibility for human trafficking. Victims of trafficking need to be provided with assistance; victims who crossed international borders need to be deported after a short recovery period, or allowed to stay if they face danger back home. There is a need for tougher border controls to stop victims from crossing borders and tougher law enforcement to tackle criminals. All European countries should criminalise the purchase of sex, and countries of victims' origin should do more to increase standards of living as a way of preventing economic migration. Companies relying on trafficked labour need to be identified and prosecuted. Companies need to ensure that their workers are not exploited and paid a living wage even if this may result in higher consumer prices. More awareness-raising campaigns on human trafficking are required in the media, on the Internet, and at schools.

The outcomes of this survey, despite certain methodological and conceptual limitations, provide an answer to at least three broad questions: first, how many people are aware of human trafficking? What do people know about human trafficking, and what are their attitudes? Secondly, to what extent does the general public's understanding of human trafficking reflect the dominant media and policy representations of trafficking as a problem? And, thirdly, what is missing from the public understanding of trafficking as a problem? The answer to the last question is key in appraising the extent and the nature of power relationships involved in biopolitical policy and media productions of 'truth' about human trafficking.

As noted earlier in this chapter, such 'truths' continue to represent trafficking as a problem of crime, immigration and prostitution that can be eliminated only by identifying and prosecuting 'criminals', and rescuing and rehabilitating narrowly defined 'genuine' victims. The location of human trafficking as we learn about it from specific media and policy representations vis-à-vis neoliberal reliance on unfree labour, and vis-à-vis broader issues of social, economic and, increasingly, environmental (in)justice, does not, in most cases, enter policy, media, public or private discussions of human trafficking. Human trafficking, from this perspective, represents a domain where the intersections of power, knowledge and ignorance, on the one hand, and who is privileged and disadvantaged by such knowledge and ignorance, on the other hand, can be studied in an attempt to highlight the role of neoliberal governmentality and its economic and political power in the construction of what we come to accept as 'knowledge', and how we choose to act on such knowledge.

The recorded variation in the level of public knowledge of human trafficking in the three countries cannot be fully explained within the context of this particular study. However, the fact that almost one in five respondents in Hungary and Great Britain were unable to explain, in their own words, what human trafficking was in comparison with one in ten respondents in Ukraine is notable especially within the context of the media and policy brouhaha surrounding the issue of 'modern slavery' in the United Kingdom. The question also remains as to the extent to which respondents who were not familiar with the phenomenon of human trafficking could be vulnerable to becoming victims of trafficking themselves; or unable to identify a potential victim if, in their daily life, they come across someone trafficked and/or exploited; or unable to think of themselves not as consumers, making 'ethical' choices, but as citizens working to change broader policy and larger social institutions.

In responding to the second question on whether predominant public understanding reflects specific media and policy representations of human trafficking, the survey outcomes suggest that this may well be the case. The majority of respondents in the three countries understand trafficking as a crime involving, in most cases, sexually exploited women and children, irregular immigration, prostitution and abuse. The relationship between public opinion, government policies and mass media remains a contentious issue with no universally accepted or infallible quantitative and/or qualitative methodology available for such assessments. Nevertheless, survey outcomes suggest that media and policy representations of human trafficking exert significant influence on public understanding of the phenomena, problematised by the governments and the media as ethereal yet, in the words of the UK Home Office, 'closer than you think' (UK Government 2014b).

The outcomes of the survey highlight the conspicuous absence of human trafficking as an issue of concern from the daily lives of 'ordinary' consumer-citizens. It appears that the 'information deficit model', increasingly relied upon by anti-trafficking 'stakeholders' in calling for more awareness campaigns, may be irrelevant in a situation where the majority of respondents are aware of human trafficking, its exploitative contexts, declare their preparedness to act 'ethically', and are supportive of measures to hold businesses and corporations to account for unfree labour. At the same time, most respondents continue to think of and imagine human trafficking as a phenomenon of unabated crime, 'illegal' immigration and sexual abuse, and, therefore, as something that remains outside their everyday life and 'normal' reality. Drawing upon theoretical frameworks of socially organised denial (Norgaard 2011) and agnotology (Proctor and Schiebinger 2008), one of the suggestions that emerge from the outcomes of this study is that the general public's non-response to human trafficking should be understood as a biopolitical phenomenon of socially organised denial, shaped and produced within the context of neoliberal capitalism and its ideology of 'living well for less (at any price)'. Within this context, the importance of making and theorising a link between human trafficking, unfree labour, consumption and profit-driven neoliberal accumulation should not be underestimated, whilst the role of the public response to social issues, including social movements, behavioural changes and public pressure on governments and corporations should not be discounted in discussions of strategies to eradicate trafficking.

Conclusion

The study discussed in this chapter has been designed to explore public understanding of human trafficking in response to an implicit assumption that underlies most of the anti-trafficking prevention initiatives: 'if only people knew' what human trafficking or 'modern slavery' were, they would behave differently. The 'information deficit' approaches emphasise lack of information as a limiting factor in changing individual behaviour. 'If only potential victims knew', they would never have fallen victim to criminals. 'Victims' in such discussions are, in most cases, assumed to be naive and uninformed 'womenandchildren'[11] duped by cunning criminals, rather than people who exercise individual agency – even if severely constrained by conflicts, violence, environmental degradation, poverty – to move across or within national borders knowing that such decisions may result in heavy restrictions on their freedom (see O'Connell Davidson 2010, 2013). In policy and media discussions of human trafficking, recognising and responding to the continuums of labour, migration and agency is effectively cancelled out by simplistic yet powerful binaries of choice–coercion, naive–deceitful, innocent–evil, genuine–not genuine, freedom–slavery, victim–criminal, legal–illegal. These binaries remain reflective of the biopolitical mode of governing, which actively inserts and normalises the narratives of threat within the everyday life of consumer-citizens, disciplines the 'wrong people',[12] and constructs the 'illegal' and dangerous 'Other'.

In addition to the populations constituted as 'vulnerable' to human trafficking, the general public – approached as if made up of individual consumer-citizens – has become another target audience for awareness campaigns run by governments and NGOs. Recognise and report 'victims' and 'criminals'; make a donation to rescue 'victims'; consume 'ethically'; anti-trafficking 'experts' and celebrity 'expert-advocates' tell us, as they regurgitate time and time again the imagery of chained and luggage-tagged hands, crying children, and of beautiful women's wounded and dead bodies (Andrijasevic 2007).

The survey outcomes discussed in this chapter demonstrate that, despite an implicit assumption 'if only people know' built into the majority of such awareness campaigns, the majority of people are familiar with the concept of human trafficking and of the exploitative contexts in which it happens. With high levels of recognition of human trafficking as a national problem and of support towards more law enforcement, immigration control, disciplining of companies that rely on unfree labour, rehabilitation of victims and a declaration of preparedness to consume 'ethically', an overall picture of well-informed and ready-to-act populations emerges. However, equally high levels of failing to recognise human trafficking as a problem that affects the everyday life of consumer-citizens suggest that individual awareness of human trafficking co-exists with individual denial of involvement and responsibility. The biopolitics of human trafficking within the context of neoliberal accumulation and its reliance on unfree labour operates through technologies of containment, discipline and risk management. It relies on a range of biopolitical tools and neoliberal solutions to displace responsibility for social ills that can be directly attributed to the operation of neoliberal capitalism onto selected and 'Othered' individuals as it simultaneously engineers and embeds fear, ignorance and uncertainty into public imaginations of consumer-citizens. The 'accelerating individualization of responsibility' (Maniates 2002: 46) depoliticises human trafficking and exploitation, narrows our imagination and undermines our capacity to initiate and sustain structural interventions. The 'wholesale' production of ignorance around human trafficking at the level of populations appears to be paralleled by the social production of denial at the individual level. To ignore something, Norgaard (2011: 197) notes, is 'essentially to manage emotion. Thinking, feeling and talking are linked and socially structured; therefore ignoring is also a social process.' It appears that for the majority of respondents, awareness of human trafficking and its exploitative contexts does not result in a sense of reality in which exploitation of other people is visible in their everyday life – it happens to someone else in far-away places. Further research may be needed to explore how day-to-day norms of emotion, attention and conversation in our biopolitically governed realities stifle opportunities for challenging the way in which the politics and ethics of encounter with the 'Other' are channelled through and framed by the politics of fear, denial and consumption, and (re)-produced through cultural practices of everyday life. Further and immediate action is required to account for and confront the dynamics of modern capitalism which restructures time and space such that although every aspect of our daily life links us to the hardships and poverty of people in other parts of the world or in a factory or a farm nearby, we remain aware of these links, but fail to imagine the reality of our current situation and act upon it as citizen-consumers rather than consumer-citizens.

Annex 1. Survey methodological details for case study countries

	Ukraine	Hungary	Great Britain
Methodology and date	Omnibus face-to-face, PAPI (paper-and-pencil interviewing), January 2014.	Omnibus face-to-face, PAPI, December 2013.	Omnibus face-to-face, CAPI (computer-assisted personal interviewing), January 2014.
Sample size	1,000 representative of national population within the specified age range.	1,000 representative of national population within the specified age range.	1,000 representative of GB population within the specified age range.
Sampling	Multi-stage sample based on random probability approach with respondents selected by the random route technique with the 'last birthday' method employed at the end stage of selection.	Multi-stage sample selected with proportional stratification with final respondents selected by random walking sampling.	Multi-stage sample – 125–50 sample points per survey week at the first stage; addresses were then randomly selected from the Post Office Address file (PAF); residents were interviewed according to interlocking quotas on sex, working status and presence of children.
Age range	15–59	18 and older	16 and older
Coverage	Ukraine, national, six regions singled out on a geographic and economic basis.	Hungary, national, eight regions.	Great Britain, south of the Caledonian Canal.
Weighting	Quota and weight.	By gender, age group, type of settlement and educational level.	By gender, age group, social class and region.
Quality control	4 per cent of completed interviews controlled by face-to-face method and 6 per	Multiple techniques, including random visits by regional instructors (10 per cent), postal or by	10 per cent back-check.

Annex 1. (*cont.*)

	Ukraine	Hungary	Great Britain
Quality control (cont.)	cent by telephone (100 interviews).	telephone post-survey quality control when required.	
Company used	GfK Ukraine (www.gfk.ua).	TARKI (www.tarki.hu/en).	UK-based market-research company; name not released for contractual reasons.
Representation	Representative of the national population, age range 15–59, margin of error (95 per cent confidence level) ±3.1 percentage points.	Representative of the national population, age range 18+, margin of error (95 per cent confidence level) ±3.1 percentage points.	Representative of the national population, age range 16+, margin of error (95 per cent confidence level) ±3.1 percentage points.

Notes

1. Inverted commas are used to highlight the contested meaning of a term or concept without providing a discussion of their contested nature.
2. The concept of 'unfree labour' referred to throughout this chapter should be understood as theorised by Robert Miles (1987) and Tom Brass (1999), with the latter noting that 'unfree labour is not only compatible with relatively advanced productive forces but also fulfils the same role as technology in the class struggle: capital uses both to cheapen, to discipline or as substitutes for free wage labour' (1999: 9).
3. The concept of 'labour exploitation' referred to throughout this chapter should be understood as theorised by Skrivankova (2010) as a 'continuum of exploitation': from decent work to forced labour.
4. See, for example, Mike Dottridge's critical commentary on the use of the term 'modern slavery' (Dottridge 2014).
5. Attention should be drawn to the problematic nature of using the term 'anti-trafficking community', which implies unity within the context of a deeply divided movement.
6. For more details, see, for example, issue 3 of the *Anti-Trafficking Review*, which focuses on money trails in the anti-trafficking sector, available at: http://gaatw.org/ATR/AntiTraffickingReview_Issue3.2014.Following_the_Money.pdf.
7. Melanie White, for example, comments on how neoliberalism creates 'citizen-consumers': 'It extends political agency to producers, consum-

ers and entrepreneurs at the same time as it marginalises the poor, the working poor and the otherwise disenfranchised' (1999: 57).

8. A marketing campaign slogan by one of the largest supermarket chains in the United Kingdom, which promotes 'making the most of the good things in life . . . without paying the earth for it'.

9. Research presented in this chapter received funding from the People Programme (Marie Curie Actions) of the European Union's Seventh Framework Programme FP7/2007-2013 under REA grant agreement No. PIEF-GA-2011-298401. More information available at: http://cps. ceu.edu/research/trafficking-in-human-beings.

10. No data have been made available specific to the EU, other than 'developed economies and European Union'.

11. A term coined by Enloe (1990) referring to the infantilised collective subject 'womenandchildren' accustomed to being 'helped' by society or men.

12. A reference to 'the wrong people' is based on the language used by the UK Government in its 2011 Human Trafficking Strategy. In advocating the strengthening of the UK border as one of the primary means of combating human trafficking, the Strategy suggests that only 'the right people' should be 'allowed to come to the UK', making the UK border impenetrable for, one may assume, 'the wrong people' (see UK Government 2011).

References

Agustin, L. (2007), *Sex at the Margins: Migration, Labour Markets and the Rescue Industry*, London: Zed Books.

Andrijasevic, R. (2007), 'Beautiful dead bodies: gender, migration and representation in anti-trafficking campaigns', *Feminist Review*, 86: 24–44.

Ardau, C. (2004), 'The perverse politics of four-letter words: risk and pity in the securitisation of human trafficking', *Millennium – Journal of International Studies*, 33(2): 251–77.

Bauman, Z. (1998), *Globalization: The Human Consequences*, Cambridge: Polity Press.

Berman, J. (2010), 'Biopolitical management, economic calculation and "trafficked women"', *International Migration*, 48(4): 84–113.

Brass, T. (1999), *Towards a Comparative Political Economy of Unfree Labour: Case Studies and Debates*, London: Frank Cass.

Buckley, M. (2009), 'Public opinion in Russia on the politics of human trafficking', *Europe–Asia Studies*, 61(2): 213–48.

Department for Environment, Food and Rural Affairs (DEFRA) (2010), *Omnibus Survey on Public Attitudes and Behaviours towards the Environment: Data Tables 2010*, available at: http://www.defra.gov.uk/ evidence/statistics/environment/pubatt/download/omnibus-datatable.pdf, last accessed 10 October 2014.

Deva, S. (2013), *Regulating Corporate Human Rights Violations: Humanizing Business*, London: Routledge.

Dottridge, M. (2014), *Some Implications of Using the Term 'Modern Slavery'*, available at: https://thetraffickingresearchproject.word-press.com/2014/02/28/some-implications-of-using-the-term-modern-slavery, last accessed 18 February 2015.

Eisenstein, H. (2010), *Feminism Seduced: How Global Elites Use Women's Labor and Ideas to Exploit the World*, Boulder, CO: Paradigm Publishers.

Enloe, C. (1990), 'Womenandchildren: making feminist sense of the Persian Gulf crisis', *The Village Voice*, 25 September.

European Commission (2012), *The EU Strategy towards the Eradication of Trafficking in Human Beings 2012–2016*, Brussels: European Commission.

European Parliament (1989), Resolution on the Exploitation of Prostitution and the Traffic in Human Beings, Doc. A2-52/89, *Official Journal of the European Communities*, No. C120, pp. 352–5.

European Parliament (2011), Directive 2011/36/EU of the European Parliament and of the Council on Preventing and Combating Trafficking in Human Beings and Protecting its Victims, and Replacing Council Framework Decision 2002/629/JHA, *Official Journal of the European Union*, L 101/1-11, 15 April 2011.

Eurostat (2013), *Trafficking in Human Beings*, Eurostat Methodologies and Working Papers, Luxembourg: Publications Office of the European Union.

Eurostat (2014), *Trafficking in Human Beings*, Eurostat Statistical Working Papers, Luxembourg: Publications Office of the European Union.

FitzGerald, S. (2010), 'Biopolitics and the regulation of vulnerability: the case of the female trafficked migrant', *International Journal of Law in Context*, 6(3): 277–94.

FitzGerald, S. (2012), 'Vulnerability and sex trafficking in the United Kingdom', in S. FitzGerald (ed.), *Regulating the International Movement of Women: From Protection to Control*, New York: Routledge, pp. 154–74.

Foucault, M. (1979), 'On governmentality', *Ideology and Consciousness*, 6: 5–22.

Goodey, J. (2008), 'Human trafficking: sketchy data and policy responses', *Criminology and Criminal Justice*, 8(4): 421–42.

Haynes, D. F. (2014), 'The celebritization of human trafficking', *Annals of the American Academy of Political and Social Science*, 653(1): 25–45.

International Labour Office (ILO) (2012), *Global Estimate of Forced Labour*, available at: http://www.ilo.org/washington/areas/elimination-of-forced-labor/WCMS_182004/lang--en/index.htm, last accessed 18 February 2015.

International Labour Office (ILO) (2014), *Profits and Poverty: The Economics of Forced Labour*, available at: http://www.ilo.org/wcmsp5/groups/public/---ed_norm/---declaration/documents/publication/wcms_243391.pdf, last accessed 18 February 2015.

Kapur, R. (2005), 'Cross-border movements and the law: renegotiating the boundaries of difference', in K. Kempadoo (ed.), *Trafficking and Prostitution Reconsidered: New Perspectives on Migration, Sex, Work, and Human Rights*, Boulder, CO: Paradigm Publishers, pp. 25–41.

McRedmond, P. and G. Wylie (2010), 'Introduction: human trafficking in Europe', in G. Wylie and P. McRedmond (eds), *Human Trafficking in Europe: Character, Causes and Consequences*, Basingstoke: Palgrave Macmillan, pp. 1–16.

Maniates, M. (2002), 'Individualization: plant a tree, buy a bike, save the world?' in T. Princen, M. Maniates and K. Conca (eds), *Confronting Consumption*, Cambridge, MA: MIT Press, pp. 43–66.

Miles, R. (1987), *Capitalism and Unfree Labour: Anomaly or Necessity?* London: Tavistock Publications.

Nadesan, M. H. (2008), *Governmentality, Biopower, and Everyday Life*, New York and London: Routledge.

National Crime Agency (NCA) (2014), *Strategic Assessment: The Nature and Scale of Human Trafficking in 2013*, available at: http://www.nationalcrimeagency.gov.uk/publications/399-nca-strategic-assessment-the-nature-and-scale-of-human-trafficking-in-2013/file, last accessed 2 October 2014.

Norgaard, K. M. (2011), *Living in Denial: Climate Change, Emotions, and Everyday Life*, Cambridge, MA: MIT Press.

O'Brien, E., S. Hayes and B. Carpenter (2013), *The Politics of Sex Trafficking: A Moral Geography*, Basingstoke: Palgrave Macmillan.

O'Connell Davidson, J. (2010), 'New slavery, old binaries: human trafficking and the borders of "freedom"', *Global Networks: Journal of Transnational Affairs*, 10(2): 244–61.

O'Connell Davidson, J. (2013), 'Troubling freedom: migration, debt, and modern slavery', *Migration Studies*, 1(2): 176–95.

Page, B. I. (2002), 'The semi-sovereign public', in J. Manza, F. L. Cook and B. I. Page (eds), *Navigating Public Opinion: Polls, Policy and the Future of American Democracy*, New York: Oxford University Press, pp. 325–44.

Povinelli, E. A. (2011), *Economies of Abandonment: Social Belonging and Endurance in Late Liberalism*, Durham, NC: Duke University Press.

Proctor, R. N. and L. Schiebinger (eds) (2008), *Agnotology: The Making and Unmaking of Ignorance*, Palo Alto, CA: Stanford University Press.

Rajak, D. (2011), 'Theatres of virtue: collaboration, consensus, and the social life of corporate social responsibility', *Focaal – Journal of Global and Historical Anthropology*, 60: 9–20.

Sharapov, K. (2014), 'Giving us the "biggest bang for the buck" (or not): anti-trafficking government funding in Ukraine and the United Kingdom', *Anti-Trafficking Review*, 3: 16–40.

Skrivankova, C. (2010), *Between Decent Work and Forced Labour: Examining the Continuum of Exploitation*, York: Joseph Rowntree Foundation.

Small, J. L. (2012), 'Trafficking in truth: media, sexuality, and human rights evidence', *Feminist Studies*, 38(2): 415–43.

Steele, S. L. and T. Shores (2014), 'Real and unreal masculinities: the celebrity image in anti-trafficking campaigns', *Journal of Gender Studies*, doi: 10.1080/09589236.2014.959477.

Strauss, K. and J. Fudge (2013), 'Temporary work, agencies and unfree labour: insecurity in the new world of work', in J. Fudge and K. Strauss (eds), *Temporary Work, Agencies and Unfree Labour: Insecurity in the New World of Work*, London: Routledge, pp. 118–43.

Stromback, J. (2012), 'The media and their use of opinion polls: reflecting and shaping public opinion', in C. Holtz-Bacha and J. Stromback (eds), *Opinion Polls and the Media: Reflecting and Shaping Public Opinion*, Basingstoke: Palgrave Macmillan, pp. 1–24.

Taylor, H. (2002), 'The value of polls in promoting good government and democracy', in J. Manza, F. L. Cook and B. I. Page (eds), *Navigating Public Opinion: Polls, Policy and the Future of American Democracy*, New York: Oxford University Press, pp. 315–24.

Tyler, I. (2010), 'Designed to fail: a biopolitics of British citizenship', *Citizenship Studies*, 14(1): 61–74.

UK Government (2011), *Human Trafficking: The Government's Strategy*, London: The Stationery Office.

UK Government (2014a), *Promotional Material: Modern Slavery is Closer than You Think*, available at: https://www.gov.uk/government/publications/modern-slavery-closer-than-you-think, last accessed 18 February 2015.

UK Government (2014b), *Modern Slavery: How the UK is Leading the Fight*, available at: https://www.gov.uk/government/uploads/system/uploads/attachment_data/file/328096/Modern_slavery_booklet_v12_WEB__2_.pdf, last accessed 18 February 2015.

UNHCR (2015), 'Ukraine internal displacement nears 1 million as fighting escalates in Donetsk region', News Stories, 6 February 2015, available at: http://www.unhcr.org/54d4a2889.html, last accessed 18 February 2015.

United Nations (2000), Protocol to Prevent, Suppress and Punish Trafficking in Persons, Especially Women and Children, Supplementing the United Nations Convention against Transnational Organized Crime, General Assembly, New York, 15 November 2000.

Weisberg, H. F. (2008), 'The methodological strengths and weaknesses of survey research', in W. Donsbach and M. W. Traugott (eds), *The Sage Handbook of Public Opinion Research*, London: Sage, pp. 223–31.

White, M. (1999), 'Neo-liberalism and the rise of the citizen as consumer', in D. Broad and W. Antony (eds), *Citizens or Consumers? Social Policy in a Market Society*, Halifax, Canada: Fernwood Publishing, pp. 56–64.

3 The Application of International Legislation: Is the Federalisation of Anti-trafficking Legislation in Europe Working for Trafficking Victims?

Adam Weiss

Luminata was born and raised in Moldova. At the age of 25, she was living and working (entirely lawfully) at a restaurant in Italy. She began dating a frequent customer. After a few months, they got engaged. She met his family. He met hers. He travelled frequently to the United Kingdom for work and told her that he had a business in Glasgow: a restaurant that he wanted her to help him run. They flew to Scotland. Soon after arriving, Luminata became a prisoner in a brothel. After a few weeks of brutal grooming (by her 'fiancé' and others), she was forced to have sex with fifteen men a day. She escaped by assaulting one of the clients (injuring him quite badly), stealing his wallet and sneaking out late at night. She took a train to Aberdeen and lived in a hotel room, using the stolen money. She was caught shoplifting and eventually disclosed her story to the police.[1]

Luminata has many months of legal battles ahead of her. She may be prosecuted for assault and shoplifting. If her trafficker is investigated, and she is willing to cooperate, she will probably be the key witness in the case against him. She may seek compensation from her trafficker. She may seek asylum in the United Kingdom. She may need social support in Scotland, which will be linked to her residence status (or lack of residence status) and her asylum claim.

Luminata's situation places her at the centre of five geographically concentric legal orders: Scottish law, UK law, European Union (EU) law, Council of Europe law and United Nations (UN) law. All of these legal orders have introduced norms designed to protect her and punish her traffickers; some of these legal orders also pose obstacles to those goals.

Scottish criminal law (and perhaps also Italian criminal law) will apply to the investigation and prosecution of the trafficker (see, for example, the Criminal Justice (Scotland) Act 2002); it will also apply to the decision on whether to prosecute Luminata for assault.[2] EU asylum law,[3] as transposed into UK law, will, to some extent, determine whether Luminata can stay in the United Kingdom. The United Kingdom agreed to participate in the first round of EU asylum legislation (setting minimum standards in the EU for the qualification of asylum seekers as refugees, for reception conditions of asylum seekers and for asylum procedures), but has opted out of the second round of directives, which seek to introduce common standards. The government currently accept that they remain bound by the first set of directives (UK Government 2014). Luminata can also seek residence status under UK immigration law, although there is no specific residence category for trafficking victims. However, the Secretary of State for the Home Department (Home Secretary) can grant 'discretionary leave to remain'.[4] Because of a UK opt-out, Luminata cannot seek residence status under the EU directive on granting residence permits to trafficking victims, otherwise, as a result of UK immigration law, Luminata will be required to leave Britain; there is in fact an instrument of EU law designed to hasten her return to Italy to have her asylum claim considered there.[5] EU Directive 2011/36[6] ('the EU Directive') on combating human trafficking nonetheless ensures that she will get a certain level of social protection as long as she stays, and also sets out certain requirements for the investigation and prosecution of her trafficker (including prohibiting making the investigation dependent on Luminata's report or accusation, Article 9). Article 4 of the European Convention on Human Rights (a Council of Europe[7] instrument), as interpreted by the European Court of Human Rights,[8] requires the authorities to protect Luminata from being trafficked again and to carry out an effective investigation into the trafficking; indeed, depending on the circumstances, the authorities in Italy and/or Scotland may have already violated Article 4 by not taking the necessary steps to prevent Luminata from being trafficked in the first place.[9] There is another, even more specific anti-trafficking instrument at Council of Europe level; the United Kingdom has ratified (but not explicitly incorporated into domestic law) the Council of Europe Convention on Action Against Trafficking in Human Beings ('the Council of Europe Convention') a comprehensive framework for the prevention of trafficking, the protection of victims and potential victims, and the investigation and prosecution of traffickers. There has been no specific Act of Parliament designed to incorporate the Council of Europe Convention into national law (Council of Europe Group of Experts on Action against Trafficking in Human Beings 2012: 23).

As a matter of UK law, if the Convention has not been incorporated, it remains an 'unincorporated treaty', meaning in general that it cannot be directly relied on in Scottish courts.[10] There is considerable overlap between the Council of Europe Convention and the EU Directive; for example, both have provisions on the non-prosecution of trafficking victims. The EU Member States negotiated a disconnection clause into the Council of Europe Convention to deal with any problems that might result from these overlaps. Article 40(3) states: 'Parties which are members of the European Union shall, in their mutual relations, apply Community and European Union rules insofar as there are Community or European Union rules governing the particular subject concerned and applicable to the specific case, without prejudice to the object and purpose of the present Convention and without prejudice to its full application with other Parties.' Luminata's legal representatives may also seek to rely on the United Nations Protocol to Prevent, Suppress and Punish Trafficking in Persons, Especially Women and Children, supplementing the United Nations Convention Against Transnational Organized Crime ('the UN Protocol').[11] The UN Protocol has its own provision on social support, for example Article 6(3).

The legal provisions affecting the situation of a victim of human trafficking in Scotland (and anywhere in Europe) are a case study in federalism, understood here as the division of power between central and local governing authorities (Kreimer 2001). The purpose of this chapter is to examine how these concentric legal orders with their overlapping provisions affect victims of trafficking. This chapter's point of departure is a victim-centred approach; the question is whether the federalisation of anti-trafficking law is working to support and protect victims of trafficking.

The first part of this chapter examines how the layers of law described above interact for trafficking victims in a concrete case. This part examines Luminata's situation in the light of what are the two most serious legal issues she will probably face: her prosecution for offences linked to the trafficking; and her residence status. This part also briefly touches on other legal issues that trafficking victims face. The second part of this chapter pulls back to consider whether and how federalism is working for or against trafficking victims in Europe in the light of these examples. It finds that higher level instruments fail when national and local actors put their institutional priorities before the needs of trafficking victims, and work best when they enable national and local institutions to understand that they play a key, albeit partial, role in combating human trafficking. The third part of this chapter recommends that those who want to see the higher level instruments implemented properly analyse the dilemmas national and local institutions face and introduce incentives that enable those institutions to grasp their key role in combating trafficking.

The chapter's perspective is British. Many of the observations (about criminal law and immigration law in particular) will be particular to the UK (and in particular the Scottish) context. However, the recommendations are designed to draw from this context to be applicable at European level.

Luminata's situation

Prosecution

Trafficking victims such as Luminata sometimes commit crimes as part of their trafficking. In Luminata's case, she risks being accused of the common law offence of assault (putting aside her shoplifting). Although the UN Protocol is silent about the prosecution of trafficking victims, the matter is dealt with in Council of Europe law and European Union law:

> Council of Europe Convention, Article 26:
> Each Party shall, in accordance with the basic principles of its legal system, provide for the possibility of not imposing penalties on victims for their involvement in unlawful activities, to the extent that they have been compelled to do so.

> EU Directive, Article 8:
> Member States shall, in accordance with the basic principles of their legal systems, take the necessary measures to ensure that competent national authorities are entitled not to prosecute or impose penalties on victims of trafficking in human beings for their involvement in criminal activities which they have been compelled to commit as a direct consequence of being subjected to [human trafficking].

Reading these provisions side by side raises various questions of interpretation. The Council of Europe Convention only (explicitly) addresses the question of 'imposing penalties', while the EU Directive requires *either* the possibility of non-prosecution *or* the possibility of not imposing penalties. One reading, then, is that the Council of Europe Convention makes it mandatory to allow judges (or juries) to impose no penalties on trafficking victims for crimes they were compelled to commit, whereas under EU law Member States have a choice between this option or giving prosecutors the discretion not to prosecute trafficking victims in the first place. The explanatory report to the Council of Europe Convention, normally verbose, provides little guidance on the interpretation of this provision:

> Article 26 constitutes an obligation on Parties to adopt and/or implement legislative measures providing for the possibility of not imposing penalties on victims, on the grounds indicated in the same Article. In particular, the requirement that victims have been compelled to be involved in unlawful activities shall be understood as comprising, at a minimum, victims that have been subject to any of the illicit means referred to in Article 4, when such involvement results from compulsion. Each Party can comply with the obligation established in Article 26, by providing for a substantive criminal or procedural criminal law provision, or any other measure, allowing for the possibility of not punishing victims when the above-mentioned legal requirements are met, in accordance with the basic principles of every national legal system.

The relevant recital to the EU Directive, No. 14, provides some support for this disjunctive reading:

> Victims of trafficking in human beings should, in accordance with the basic principles of the legal systems of the relevant Member States, be protected from prosecution *or* punishment for criminal activities such as the use of false documents, or offences under legislation on prostitution or immigration, that they have been compelled to commit as a direct consequence of being subject to trafficking. The aim of such protection is to safeguard the human rights of victims, to avoid further victimisation and to encourage them to act as witnesses in criminal proceedings against the perpetrators. This safeguard should not exclude prosecution or punishment for offences that a person has voluntarily committed or participated in. (emphasis added)

If the mere existence of prosecutorial discretion (subject to whatever form of review exists in the national legal system) is enough to satisfy Article 8 of the EU Directive, Scotland is in compliance with the Directive (Leverick 2006). Is Scotland bound therefore by the further requirement in Article 26 to provide for the possibility of non-punishment? It is only a theoretical question for Luminata, as there is no mandatory minimum sentence for assault (Sentencing Commission for Scotland 2006, para. 4.2), but to answer it in practice would trigger a number of questions: is this a situation where the disconnection clause applies?,[12] does it matter, given that the Council of Europe Convention is, from a UK and Scottish law perspective, an unincorporated treaty? In any event, both provisions make reference to national law, signalling that states have considerable discretion in how they deal with this provision and, in the case of Article 8 of the EU Directive, reducing the oversight of the Court of Justice of the EU (CJEU).[13]

Both provisions also include a 'compelled to commit' standard. Luminata's case shows the difficulties in applying that standard: she was not compelled to assault the 'client', assuming she could be expected to stay in the brothel or find another means of escape. Does she have to prove that her mental state, after months of abuse, left her subjectively believing there was no other choice? The Scottish courts recognise a defence of necessity, even if it is unlikely to be of assistance to Luminata;[14] is that enough to satisfy Council of Europe and EU law?

Scotland recently had the Human Trafficking and Exploitation (Scotland) Act going through the parliamentary process (Scottish Parliament 2014), with provision for the Lord Advocate to publish instructions around the prosecution of victims. The Procurator Fiscal's current guidance (Crown Office and Procurator Fiscal Service n.d.) on the prosecution of trafficking offences refers to Article 26 but not Article 8, even though there is a much stronger argument that Luminata can invoke the EU Directive (as opposed to the Council of Europe Convention) in the Scottish courts.[15] The guidance, predictably, gives effect to Article 26 by invoking the principle of prosecutorial discretion. It indicates that the Procurator Fiscal's policy is to apply a 'strong [rebuttable] presumption against the prosecution of a credible trafficked victim for crimes that arise as a consequence of the accused being a credible trafficking victim'. The guidance also sets out the Procurator Fiscal's responsibilities in relation to identifying victims.

The guidance relies heavily on one English case, that of *R* v. *O*,[16] where the Court of Appeal of England and Wales reversed the conviction of a trafficking victim for an identity document offence. The Court of Appeal based its judgment on the failure of the prosecution and the trial court to make proper enquiries into the accused's status as a trafficking victim. There has since been an even more noteworthy case south of the border from the Court of Appeal: that of *L and Others* v. *R*,[17] in which the Court of Appeal overturned the conviction of trafficking victims whose traffickers were making them grow cannabis; they had been successfully prosecuted for cannabis cultivation. The Court of Appeal had no difficulty relying on Article 26 (which it seemed to believe applied to prosecutions, and not merely punishments) and Article 8, via English law principles. While there is no specific defence available to trafficking victims, the Court of Appeal found, and although trafficking victims do not enjoy a blanket ban on prosecution:

when there is evidence that victims of trafficking have been involved in criminal activities, the investigation and the decision whether there should be a prosecution, and, if so, any subsequent proceedings require to be approached with the greatest sensitivity . . . The criminality, or putting it another way, the culpability, of any victim of trafficking may be significantly diminished, and in some cases effectively extinguished, not merely because of age (always a relevant factor in the case of a child defendant) but because no realistic alternative was available to the exploited victim but to comply with the dominant force of another individual, or group of individuals . . . What . . . is required in the context of the prosecutorial decision to proceed is a level of protection from prosecution or punishment for trafficked victims who have been compelled to commit criminal offences. These arrangements should follow the 'basic principles' of our legal system. In this jurisdiction that protection is provided by the exercise of the 'abuse of process' jurisdiction.[18]

The position in English law has been summed up in the *obiter dicta* of a minority opinion in a judgment of the Supreme Court of the United Kingdom: 'The trafficked victim, assuming that is what she is, is not relieved of criminal liability for an offence which she has committed. If, however, she was compelled to commit it as a direct consequence of being trafficked, careful consideration ought to be given to whether it is in the public interest to prosecute her.'[19] A Scottish court would naturally give careful consideration to the English position.

How does this affect Luminata? Overall, the effect appears to be positive. If prosecuted and forced to rely solely on the common law defence of necessity, Luminata would probably not fare well: while her options for escaping were limited, a Scottish court would probably find that she had 'an alternative course of action which was lawful'.[20] Luminata's offence was nonetheless, in the words of the Procurator Fiscal's guidance, 'a consequence of the accused being a credible trafficking victim'; thanks to this interpretation of Article 26, there is therefore a presumption against prosecuting her. Even if the prosecution does go ahead, there are some limits, already recognised by the English courts and enforceable through the abuse-of-process doctrine, on her prosecution. In such proceedings, she could even seek to obtain a reference to the CJEU about the correct application of Article 8. Things will be even brighter for victims like Luminata in the future: following the English case law, which itself was highly influenced by European law, legislation recently enacted in the Westminster Parliament introduced a statutory defence for trafficking victims coerced or forced to commit crimes in England and Wales (House of Commons 2015). Scotland's Act, as introduced, does not contain provision for a statutory defence.

There is still considerable uncertainty for Luminata. Unlike in *L and Others* v. *R*, the conduct of which Luminata is accused – assault – was not the purpose of trafficking her, perhaps making it harder to show that she was 'compelled' (although her case does bear some similarities to *R* v. *O*). In any event, until the introduction of a statutory defence, her situation remains subject to the discretion of prosecutors. Even after a statutory defence is introduced for trafficking victims, it is unclear whether someone in her position can claim to have been coerced or forced to commit the offence she committed. As the English courts have ruled, there is no blanket defence for trafficking victims. Given that criminal law remains essentially a matter for individual states in the EU and Council of Europe systems, this is perhaps the most that victims like Luminata can expect from European law.

Residence status

The problem of trafficking victims without residence rights in the destination country features in anti-trafficking law at UN, Council of Europe and European Union levels:

> The Palermo Protocol, Article 7:
> 1. In addition to taking measures pursuant to Article 6 of this Protocol, each State Party shall consider adopting legislative or other appropriate measures that permit victims of trafficking in persons to remain in its territory, temporarily or permanently, in appropriate cases. 2. In implementing the provision contained in paragraph 1 of this Article, each State Party shall give appropriate consideration to humanitarian and compassionate factors.

> Council of Europe Convention, Article 14:
> 1. Each Party shall issue a renewable residence permit to victims, in one or other of the two following situations or in both: (a) the competent authority considers that their stay is necessary owing to their personal situation; (b) the competent authority considers that their stay is necessary for the purpose of their cooperation with the competent authorities in investigation or criminal proceedings.[21]

Article 13 of the Council of Europe Convention also ensures that victims enjoy a thirty-day recovery and reflection period during which no immigration action can be taken against them. Although the EU Directive does not deal with residence permits, an earlier directive, Directive 2004/81,[22] sets out the conditions for granting residence permits to trafficking victims:

1. After the expiry of the reflection period, or earlier if the competent authorities are of the view that the third-country national concerned has already fulfilled the criterion set out in subparagraph (b), Member States shall consider: (a) the opportunity presented by prolonging his/her stay on its territory for the investigations or the judicial proceedings, and (b) whether he/she has shown a clear intention to cooperate and (c) whether he/she has severed all relations with those suspected of acts that might be included among the offences referred to in Article 2(b) and (c).

2. For the issue of the residence permit and without prejudice to the reasons relating to public policy and to the protection of national security, the fulfilment of the conditions referred to in paragraph 1 shall be required.

3. Without prejudice to the provisions on withdrawal referred to in Article 14, the residence permit shall be valid for at least six months. It shall be renewed if the conditions set out in paragraph 2 of this Article continue to be satisfied.

As in the case of criminal prosecution, these provisions interfere with the state's ability to take action against a trafficking victim pursuant to its own legislation. The language becomes more specific and binding as it moves from the international level towards the national level.

Unfortunately for Luminata, however, EU Directive 2004/81 is not applicable in Scotland: the United Kingdom opted out from this immigration measure.[23] Even if the United Kingdom had participated in Directive 2004/81, there is still the risk it would not apply to Luminata if it turned out that she was an EU citizen, for example, if she also had Romanian or Italian nationality. She would then have to rely on EU law on the free movement of persons to assert residence rights in Scotland.

Although no legislation has been enacted in the United Kingdom to give effect to Article 14 of the Council of Europe Convention, there is a policy for providing residence permits to recognised victims of trafficking in line with that provision.[24] The UK policy even goes beyond the text of Article 14, recognising that it may be appropriate to grant leave to trafficking victims so that they can make compensation claims. Unfortunately for Luminata, in the United Kingdom, immigration (unlike crime) is not a devolved matter. As a result, those public authorities who are best placed to assess whether she meets the conditions under Article 14 (the local social workers, healthcare workers and others who are in contact with her, for Article 14(1)(a), or the police, for Article 14(1)(b)) operate at a different level of government (Scotland) than those making the decision about whether to grant her discretionary leave to remain (United Kingdom).

This is not just a problem in Scotland. The United Kingdom has been criticised for assigning responsibility to the immigration service for deciding whether people like Luminata (that is, trafficking victims without residence status) meet the definition to be considered victims of human trafficking (Anti-Trafficking Monitoring Group 2013). Since immigration control is the main task of the institution making the decision, there is a potential conflict of interest.

This conflict of interest is often heightened when trafficking victims claim asylum, a possibility for Luminata given that the first country-guidance case in the UK immigration tribunals about trafficking victims claiming asylum recognised that trafficking victims from Moldova were a 'particular social group'.[25] Article 14 of the Council of Europe Convention explicitly states that it is without prejudice to the right to claim asylum.[26] Asylum (or, rather, international protection) is governed by its own concentric circles of law, including, but not limited to, the UN Refugee Convention, the applicable case law of the European Court of Human Rights, the EU's asylum *acquis*,[27] and national law. Without going into the details of how that body of law applies to trafficking victims (UNHCR 2006), it is enough to note that it has developed outside the influence of the anti-trafficking law that is the subject of this chapter. In the absence of a residence permit, Luminata's asylum claim and what it is meant to prevent – her forced expulsion to Moldova – can overshadow everything else in her case, disrupting her collaboration with the authorities (notably the Scottish police) and her recovery. European Union law also includes a mechanism that could make things much more difficult for Luminata: the Dublin Regulation (regulation 604/2013), the single piece of the second-generation EU asylum *acquis* in which the United Kingdom has agreed to participate. Italy is likely the EU Member State responsible under that regulation for determining Luminata's asylum claim, given that she has had a residence permit there (see Article 12). The regulation sets out procedures for returning Luminata there and requires Italy to take her back. The United Kingdom is not required to send Luminata to Italy (see Article 17), and the case law[28] is now clear that returns under the Dublin system are not permitted if they violate human rights. However, the temptation of a speedy Dublin transfer will heighten the conflict of interest on the part of the immigration official responsible for deciding whether Luminata meets the definition of a trafficking victim.

To some extent, the effect of international and European law in this area is positive: the Council of Europe Convention forces the national authorities to decide how to adjust their immigration enforcement systems to cope with the needs of victims of trafficking. The introduction of trafficking considerations into the UK's discretionary leave policy is clearly a positive result of the UK's ratification of the Council of Europe Convention. The situation for Luminata nonetheless seems more menacing than it does in relation to prosecution. When it comes to Luminata's prosecution, the authorities (police, prosecutors, criminal courts) have a complex relationship with her: she is potentially both a criminal and a victim of crime. They can justify a decision not to prosecute in the light of their responsibility towards her as a victim and in the light of their duty, and priority, to dedicate resources to pursuing the traffickers. In the case of immigration laws, those responsible have a much simpler relationship with Luminata: for them she is a third-country national with no claim to stay in Britain unless she can demonstrate a need for protection. Were Directive 2004/81 in force in the United Kingdom, there might be a more formal role for the Scottish police in making the decision about her immigration status; the UK authorities would be obliged to consider the 'opportunity' for prolonging stay for the purposes of judicial proceedings. As it is, the decision is in the hands of officials for whom her continued presence in the United Kingdom (and not her trafficking) is little more than a problem to be solved.

Other issues

Other legal issues trafficking victims face involve similar cascading and colliding provisions of international, European and domestic law. These various layers of law all have various things to say; for example, about compensation for trafficking victims: the UN Protocol (Article 6(6)), the Council of Europe Convention (Article 15 (3)–(4)), and the EU Directive (Article 17) have provisions requiring states to provide access to compensation for victims. They are all worded slightly differently and so are open to different interpretations if Luminata is refused compensation. This is a real possibility; Luminata should be able to secure compensation in Scotland under UK-wide legislation for victims of violent crime via the Criminal Injuries Compensation Act 1995, but will be refused if she is convicted of assault (Ministry of Justice 2012, annex D). The EU Directive states that 'Member States shall ensure that victims of trafficking in human beings have access to existing schemes of compensation to victims of violent crimes of intent.' Does that mean that the UK authorities must allow Luminata to receive compensation even though her conviction would block a payment under domestic law?

Social assistance is also a fraught issue. Again, it is dealt with in the UN Protocol (Article 6(3)), the Council of Europe Convention (Article 12) and the EU Directive (Article 11), all in slightly different language. For example, the Council of Europe Convention requires assistance to any victims on the territory of the state, whereas the EU Directive connects assistance to the existence of criminal proceedings against the traffickers.[29] In the United Kingdom, beyond the recovery-and-reflection period, access to social support is administered through the ordinary welfare system. If their residence status is not resolved in a way that ensures access to social assistance, those who are not asylum seekers and do not have a 'right to reside'[30] in the United Kingdom (including many EU citizens) face destitution after the recovery-and-reflection period ends. They will nonetheless remain eligible for free treatment from the National Health Service, thanks to explicit amendments to the charging regulations.[31]

Federalisation of anti-trafficking law in Europe

There is a theory (largely developed in the United States) that federalism is conducive to individual freedom and respect for fundamental rights (Kreimer 2001). It is not a theory that applies well to trafficking victims, because it depends on principles such as freedom of movement between devolved territorial units with their own norm-producing capabilities. The discussions above nonetheless suggest some ways though in which the federalisation of anti-trafficking law in Europe may be helpful to victims of trafficking. There are two, related, aspects of the concentric legal protections for trafficking victims that are striking:

- They have been introduced from the top down. The first comprehensive legal instrument on trafficking victims came from the UN in 2000. The Council of Europe Convention followed in 2005. Although there was an earlier EU Framework Decision on human trafficking,[32] it lacked the comprehensive character of the other instruments, such as provisions on victim protection where Article 7 covered protection and assistance in brief terms, dealing mainly with children and ensuring that prosecution was not dependent on the victim's accusation or report; it was not until 2011 that the EU introduced its directive. The United Kingdom is now a pioneer in Europe, introducing comprehensive legislation at national level to address human trafficking (House of Commons 2014). (This top-down history makes the laboratory-of-democracy theory[33] of how federalism enhances individual rights inapplicable: higher legislation was not the result of democratic experimentation at the lower levels.)
- The higher level legal orders are more likely to introduce wide-ranging instruments whose aim is to tackle human trafficking

comprehensively in a single text. This is necessarily related to the first observation: until the United Kingdom introduces its comprehensive anti-trafficking legislation, protection will necessarily be spread across multiple areas of domestic law. However, even after that legislation is introduced, lawyers acting for trafficking victims in Britain will still have to look across an array of legislation, mostly criminal and immigration statutes, when looking after the interests of trafficking victims, because the effect of the proposed legislation is to amend various other pieces of primary legislation. The step down from Council of Europe to EU level is particularly interesting. Although the EU Directive contains provisions equivalent to most of those in the Council of Europe Convention, Article 14 of the Council of Europe Convention (on residence permits) finds its equivalent in a separate instrument: EU law in Directive 2004/81. There is a good lawyer's answer to the question of why the EU Directive is comprehensive: competence in the area of criminal law (the subject of the EU Directive) is derived from Chapter 3 of Title V of the Treaty on the Functioning of the European Union, whereas competence in immigration matters (the subject of Directive 2004/81) is derived from Chapter 2 of Title V. Directive 2004/81 could nonetheless have been repealed and folded into Directive 2011/36. The failure to do so suggests an unwillingness to uncouple residence status from 'the opportunity presented by prolonging [the victim's] stay on its territory for the investigations or the judicial proceedings' (Directive 2004/81, Article 8) and instead connect it to the 'integrated, holistic, and human rights approach to the fight against trafficking in human beings'.[34] As a result, Article 14(1)(a) of the Council of Europe Convention (on providing residence permits to trafficking victims when it is 'necessary owing to their personal situation') still has no counterpart in EU law. Likewise, the House of Commons Library notes that the Modern Slavery Bill has failed to deal with the problem of domestic-worker visas, an immigration issue closely connected to the protection of trafficking victims.

These two related trends show how taking a victim-centred approach to the legal issues involved in human trafficking is easier at higher levels of (federalist) abstraction. At the higher levels of European and international federalism, there is a clearly defined specialised body of anti-trafficking law. As it arrives closer to the national and local levels, that specialised body of law fragments, embedding itself into, but also being overtaken by, national law (notably criminal law, immigration law and social welfare law). The benefit of the federalisation of anti-trafficking law in Europe is that the higher levels provide a space where all (or more) of the problems that affect victims of trafficking can be considered together; these higher levels are undisturbed by the practical reality that trafficking touches on so many spheres of life and law, involving a wide range of state actors, none or only a few of whom will prioritise a victim's situation and status as a trafficking victim. Indeed, the primacy of patient care to health officials perhaps explains why free-of-charge healthcare, but no other social security or social assistance benefits, has been extended to all trafficking victims in the United Kingdom, regardless of their residence status. When it comes to welfare benefits, other concerns seem to overshadow worries about the impact of entitlement restrictions on trafficking victims.

The disadvantage of this federalised approach is that lower level entities will resist incorporating comprehensive higher level instruments into their law in a uniform way. This is what happened to some extent at the EU level: the residence rights of trafficking victims are dealt with outside the EU Directive and, arguably, inadequately, in the light of Article 14(1)(a) of the Council of Europe Convention.[35] This has happened to a much greater extent in the United Kingdom and other European states, which lack comprehensive anti-trafficking legislation and state institutions dedicated to dealing with all aspects of human trafficking.

Many fundamental rights instruments agreed at European and international levels that target one specific matter other than human trafficking (for example, data protection[36]) are susceptible to implementation through a single, concentrated legal act at national level and overseen by a single authority. Like human rights law generally, the higher level legal instruments that deal with human trafficking act instead like a UV lamp passing over a collection of objects and trying to illuminate them; some luminesce while others stubbornly remain dark. The earlier discussion of Luminata's situation in particular and of the interaction of the various legal orders dealing with the rights of victims of trafficking in general, suggests what causes some officials and institutions to light up while others remain inert.

Because of the nature of human trafficking – touching mainly on crime, immigration and welfare – and the absence of a coordinating state institution, the protection needs of trafficking victims frequently create a dilemma for state institutions, which are likely to prioritise other obligations unrelated to human trafficking. In Luminata's case, those other priorities include punishing people who commit assault and maintaining an effective system of immigration control.

The higher level, more comprehensive trafficking instruments succeed in ensuring protection for victims when they enable those conflicted state institutions to understand the key role they play in fighting human trafficking by protecting its victims and, in that way, see fighting human trafficking as a priority above other concerns.

In the criminal sphere, in the United Kingdom, this has worked[37]: prosecutors in Scotland otherwise determined to secure convictions have set out a presumption against the prosecution of trafficking victims. The Scottish guidance goes beyond the compelled-to-commit standard in the Council of Europe Convention and the EU Directive to cover offences 'that arise as a consequence of the accused being a credible trafficking victim', demonstrating a clear commitment to victim protection. The English courts, exercising their criminal jurisdiction, have recognised that the trafficking situation can 'extinguish' culpability (even in a case involving drugs)[38] despite the absence of necessity or duress as those terms are normally understood in English criminal law. Article 26 of the Council of Europe Convention and Article 8 of the EU Directive worked here because they enabled prosecutors and criminal courts in the United Kingdom to see how by stopping prosecution, they play a key role in fighting human trafficking.

The Procurator Fiscal and the English criminal courts fluoresced under the glow of these instruments because it is easy for them to see how refraining from prosecution serves their institutional purposes as well: the accused become victims and witnesses in much larger anti-trafficking cases or, at least, they are less likely to be re-trafficked, reducing future crime. The same will probably be true for those officials responsible for criminal injuries compensation: by ensuring victims such as Luminata receive compensation, they encourage victims to come forward and (depending on the source of the funds) may create financial incentives for traffickers to stop. Unsurprisingly, the UK authority has distributed a brochure specifically encouraging victims of trafficking to come forward (Criminal Injuries Compensation Authority n.d.).

In the areas of immigration and welfare in the United Kingdom, though, the glow of higher level comprehensive instruments is less stimulating. If the theory set out above is correct, it is because these instruments do not enable these institutions to prioritise fighting trafficking by understanding their key role in combating it. There is a growing recognition in the courts that immigration authorities play such a role. According to the European Court of Human Rights, 'a State's immigration rules must address relevant concerns relating to encouragement, facilitation or tolerance of trafficking'.[39] Lord Justice Sedley of the Court of Appeal of England and Wales, deciding in 2007 to grant permission to a trafficking victim to appeal against her refusal of asylum, remarked as follows:

This woman was brought to this country by a criminal who should not have been allowed in, and was compelled by force to provide sexual services to men living here. Her reward, now that she has finally escaped, is to be returned to a country where she will certainly be without social or familial support, will be expected to move to a strange region and try to find work there and might still be at risk from the same predator. Some might think she is owed better than this.[40]

In the United Kingdom and in the EU institutions (which declined to fold Directive 2004/81 into Directive 2011/36 or to ensure trafficking victims would not get caught up in the Dublin III Regulation), the higher level, comprehensive instruments have not enabled immigration authorities to recognise their role in combating trafficking by respecting victims' rights. Article 6(3)(c) of the Dublin III Regulation (regulation 604/2013) requires states to take into account the risk that a child has been trafficked when dealing with the best interests of children in Dublin proceedings, but the consequences of this consideration are not spelled out, and the regulation is silent about trafficked adults. The situation may be different in countries where the police are responsible for immigration control and decisions concerning residence permits; Directive 2004/81 and Article 14(1)(b) of the Council of Europe Convention are properly aimed at them, but not at immigration officials in the United Kingdom. Article 14(1)(a) of the Council of Europe Convention currently requires immigration officials to grant residence permits when they consider it 'is necessary owing to [the victims'] personal situation'. This vague language does little to ensure that the immigration official resolves the dilemma between protecting the trafficking victim and enforcing immigration laws against him or her in the victim's favour. It encourages immigration officials to see victim protection as a question of individual benevolence, instead of a crucial element of fighting human trafficking. The provision would be more effective if it required permits to be granted when 'there is a real risk that victims would otherwise be re-trafficked', and where it 'is necessary to ensure victims can exercise the other rights in this Convention'. Indeed, the UK immigration authorities are starting to show signs of understanding this latter role: as mentioned above, the UK authorities will now consider granting trafficking victims discretionary leave to remain in order to pursue compensation claims, even though the European and international anti-trafficking instruments do not explicitly mention the issue.

Recommendations

What can be done within a framework that has come, in federalist terms, from the top down, where legal orders have introduced potentially confusing variations on similar themes, and where the specialised body of law devoted to combating human trafficking gives way to the priorities of national law the closer we get to the ground?

Attention on the rights of victims is most concentrated at the higher levels. Protection failures that happen at national and local levels occur because of the lack of national legislation and state institutions for which human trafficking is an overriding priority. The higher level instruments therefore create dilemmas for state institutions and officials between their ordinary priorities and victims' rights; those dilemmas are often resolved against the victim. Anyone interested in seeing the promise of the higher level instruments fulfilled (UN, Council of Europe and European Union anti-trafficking officials, as well as NGOs and lawyers), should identify the state officials for whom these instruments pose dilemmas and examine how those dilemmas are being resolved. In the United Kingdom, for instance, those interested in the implementation of Article 26 of the Council of Europe Convention or Article 8 of the EU Directive should look at prosecutors and criminal courts. They would have reason to be encouraged by the developments in the English courts as well as the UK's prosecution services: those institutions are resolving the dilemma between prosecuting offences trafficking victims may have committed and supporting victim recovery in favour of the latter. They would likely be more dismayed at the way UK immigration officials are resolving the dilemma between victim protection and immigration control. The same would be true if they saw the way those responsible for legislating and administering welfare provision deal with trafficking victims in Britain who have neither claimed asylum nor have any other basis for exercising residence rights. They should then think about what incentives they can give those officials to see their work in protecting victims as part of the broader fight against human trafficking. If the instruments themselves cannot be changed, international and European officials can nonetheless guide their interpretation; for example, Council of Europe officials might insist that Article 14(1)(a) of the Council of Europe Convention should be interpreted as covering circumstances where victims will not be able to exercise their other rights in the Convention without a residence permit.

Elsewhere in Europe, different dilemmas will arise and the same dilemmas will inevitably be resolved differently. Whatever they observe happening at national and local levels, those who are seeking implementation of the higher level legal instruments should formulate arguments that force the state officials facing these dilemmas to recognise the seriousness of human trafficking and to understand how respecting victims' rights enables them to combat trafficking. In the absence of comprehensive national legislation and centralised national institutions dedicated to dealing with all aspects of trafficking, the instruments that exist above national level must be used to make national officials realise that they are a crucial part of a diffuse team working (or not) to combat a single evil.

The current setup will continue to engender these dilemmas between victims' rights and other priorities, resulting in disputes between trafficking victims and state officials. Lawyers and courts therefore have a significant role to play. The job of lawyers acting for trafficking victims is to make courts realise that the higher level instruments provide comprehensive guidance for resolving these dilemmas, and that recourse to these instruments is necessary because of the splintered approach at national level.

A final recommendation for those who want to see the higher level instruments implemented at national level is to work to complete the pattern. The EU almost has comprehensive legislation on trafficking; if Directive 2011/36 is ever recast, it should incorporate and build on the provisions of Directive 2004/81. At national level, comprehensive legislation designed with trafficking victims in mind will reduce the possibility of dilemmas between victims' rights and other demands arising, and concentrate responsibility for combating trafficking in fewer institutions giving trafficking victims higher priority.

Notes

1. This is a fictional story, inspired in large part by the events in the case of *L.R.* v. *United Kingdom* (Application No. 49113/09), which led to a friendly settlement in the European Court of Human Rights (Decision, 14 June 2011).
2. Assault is a common law offence in Scotland. See, for example, Lord Advocate's Reference No. 2 of 1992, 1993 SLT 460.
3. The EU asylum *acquis* consists of a suite of measures adopted pursuant to Article 78 of the Treaty on the Functioning of the European Union.
4. There is no specific residence category for trafficking victims. However, the Home Secretary can grant 'discretionary leave to remain'. The current policy on discretionary leave to remain as it relates to trafficking victims and others can be found at: https://www.gov.uk/government/uploads/system/uploads/attachment_data/file/312346/discretionaryleave.pdf, last accessed 10 October 2014.

5. See regulation (EU) 604/2003 of the European Parliament and of the Council, 26 June 2013, establishing the criteria and mechanisms for determining the Member State responsible for examining an application for international protection lodged in one of the Member States by a third-country national or a stateless person (recast) (the so-called 'Dublin III Regulation').

6. Directive (EU) 2011/36, 5 April 2011, on preventing and combating trafficking in human beings and protecting its victims, and replacing Council Framework Decision 2002/629/JHA.

7. The Council of Europe is a separate body from the European Union; the former has forty-seven member states, whereas the latter has twenty-eight.

8. *Rantsev* v. *Cyprus and Russia*, application No. 25065/04, judgment of the European Court of Human Rights (First Section), 10 May 2010, paras 283–9.

9. *Ibid.*, para. 284.

10. See, for example, *Graeme Donaldson* v. *Scottish Legal Aid Board* [2014] CSIH 31, para. 37 (refusing to order legal aid to be provided to take a case to the European Court of Human Rights, because 'to hold that the phrase "the application of Scots law" . . . extends to . . . unincorporated European treaty and convention provisions would be a major innovation in the proper approach to the construction of Scottish legislation which cannot, in our view, be justified').

11. Protocol to Prevent, Suppress and Punish Trafficking in Persons, Especially Women and Children, supplementing the United Nations Convention against Transnational Organized Crime, New York, 15 November 2000.

12. Presumably it is not, as this has nothing to do with the 'mutual relations' between EU Member States. Article 40(3) of the Council of Europe Convention states: 'Parties which are members of the European Union shall, in their mutual relations, apply Community and European Union rules insofar as there are Community or European Union rules governing the particular subject concerned and applicable to the specific case, without prejudice to the object and purpose of the present Convention and without prejudice to its full application with other Parties.'

13. Case C-571/10, *Kamberaj*, judgment of the Court of Justice of the European Union, 24 April 2012 (Grand Chamber), para. 77: 'when the European Union legislature has made an express reference to national law, as in Article 11(1)(d) of Directive 2003/109, it is not for the Court to give the terms concerned an autonomous and uniform definition under European Union law (see, to that effect, Case 327/82 *Ekro* [1984] ECR 107, para. 14). Such a reference means that the European Union legislature wished to respect the differences between the Member States concerning the meaning and exact scope of the concepts in question.'

14. See, for example, *Moss* v. *Howdle*, 1997 SCCR 215 ('if Mr Moss had

had an alternative course of action which was lawful, the defence could not apply').

15. EU Directives have 'direct effect' in the legal orders of the Member States (that is, they can be relied on directly in national courts) under certain conditions. See Case 26/62, judgment of the Court of Justice of the European Communities, 5 February 1963. The Council of Europe Convention, on the other hand, should be incorporated into law by the UK Parliament or the Scottish Parliament in order to be directly applicable in the Scottish courts. See above, n. 14.

16. [2008] EWCA Crim 2835.

17. [2013] EWCA Crim 991.

18. *L and Others*, para. 14.

19. *Hounga (Appellant)* v. *Allen and Another (Respondents)*, 2014 UKSC 47, para. 64.

20. See, e.g., *Moss* v. *Howdle*, 1997 SCCR 215: 'if Mr Moss had had an alternative course of action which was lawful, the defence could not apply'.

21. The intended binding nature of the provision is made clear further in the Article, through a caveat: '4. The non-renewal or withdrawal of a residence permit is subject to the conditions provided for by the internal law of the Party.'

22. Council Directive 2004/81/EC, 29 April 2004, on the residence permit issued to third-country nationals who are victims of trafficking in human beings or who have been the subject of an action to facilitate illegal immigration, who cooperate with the competent authorities.

23. The United Kingdom nearly also opted-out of Directive 2011/36, as it enjoys an opt-out from EU criminal legislation (Home Office 2011).

24. See above, n. 6.

25. SB (PSG, Protection Regulations, reg. 6), *Moldova CG* [2008] UKAIT 00002 (26 November 2007).

26. Article 14(5): 'Having regard to the obligations of Parties to which Article 40 of this Convention refers, each Party shall ensure that granting of a permit according to this provision shall be without prejudice to the right to seek and enjoy asylum.'

27. The United Kingdom opted-in to the first generation of that legislation, but has opted-out of most of the second generation (Costello and Hancox 2014).

28. *M.S.S.* v. *Belgium and Greece*, Application No. 30696/99, judgment of the Grand Chamber of the European Court of Human Rights, 21 January 2011.

29. See recital 18 to the EU Directive.

30. Exclusion from most mainstream benefits, such as Housing Benefit, is the result of the Social Security (Habitual Residence) Amendment Regulations 2004. Exclusion, in England, from homelessness assistance is the result of the Allocation of Housing and Homelessness (Eligibility) (England) Regulations 2006.

31. The National Health Service (Charges to Overseas Visitors)

(Amendment) Regulations 2008; National Health Service (Charges to Overseas Visitors) (Scotland) Amendment Regulations 2008; National Health Service (Charges to Overseas Visitors) (Wales) (Amendment) Regulations 2008; Provision of Health Services to Persons not Ordinarily Resident (Amendment) Regulations (Northern Ireland) 2008.

32. Council Framework Decision 2002/629/JHA, 19 July 2002, on combating trafficking in human beings.

33. *New State Ice Co.* v. *Liebmann* 285 US 262 (1932), *per* Justice Brandeis: 'It is one of the happy incidents of the federal system that a single courageous state may, if its citizens choose, serve as a laboratory; and try novel social and economic experiments without risk to the rest of the country.'

34. This language is contained in the EU Directive's, recital 7.

35. The EU is not a party to the Council of Europe Convention or the UN Protocol, and so is not bound by them. However, the Directive was clearly drafted with those instruments – and Member States' obligations under them – in mind. See recital 9 to the Directive.

36. Complementing Council of Europe instruments, the EU has its own Directive 95/46/EC of the European Parliament and of the Council, 24 October 1995, on the protection of individuals with regard to the processing of personal data and on the free movement of such data. Directive 95/46 requires Member States to put in place an independent supervisory authority or authorities. The individual rights are transposed in the United Kingdom via the Data Protection Act 1998, which created the Information Commissioner's Office, responsible for ensuring respect for individual data protection rights.

37. See above, Part A.

38. [2013] EWCA Crim 991, para. 13.

39. *Rantsev*, para. 284.

40. *PO (Nigeria)* v. *Secretary of State for the Home Department* [2007] EWCA Civ 1183, para. 9.

References

Anti-Trafficking Monitoring Group (2013), *Hidden in Plain Sight. Three Years On: Updated Analysis of UK Measures to Protect Trafficked Persons*, October, available at: http://www.antislavery.org/includes/documents/cm_docs/2013/h/hidden_in_plain_sight.pdf, last accessed 10 October 2014.

Costello, C. and H. Hancox (2014), *The UK, EU Citizenship and Free Movement of Persons, Migration Observatory Policy Primer*, May, Oxford: COMPAS.

Council of Europe Group of Experts on Action against Trafficking in Human Beings (2012), *Report Concerning the Implementation of the Council of Europe Convention on Action against Trafficking in Human Beings by the United Kingdom*, Strasbourg, 12 September, available at:

http://www.coe.int/t/dghl/monitoring/trafficking/docs/Reports/GRETA_
2012_6_FGR_GBR_en.pdf, last accessed 10 October 2014.

Criminal Injuries Compensation Authority (n.d.), *Victims of Human
Trafficking and the Criminal Injuries Compensation Scheme*, available
at: https://www.gov.uk/government/uploads/system/uploads/attachment_
data/file/351337/human-trafficking-leaflet.pdf, last accessed 10 October
2014.

Crown Office and Procurator Fiscal Service (n.d.), *Guidance on Human
Trafficking Offences*, available at: http://www.copfs.gov.uk/images/
Documents/Prosecution_Policy_Guidance/Guidelines_and_Policy/
Guidance%20on%20Human%20Trafficking%20Offences.pdf, last acc-
essed 10 October 2014.

Home Office (2011), *EU Directive on Human Trafficking*, 22 March 2011,
available at: https://www.gov.uk/government/speeches/eu-directive-on-
human-trafficking, last accessed 10 October 2014.

House of Commons (2015), *Modern Slavery Act*, London: The Stationery
Office.

Kreimer, S. (2001), 'Federalism and freedom', *Annals of the American
Academy of Political and Social Science*, 547(1): 66–80.

Leverick, F. (2006), 'Plea and confession bargaining in Scotland', *Electronic
Journal of Comparative Law*, 10: 3.

Ministry of Justice (2012), *The Criminal Compensation Scheme 2012*,
available at: https://www.justice.gov.uk/downloads/victims-and-wit
nesses/cic-a/am-i-eligible/_criminal-injuries-comp-scheme-2012.pdf, last
accessed 10 October 2014.

Scottish Government (2014), 'New Human Trafficking Bill for Scotland',
17 March, available at: http://news.scotland.gov.uk/News/New-human-
trafficking-bill-for-Scotland-a76.aspx, last accessed 10 October 2014.

Scottish Parliament (2014), Human Trafficking and Exploitation (Scotland)
Bill, available at: http://www.scottish.parliament.uk/parliamentarybusi
ness/Bills/84356.aspx, last accessed 31 January 2015.

Sentencing Commission for Scotland (2006), *The Scope to Improve
Consistency in Sentencing*, available at: http://www.scotland.gov.uk/
Resource/Doc/925/0116783.pdf, last accessed 10 October 2014.

UK Government (2014), *Review of the Balance of Competences between the
United Kingdom and the European Union: Asylum & Non-EU Migration*,
February, available at: https://www.gov.uk/government/uploads/system/
uploads/attachment_data/file/279096/BoC_AsylumImmigration.pdf, last
accessed 10 October 2014.

UNHCR (2006), *Guidelines on International Protection: The Application
of Article 1A(2) of the 1951 Convention and/or 1967 Protocol relating
to the Status of Refugees to Victims of Trafficking and Persons at Risk of
being Trafficked*, 7 April, available at: http://www.unhcr.org/443b626b2.
html, last accessed on 10 October 2014.

4 International and European Standards in Relation to Victims and Survivors of Human Trafficking

Kirsty Thomson

While the previous chapter outlined the relevant international and European standards that apply in the area of human trafficking, this chapter further considers these standards in the specific context of how states respond to victims and survivors of human trafficking.[1] It will look at some of the key concepts contained within international law before outlining victims' rights within this area. The chapter will then focus on how such standards are implemented within Scotland and consider some of the difficulties that have arisen with this implementation based on my experiences as a Scottish solicitor managing a department directly working with victims of human trafficking across Scotland in the last eight years.

Summary of the relevant international and European legal standards

As noted in Chapter 3, there are a number of international standards from the United Nations (UN) and the International Labour Organisation (ILO) which are directly applicable to a state's response to victims of human trafficking. These include the UN Convention on the Elimination of All Forms of Discrimination against Women, the UN Convention on the Rights of the Child, the ILO Forced Labour Convention (1930) and the ILO Worst Forms of Child Labour Convention (1999).

The UN Protocol to Prevent, Suppress and Punish Trafficking in Persons, Especially Women and Children (the 'Trafficking Protocol') supplements the UN Convention against Transnational Organized

Crime. It provides a definition of trafficking in persons which has since been widely adopted in the international community.

These standards are supplemented by legal instruments created within the two legal systems operating in Europe: the Council of Europe and the European Union (EU). In terms of the first system, the Council of Europe Convention on Action against Trafficking in Human Beings (the 'Trafficking Convention') is a key standard in this area. It provides increased protection to victims by expanding the definition of human trafficking and providing a comprehensive framework for the identification, protection and promotion of victims' rights within its Chapter III.

The European Convention of Human Rights (ECHR) is another key European standard from the Council of Europe in the area of victim protection. Human trafficking, as defined within the Trafficking Protocol and the Trafficking Convention, is specifically prohibited by Article 4[2] of this Convention (*Rantsev* v. *Cyprus and Russia*[3]). Other rights protected by the ECHR may also be engaged when looking at a state's responsibilities to victims of human trafficking.

The EU also has a Charter of Human Rights that expressly prohibits human trafficking, and has increasingly adopted legal measures that seek to strengthen protection for victims of human trafficking in the areas of compensation, residence permits and protection afforded to witnesses in criminal proceedings. However, the main EU legal standard is Council Directive 2011/36/EU of 5 April 2011 on preventing and combating trafficking in human beings and protecting its victims (the 'Trafficking Directive') which should have been transposed in April 2013. The extent to which all of it has been transposed is arguable, particularly in relation to victim protection. The Trafficking Directive further extends the definition of human trafficking as well as establishing a set of protection measures which states must ensure are in place for victims. The Trafficking Directive is binding as to the results Member States must achieve, but states have discretion as to how they implement the Directive in order to obtain these results. An EU Directive therefore may not always result in new legislation within the United Kingdom if its terms are already contained within UK law.

Key concepts from the international and European standards in the area of victim protection

A human rights-based approach

A human rights-based approach, placing the victim at the centre, is fundamental to any state response to human trafficking. However, when working with international and European standards in this area, it is important to appreciate and understand their context. The Trafficking Protocol and the Trafficking Directive are largely framed against a criminal justice background. Their primary aim is therefore the criminal prosecution of the perpetrators of human trafficking and the standards of victim protection contained within them must be viewed against this background. This is in contrast to the Council of Europe standards, which are entirely located within a human rights framework and consequently are often where the greatest protection for victims is found.

It is perhaps not unsurprising therefore that law enforcement often takes priority in a state's response to human trafficking, as this in part reflects the background of some of the key international legal standards. However, even the criminal justice standards recognise that the best means to achieve criminal prosecutions is to provide for the protection of victims in a way that respects their human rights. Therefore, the failure of a state to prioritise the human rights of a victim is a failure to act in compliance with international law.

Due diligence

Human trafficking is a crime largely perpetrated by individuals and not states. However, international law and the jurisprudence from the European Court of Human Rights makes it clear that public authorities within Member States must act with 'due diligence'. Therefore, whilst states cannot be held responsible for the acts of private individuals, they can be held to account for their own failures to prevent, protect and prosecute acts of human trafficking. The European Court of Human Rights, in *Siliadin* v. *France*[4] and *Rantsev* v. *Cyprus and Russia*, has made it clear that in order to meet the standard of due diligence in the area of human trafficking, states have positive legal responsibilities to ensure that:

- individuals are identified and protected from trafficking (which at a minimum would include the rights contained within Chapter III of the Trafficking Convention);
- human trafficking is investigated and if possible prosecuted; and
- a legislative and administrative framework is in place designed to punish traffickers.

These positive obligations provide victims with a powerful tool to ensure that states do indeed prioritise their human rights within any anti-trafficking response. Failure to do so can result in damages being paid.

The concept of a victim

In order to ensure that an individual obtains the relevant protections they are entitled to under international law, they must be recognised by the state as a victim. This is not a straightforward process, with barriers to recognition stemming from problems with the ways in which human trafficking is defined as well as difficulties with the identification mechanisms in place within states to support such recognition. These difficulties will be examined in turn.

Definition

For trafficking to have occurred, three constituent elements must be present, namely, an act (what is done), the means (how the act is done) and the exploitation or intention to exploit (why it is done). For children, defined in international law as those aged 18 and under, it is not necessary to establish the 'means'. The Trafficking Protocol, commonly used to define trafficking, links its definition to organised crime across borders. The Trafficking Convention enhanced victim protection by removing these restrictions. Therefore, within Council of Europe member states, an international link to organised crime is no longer required in order for a situation of exploitation or intended exploitation to be defined as human trafficking. The Trafficking Directive extended the Trafficking Convention definition further by applying it to other types of exploitation, including forced begging, the exploitation of an individual in criminal activities, as well as illegal adoption and forced marriage.

The definition of what constitutes human trafficking has continued to expand in response to the continuously evolving nature of a trafficker's modus operandi. However, the evolving nature of this phenomenon can take time to filter down to the competent authorities tasked with ensuring that a state's legal responsibilities are complied with, and it can take time for the relevant knowledge to build and responses to be properly implemented. Problems can arise for front-line practitioners in ensuring that the definition is applied to victims of human trafficking who (1) have not moved across international borders and/or (2) are being exploited by private individuals instead of by organised crime. Furthermore, in identifying victims, there can be an overemphasis on the 'movement' of a victim and a lack of understanding and awareness regarding the other elements that can constitute a trafficking act, such as recruitment and harbouring.

Gaps remain in knowledge of how traffickers control victims. It is commonly misunderstood that such control is always physical, with victims being kidnapped or deceived into a situation of exploitation and then prevented from leaving this situation by having their freedom of movement curtailed by force. However, this is not representative of how traffickers operate, with control increasingly exercised through psychological means, such as isolation, threats regarding immigration status or made against family members. Concepts such as 'abuse of a position of vulnerability' contained within the definition become increasingly important; however, knowledge and understanding of what this means in practice remains limited.

Identification of victims

Key to a state meeting its international obligations, and therefore the cornerstone of victim protection, is the early identification of victims of human trafficking. Within most European states, victims are recognised as such through formal identification systems called National Referral Mechanisms (NRMs). An NRM is a framework for identification and support established by the Office for Democratic Institutions and Human Rights (ODIHR) at the Organization for Security and Co-operation in Europe (OSCE). The basic aim of an NRM, as defined by the OSCE (2004), is to ensure that the human rights of trafficked persons are respected and to provide an effective way to refer victims of trafficking to essential services required for their recovery and protection.[5]

Many countries have adopted identification mechanisms (referred to as NRMs), but which vary in how closely aligned they actually are to the OSCE principles. Many are law enforcement-led, which can limit the access that victims have to the rights and protections they are entitled to under international law. The situation can therefore arise where an individual is not recognised as a victim unless that status has been formally conferred on him or her through a formal framework such as an NRM. This is despite clear international and European legal standards stating that where an individual meets the definition of a victim of human trafficking, they are to be recognised as a victim with all the rights and responsibilities that this entails. Such rights do not stem from a formal status conferred on a victim, but from the victim's experiences.

Rights and responsibilities within victim protection in international law

In order to ensure that states meet their international obligations, victims of human trafficking have an enforceable legal right under international law to effective and appropriate legal remedies, regardless of whether they have been formerly identified as a victim. It is clear from the key international and European standards in this area that the right to an effective remedy encompasses a set of procedural rights that may be criminal, civil or administrative and that include the following:

- access to information on available remedies in a language victims understand;
- access to support and assistance to facilitate rehabilitation;
- access to legal assistance and free legal aid for the duration of any criminal, civil or other action against the traffickers;
- guarantees of non-repetition (states must take all measures necessary to protect a victim, including effective prosecutions and sanctions and international protection/residence permits for foreign victims);
- access to restitution, including restoration of liberty;
- access to compensation.

These rights will be looked at in turn.

Access to information on available remedies

International law recognises that a victim of human trafficking must have access to information about legal rights. Advice services for trafficked persons are an essential element of the right to an effective remedy. Information should be provided that will enable victims to evaluate their situation and make an informed choice from the various possibilities open to them. Victims are entitled to information on:

- the type of services or organisations to which they can turn for support and how to obtain this;
- the type of support that they can obtain;
- where and how they can report an offence;
- how the criminal law system operates, including
    - the consequences of an investigation or trial,
    - the length of a trial,
    - witnesses' duties,
    - the chances of a judgment being properly enforced;
- to what extent and on what terms they have access to legal advice and legal aid;
- legal remedies available, including compensation;
- how and under what conditions they can obtain protection;

- if they are resident in another state, any special arrangements available to them in order to protect their interests; and
- the right to privacy and witness protection.

Access to information on legal rights is not the same as access to legal representation and free legal aid. This information could therefore be provided by a non-governmental organisation (NGO) and not a lawyer. However, best practice would be to ensure access to a legal representative as soon as possible, and for a lawyer to provide detailed information because of the complexity of anti-trafficking systems.

Access to support and assistance to facilitate rehabilitation

States are obliged to provide support and assistance for victims, including the provision of appropriate and safe accommodation, material assistance and necessary medical treatment, including psychological assistance. These measures are often the most pressing initial needs of a victim, and their provision in itself operates as an important remedy; that of recovery. Without the ability to recover, victims may be unable to access other rights. Therefore, international law makes it clear that these provisions are not conditional on a victim's cooperation with law enforcement and to make them so would be contrary to international law.

Access to free legal assistance

The legal standards

The Trafficking Protocol and Trafficking Directive, with their criminal justice focus, provide more limited rights for victims of trafficking than the human rights-based instruments. For instance, Article 12(2) of the Trafficking Directive states that victims must have access without delay to legal counselling and legal representation, but limits this to the duration of any ongoing criminal proceedings involving a trafficker. In such proceedings, legal representation is free of charge where the victim does not have sufficient financial resources. The widest protection in this area comes from the Trafficking Convention, which does not restrict the right to free legal representation to criminal proceedings on the basis that court and administrative procedure in this area is highly complex.[6]

In terms of accessing free legal representation, the jurisprudence of the European Court of Human Rights, Article 6, the right to a fair trial, can be helpful.[7] This jurisprudence makes it clear that, even in the absence of legislation granting free legal assistance, effective access to a court may necessitate this if someone is not in a position to present his or her case satisfactorily without the assistance of a lawyer.[8] The lack of free legal representation may also lead to violations of other fundamental rights protected by the ECHR.

In assessing whether the lack of free legal representation would jeopardise the right to a fair trial, the complexity of procedures will be examined together with the emotional character of the situation. From my own experience of representing victims, free legal assistance will nearly always be required, taking into account the novelty and complexity of the legal systems involved, the personal situation of the victim (including language barriers, fear of authorities, shame and psychological health) and the importance of the proceedings in relation to a victim's ongoing protection needs.

Early and effective legal intervention

Access to early and effective legal representation is essential for a victim to be able to realise his or her rights and to ensure that states fulfil their obligations under international and national law. Legal representation/intervention is an important tool in balancing any overt law enforcement/border control response by a state. Legal representation must therefore be provided at the earliest point possible. This should be at the victims' first point of contact with the authorities and before any formal complaint is made. To be effective, lawyers working in this area should be trained in the relevant legal standards and procedures that may be relevant to a victim of human trafficking. They must work closely with NGOs and other state actors. A human rights-based approach to the provision of legal advice should place the victim at the centre of any response. Gender and child-sensitive legal representation may also be required.

Good practice dictates that legal representatives should be available for all legal proceedings relating to the person's victim status, including criminal, civil, or labour procedures, for the purposes of compensation as well as proceedings in relation to immigration status or asylum. The rationale behind this is to increase disclosure and potential participation in criminal investigations.

Criminal proceedings

Article 6(2)(b) of the Trafficking Protocol obliges states to ensure that their domestic legal or administrative system contains measures that provide assistance to victims of trafficking to enable their views and concerns to be presented in criminal proceedings. National authorities often focus exclusively on a victim's potential role as a witness. However, such considerations should not affect a victim's rights. Every victim should be able to decide, without duress, whether to cooperate with criminal prosecutions, and to do that they need objective and impartial legal advice tailored to their situation.

During the criminal prosecution, human rights must be consistently safeguarded, and international and European standards provide specific protections in a judicial context. Article 12(4) of the Trafficking Directive states that: 'without prejudice to the rights of the defence, victims should receive specific treatment aimed at preventing secondary victimisation'. Article 30 of the Trafficking Convention also refers to procedural measures of protection within court proceedings, and Article 8 of the ECHR, the right to private life and physical and moral integrity, provides protection in this regard.[9]

Such measures ensure that the identity of trafficking victims is not publicly disclosed and that their privacy is respected and protected to the greatest extent possible. These measures are set down within the Trafficking Directive and include private hearings, minimising visual contact between the victim and the accused, and protection against inappropriate and unnecessary questions about private life or sexual history. However, in terms of criminal proceedings, such rights need to be balanced against the rights of the defence, specifically protected by Article 6 of the ECHR. Article 6 does not protect the rights of a witness in a criminal trial, such rights being protected under Article 8. It is left to each Member State to decide the appropriate balance between these competing rights.[10]

Guarantees of non-repetition: obligation to prosecute, punish and protect

Under international law, states have a duty to investigate allegations of human trafficking, prosecute and punish the perpetrators, and protect the victim. This duty specifically applies to law enforcement and immigration bodies. This means that allegations of trafficking must be investigated by police and prosecuting authorities. For foreign nationals, residence permits must be available to secure international protection and to protect the human rights of the victim.[11] Failure by the relevant authorities to take the appropriate steps to investigate and protect is a breach of international law. The European Court of Human Rights has made this position clear in its jurisprudence where states have been found to have violated Article 4 by failing to prosecute and protect in this area (see, for example, *Siladin* v. *France*, *Rantsev* v. *Cyprus and Russia*).

Restitution: restoration of liberty

International law recognises that a victim of trafficking should not be punished for acts that he or she was compelled to commit. However, the legal standards have been ambiguous in prescribing how far states should implement this principle in relation to human trafficking, reflecting disagreement and resulting in unhelpful compromise on this issue at an international level. The Trafficking Protocol does not refer to this principle at all. Article 26 of the Trafficking Convention requires states to simply provide for the 'possibility' of non-prosecution. Recital 14 of the Trafficking Directive acknowledges that victims should be protected from prosecution or punishment for crimes they have been compelled to commit as a direct consequence of being subject to trafficking. It does not, however, go as far as prohibiting states from prosecuting at all. Article 8 leaves it to individual states to ensure that they have mechanisms in place so that the relevant authorities can choose not to prosecute in such circumstances. This is a clear example of how states have prioritised law enforcement over the human rights of a victim.

Right to compensation

Compensation mechanisms exist in most European states, but for a variety of reasons only a minority of victims receive the compensation to which they are entitled, with compensation one of the weakest protected rights and often the most inaccessible. The main distinction between different compensation mechanisms is whether compensation is paid to the trafficked person by the state or by the perpetrator. The accepted principle in this area is that compensation should fall on the perpetrator who has caused the victims suffering and distress.

Article 6(6) of the Trafficking Protocol requires states to ensure that at least one type of legal procedure is available to trafficked persons to access compensation. Article 17 of the Trafficking Directive states that victims are entitled to access *existing* compensation schemes for victims of violent intentional crimes. Other EU Directives establish supplementary rights in this area.[12] Once again, the greatest protection comes from the human rights standards, with Article 15(4) of the Trafficking Convention requiring states to take steps to guarantee compensation of victims on the basis that compensation is rarely available in full from a trafficker.[13]

The ECHR also provides protection in this area, with the European Court of Human Rights recently finding a breach of the ECHR where the level of compensation awarded by a state in a situation of sexual assault provided insufficient redress.[14]

Case study: Scotland

Scotland is bound by the contents of the international and European standards set out above. However, it is the UK Government that ratified these standards and not Scotland. This can lead to areas of best practice given its smaller scale, but it can also lead to problems in terms of implementation when one considers the distinct legal system and processes Scotland has in terms of victim protection.

Devolution

The countries which make up the United Kingdom operate on a devolved basis. Devolved powers are statutory powers granted to the parliaments and administrations of Northern Ireland, Scotland and Wales. Reserved powers are those decisions that remain with the UK Parliament and Government at Westminster. Westminster is also responsible for legislation and policy in England on all matters that have been devolved. In addition, Scotland has its own unique law enforcement, legal and justice system which differs to the rest of the United Kingdom.

In terms of international and European legal standards, it is the UK Parliament that ratifies these standards on behalf of the United Kingdom, and thus Scotland is bound by such ratifications. However, these standards have differing status within the United Kingdom depending on how they have been incorporated. This can affect the ease with which victims are able to exercise their rights.

In terms of interventions in the area of human trafficking, immigration is a reserved matter. Human trafficking and the formal identification of human trafficking through an NRM are viewed by the UK Government to fall within the area of immigration and are therefore reserved matters. However, this is at odds with the fact that criminal law and victim care are devolved matters in Scotland, as are health and the safeguarding and protection of children. Therefore, the majority of public authorities tasked with victim protection operate within the devolved competency of the Scottish Parliament, yet human trafficking remains a reserved matter. This causes a tension in the area of victim protection for victims of human trafficking within Scotland, as the rest of this chapter will highlight.

The international and European legal standards

The Trafficking Protocol and the Trafficking Convention

The UK Government ratified the Trafficking Protocol in 2006. It ratified the Trafficking Convention in 2008, and it came into force within the United Kingdom, including Scotland, on 1 April 2009. Despite ratification, these legal instruments do not have direct legal effect in the United Kingdom, including Scotland, unless they have been specifically incorporated into national legislation.

Although some parts of these instruments have been incorporated, the provisions that relate to the definition of human trafficking and the victim protection measures, contained within Chapter III of the Trafficking Convention, have not all been incorporated and therefore do not have direct legal effect. These provisions provide the greatest protection for victims, but the United Kingdom, and therefore Scotland, has previously sought to comply with them through the development of policy rather than by legislation. The best that can be stated is that there is a legitimate expectation that the United Kingdom and Scotland will comply with the victim protection standards contained within these instruments.

The ECHR

The United Kingdom is also a signatory to the ECHR. The United Kingdom and Scotland have introduced legislation that gives further legal effect to certain rights, referred to as the 'Convention rights', within the ECHR in the form of the Human Rights Act 1998 and the Scotland Act 1998. The Human Rights Act ensures that all legislation must be read in a way that is compatible with the Convention rights. Furthermore, all public authorities must act compatibly with these rights. The Scotland Act ensures that any act passed by the Scottish Parliament on a devolution issue must be compatible with the Convention rights and, if not, it will be invalid. This is therefore a stronger provision than contained in the Human Rights Act. Article 4 of the ECHR is one of the rights that is given further legal effect through this legislation, and it is a powerful legal avenue for victim protection in terms of ensuring full legal implementation of the state's responsibilities as well as obtaining damages for any breach. It is also one that has been used with success in terms of the UK Government's failure to protect victims and prosecute traffickers,[15] and it is particularly powerful when the Trafficking Convention is used as a tool to interpret the positive obligations of states in this area (see *Rantsev* v. *Cyprus and Russia*).

The EU Directives

According to the UK Government, the Trafficking Directive was transposed into the United Kingdom, including Scotland, before 6 April 2013. The EU Directive on Victims of Crime (Directive 2012/220/JHA) is due to be transposed within the United Kingdom, including Scotland, by November 2015. Following transposition of the Trafficking Directive, no additional measures were implemented in terms of victim identification or care as the UK Government has taken the position that it was already in compliance with such provisions. As these are EU instruments, they do have direct legal effect within the United Kingdom, including Scotland, with EU law having supremacy over national law. These are also powerful legal tools for holding the government to account, with damages also being possible for a breach of their terms.

National legislation

To date (early 2015), no specific and comprehensive piece of legislation has been introduced, in England and Wales or by the Scottish Parliament, in relation to human trafficking. Northern Ireland has introduced the Human Trafficking and Exploitation (Criminal Justice and Support for Victims) Act (Northern Ireland) 2015.

There has been criticism of the United Kingdom regarding the legislative response, including the Scottish Parliament. In respect of Scotland specifically, this has come from the Equality and Human Rights Inquiry into Human Trafficking in Scotland (Equality and Human Rights Commission 2011) and a report by GRETA, the monitoring mechanism of the Trafficking Convention, in 2012 (GRETA 2012). The national legal standards relating to human trafficking within Scotland are found in a plethora of piecemeal national legislation focusing on law enforcement, immigration and broader standards relating to the welfare of children. However, the UK Government has introduced a Modern Day Slavery Act in front of the UK Parliament, and the Scottish Government a Human Trafficking and Exploitation (Scotland) Act into the Scottish Parliament, which aims to enhance the status of, and support to, victims of human trafficking.

Government strategy/monitoring and evaluation

In recent years, there have been a number of studies and inquiries into the issue of human trafficking in Scotland, including those by Amnesty International (2008), the Scottish Parliament Equal Opportunities Committee (Equal Opportunities Committee 2010), the Scottish Commissioner for Children and Young People (2011) and the Equality and Human Rights Commission (2011, 2013).

External monitoring has been undertaken by CEDAW (2013), the US State Department (2014), GRETA (2012) and the OSCE (2012). This monitoring has specifically examined victim protection measures.

The result of this attention in Scotland has been a recognition that human trafficking exists within Scotland (although the exact extent of the issue is unknown due to its complex and hidden nature) and an increased focus by the Scottish Government on the identification and protection of victims.

Following the EHRC inquiry in 2011 (Equality and Human Rights Commission 2011), the Scottish Government held a Summit on Human Trafficking in October 2012. From this summit, an Anti-Trafficking Progress Group was established in order to agree and take forward key actions on this issue within Scotland. This Progress Group has convened themed sub-groups, one of which is responsible for examining the issue of victim care and support. In addition, a Cross-Party Parliamentary Group on Human Trafficking was convened within the Scottish Parliament, and human trafficking is part of the National Action Plan launched by the Scottish Human Rights Commission for 2013–17.

Victim protection within Scotland

Identification

On 1 April 2009, and in order to comply with the Trafficking Convention, the UK Government introduced an NRM that would formally identify victims of human trafficking. It is important to note that the NRM emerged from policy and is not contained within any legislation in the United Kingdom, including Scotland. Indeed, its operation is largely detailed within Immigration Guidance.[16]

Under the NRM, there are only two specified bodies that can formally identify a victim of trafficking (referred to as 'competent authorities'). These are UK Visas and Immigration (for those who require leave to stay in the United Kingdom) and the UK Human Trafficking Centre, which is part of the UK National Crime Agency (for all other victims). Only certain agencies can refer potential victims of human trafficking to these bodies for identification. These agencies are referred to as 'first responders'.[17] Upon receipt of a referral from a first responder, the competent authority will make a 'reasonable grounds decision' (which has a low standard of proof of 'suspect but cannot prove'). If this decision is positive, the potential victim will be given a forty-five-day recovery and reflection period. If the victim is subject to immigration control, they cannot be removed from the United Kingdom during this period, and are entitled to access victim care and support.

Within the recovery and reflection period, the competent authority is under a proactive obligation to gather information about the individual to allow it to make a Conclusive Decision as to whether the individual has been trafficked. Information should be obtained from the first responder in order to inform the final decision, but this is the extent of the first responder's involvement in the actual identification under the NRM. If an individual is subject to immigration control and receives a positive Conclusive Grounds Decision, then a renewable one-year residence permit may be granted if:

(a) the individual's personal circumstances necessitate a permit (that is, they need to complete a course of medical treatment);
(b) the individual requires to remain in the United Kingdom in order to pursue compensation; and
(c) the individual requires to remain in the United Kingdom in order to assist with police inquiries.

The NRM system within the UK has attracted significant criticism from both internal and external monitoring bodies. It has been criticised for failing to adhere to the OSCE principles of an NRM as it is not a referral body. Its function is to receive requests and identify victims only. The EHRC inquiry in Scotland found that the NRM was too centralised, lacking in accountability, created a conflict of interest in decision-making and was ineffective in tracking outcomes for victims or identifying patterns and trends in trafficking. The NRM model was the subject of a review instigated by the Secretary of State for the Home Department (Home Secretary) and published in November 2014. This report recommended various changes to the current system of identification under the NRM.

Overview of how victim care and support is provided in Scotland

The identification and protection of child victims of human trafficking is the responsibility of local authorities. Social Work services within these authorities, through their local procedures, should ensure the provision of, or access to, accommodation, health, financial support, education and specialist counselling to children and young people. The Scottish Government also fund a specialist guardianship service for children who may have been trafficked.[18]

Where a child is deemed to be a potential victim of human trafficking, child protection procedures should be instigated; however, such procedures often apply only to children under the age of 16. For children aged 16–18 other safeguarding procedures are required, and these vary depending on the local authority area.

There can be some degree of ambiguity regarding the level and type of support provided to young people aged between 16 and 18. This is because a child is often viewed as being 16 and under within Scots law and practice. A child can be defined differently in different legal contexts within Scotland. For example, section 93(2)(a) and (b) of the Children (Scotland) Act 1995 defines a child in relation to the powers and duties of the local authority. For adult victims of human trafficking, the Scottish Government specifically fund two specialist NGOs, TARA and Migrant Help,[19] to provide victim care. The remit for both organisations is restricted to those over the age of 18.

TARA and Migrant Help act as first responders in respect of the NRM and will carry out assessments before referring service users into this system. They are also, however, specifically contracted by the Scottish Government to assist it in upholding its international legal obligations in this area. Both organisations also ensure the provision of, or access to, accommodation, health and subsistence payments for trafficking victims. Social work services and the specialist NGOs act as important 'gatekeepers' within Scotland to ensure that a victim has access to relevant information, material assistance and legal representation.

Legal representation/compensation

Routes into legal advice and representation can depend on whether victims are involved in a legal process and the nature of such process, the type of exploitation suffered and the support they are able to access. There is no formal route, protocol or procedure in place to ensure that access to early legal advice is provided to all victims of human trafficking regardless of the legal processes with which they are involved.

There is a state-funded legal aid scheme within Scotland which victims of human trafficking can access, as can any other resident. The legal aid system in Scotland therefore does ensure that, in theory, access to free legal advice and assistance is available in a broad area of legal matters that relate to human trafficking, including identification, access to material support and assistance, immigration law, international protection and compensation. Not all potential legal issues are, however, covered by the state legal aid scheme and/or are provided by knowledgeable legal aid lawyers. Legal assistance by a specialised service may be required and the Scottish Government has funded a service in this area.[20]

Victims in Scotland are therefore assisted in obtaining both residence permits because of their trafficking status and compensation as a result of their experiences. This compensation has largely derived from the state scheme on providing compensation to victims of violent crime, the Criminal Injuries Compensation Scheme.

Victims who are involved with criminal proceedings, however, have no formal standing within these proceedings in Scotland. They therefore have no right to independent legal representation on issues such as privacy, secondary victimisation and whether or not a compensation order is taken against a perpetrator. Such a right would require a change in national legislation. Free legal aid is therefore not available to those who are victims in criminal proceedings precisely because they have no standing in them.

Restitution: restoration of liberty

Victims of human trafficking, including children, have been prosecuted and have spent time in prison for offences directly linked to human trafficking. This has particularly been an issue with Vietnamese nationals and cannabis cultivation in Scotland, reflecting the wider UK picture in this area. A number of children's cases were identified in 2012 and 2013 in Scotland within the detention estate and the Legal Services Agency (LSA) acted in a number of these. Since this point, increased awareness, a shift in focus to victim protection by Police Scotland and the Lord Advocate's clearly stated presumption against prosecution in such cases appears to have improved matters on the ground. However, children have still been identified within the detention estate as recently as the end of 2014. Increased awareness and training, particularly amongst the criminal justice and legal profession, together with clearer legal instruction on this matter is still required.

Issues with victim protection and devolution

The introduction of key standards in Scotland has undoubtedly led to greater awareness of human trafficking as an issue that needs to be addressed. Gaps remain, however, in the use of current definitions of human trafficking, particularly in relation to internal human trafficking (that is, trafficking within the United Kingdom), means of control by traffickers and the varied types of exploitation involved.

In terms of victim protection, in its inquiry the EHRC found that Scotland does not yet have comprehensive high quality end-to-end services for victims of human trafficking (Equality and Human Rights Commission 2011, 2013). The GRETA report stated that further efforts are required in Scotland to ensure that victims of human trafficking (including potential victims) are provided with adequate support and assistance (GRETA 2012). The most recent US State Department Trafficking in Persons report for the UK (US State Department 2014) highlighted the need for better victim-centred responses and access to services *before* victims have to engage with law enforcement and immigration.

A recent review of support for victims in Scotland highlighted that Scotland is moving towards a more victim-centred approach (Malloch *et al.* 2012). However, this would appear to be an approach led by front-line expertise within key specialist agencies rather than a strategic government-led initiative within Scotland. This is not surprising when one considers the UK Government's clear stance on the identification of human trafficking as being a reserved matter within a formal NRM process currently restricted to UK immigration and law enforcement bodies. From my experience of working in this area, this stance has been unhelpful, incorrect and has potentially resulted in a situation where Scottish public authorities have been in breach of international law for the following reasons:

The first problem with viewing victim protection within the sphere of immigration, and therefore as a reserved matter, is that the peculiarities of the Scottish legal system in relation to victim protection get missed or forgotten about when ratifying such standards. It is well known that a Member State such as the United Kingdom will not opt-in to EU Directives or ratify other international standards unless it is confident that its legal processes are already in compliance with their terms. However, the child protection system in Scotland is arguably not in compliance with such standards. The international and European standards are clear that a young person under the age of 18 is a child victim of human trafficking. However, for the most part, a child is viewed to be 16 and under within Scotland (as noted earlier in this chapter), which could lead to differential and unlawful treatment in terms of victim protection of those aged between 16 and 18.

The second issue with this stance is the NRM and its perception within Scotland. As noted earlier in this chapter, a formal identification process can often lead to the perception that an individual is not a victim unless that status has been formally conferred on him or her through a formal identification mechanism. This is made more problematic when rights to victim care and support have largely been transposed through policy initiatives and funding arrangements, as is the case in Scotland, rather than through legislation.

Within the United Kingdom and Scotland, access to certain rights is increasingly becoming contingent on an individual being identified through the NRM process. Access to accommodation for those who require it is linked to the recovery and reflection period. Unlike in England and Wales, however, TARA and Migrant Help are able to provide accommodation and other support after the forty-five-day period as long as need is identified. Access to accommodation and welfare support past this period is, however, problematic where an individual has not made a claim for asylum and is therefore not being housed and supported by the Home Office. Access to compensation through the state-funded scheme within the United Kingdom is now linked to identification under the NRM.

Within Scotland in particular, this approach masks the fact that for the most part, many public authorities who have legal responsibilities within victim protection fall within the devolved competence of the Scottish Government (for instance, police, the legal system and local authority provision). As a result of the international and European legal standards set out earlier in this chapter, these public authorities within Scotland have a duty to identify and protect potential victims of human trafficking regardless of their identification and/or participation with the NRM. Failure to do is a breach of international law.

Based on my experience of working in this area, I would argue that this is still not properly understood within Scotland, and the existence of the NRM can itself operate as a barrier to achieving protection for a victim. Treating human trafficking as a reserved matter, which is law enforcement-led and where victim protection is a low priority area, cannot be considered compliant with the spirit of international law.

Piecemeal legislation in the area of human trafficking coupled with an unclear victim strategy found within policy documents has led to public authorities, who fall within the devolved competence of the Scottish Government, being unclear of their international legal obligations towards victims of human trafficking. This has led to breaches of international law in this area. Breaches will continue to happen unless clear statutory obligations are established in the area of victim protection coupled with improved knowledge and awareness of the needs of victims of human trafficking.

Notes

1. Throughout this chapter, survivors of human trafficking are referred to as victims to reflect the current legal and policy discourse. This is not to detract from the recognition that people who have been trafficked are survivors.
2. Article 4 prohibits slavery and forced labour.
3. (2010) 51 EHRR 1.
4. (2006) 43 EHRR 16.
5. The OSCE defines an NRM as 'a cooperative framework through which state actors fulfil their obligations to protect and promote the human rights of trafficked persons, coordinating their efforts in a strategic partnership with civil society' (OSCE 2004).
6. Explanatory Report of the Trafficking Convention 2005, para. 195.
7. *Airey* v. *Ireland* (1979) 2 EHRR 305.
8. Explanatory Report of the Trafficking Convention 2005, para. 196.
9. The Trafficking Protocol, Article 6(1) also refers to the protection of confidentiality within legal proceedings.
10. *Doorson* v. *Netherlands* (1996) 22 EHRR 330; Explanatory Report, para. 306.
11. In terms of the Convention Relating to the Status of Refugees 1951; ECHR, Articles 3 and 4; Council Directive of the European Parliament and of the Council on standards for the qualification of third-country nationals or stateless persons as beneficiaries of international protection, for a uniform status for refugees or for persons eligible for subsidiary protection, and for the content of the protection granted (Directive 2011/95/EU).
12. EU Directive 2004/80/EC, n. 7, has a requirement to establish a state scheme for victims of violent crime. EU Directive 2012/29/EU, n. 7, provides for the right to receive information from the first contact with state authorities on compensation and the right to a decision on compensation from the perpetrator in criminal proceedings.
13. Explanatory Report, paras 191–3 and 197–9.
14. *W* v. *Slovenia*, Application No. 24124/06, Council of Europe, ECHR, 23 January 2014.
15. *O.O.O. and Others* v. *Commissioner of Police for the Metropolis* [2011] EWHC 1246 (QB); *CN* v. *The United Kingdom*, n. 35. Also in April 2011, the Home Office agreed damages to a Moldovan woman trafficked to the United Kingdom for prostitution who was removed to Moldova in 2003 where she was re-trafficked back to the United Kingdom. The Home Office settled a claim for damages pursued under Articles 3 and 4 of the ECHR.

16. Home Office, Victims of Trafficking – Competent Authority Guidance, Version 1, available at: https://www.gov.uk/government/uploads/system/uploads/attachment_data/file/298421/traffickingcompetent.pdf.
17. For Scotland, these are the NGOs TARA and Migrant Help, local authorities, health, National Crime Agency, Police Scotland and UK Visas and Immigration.
18. This is not a statutory guardianship service.
19. TARA has a remit to work with adult women who have been victims of commercial sexual exploitation. Migrant Help works with all other adult victims.
20. Women's Project, Women and Young Persons' Department, Legal Services Agency.

References

Amnesty International (2008), *Scotland's Slaves: An Amnesty International Briefing on Trafficking in Scotland*, Edinburgh: Amnesty International Scotland.

CEDAW (2013), *Concluding Observations on the Seventh Periodic Report of the United Kingdom of Great Britain and Northern Ireland*, New York: United Nations.

Equal Opportunities Committee (2010), *Inquiry into Human Trafficking in Scotland*, Edinburgh: Scottish Parliament.

Equality and Human Rights Commission (2011), *Inquiry into Human Trafficking in Scotland*, Glasgow: Equality and Human Rights Commission.

Equality and Human Rights Commission (2013), *Follow Up Report into Inquiry into Human Trafficking in Scotland*, Glasgow: Equality and Human Rights Commission.

Group of Experts on Action Against Trafficking in Human Beings (GRETA) (2012), *Report on the UK*, Strasbourg: Council of Europe.

Malloch, M., T. Warden and N. Hamilton-Smith (2012), *Care and Support for Adult Victims of Human Trafficking in Human Beings*, Edinburgh: Scottish Government.

Organization for Security and Co-operation in Europe (OSCE) (2004), *National Referral Mechanisms: Joining Efforts to Protect the Rights of Trafficked Persons, A Practical Handbook*, Vienna: OSCE.

Organization for Security and Co-operation in Europe (OSCE) (2012), *Report by OSCE Special Representative and Co-ordinator for Combating Trafficking in Human Beings*, following her visit to the UK, 7–10 March 2011, Vienna: OSCE.

Scottish Commissioner for Children and Young People (SCCYP) (2011), *Scotland: A Safe Place for Child Traffickers?* Edinburgh: SCCYP.

US State Department (2014), *Trafficking in Persons Report*, Washington, DC: US Department of State.

5 Child Protection for Child Trafficking Victims

Paul Rigby and Philip Ishola

In the past 10 to 15 years, significant efforts at various levels – national, international and European – have been made to establish legal and policy frameworks capable of dealing with the complex and multifaceted issue of human trafficking. While these efforts have resulted in the development of legal, policy and practical measures to identify and address the needs of victims, they have often fallen short of creating a system that recognises the vulnerability of children, treats them as children first and foremost, and recognises their agency, age and stage. This approach has maintained what is, in practice, a two-tier system of protective services, with the defining factor often being asylum and immigration, which is at odds with the existing UK children's legislation and practice.

Within the trafficking discourse, children and young people are generally addressed as a 'sub-group' of human (adult) trafficking (Wallace and Wylie 2011), rather than autonomous human beings with their own needs and vulnerabilities. While the specific vulnerabilities of children who have been trafficked have been highlighted (Rigby *et al.* 2012a), there has also been substantial debate about the agency of children in decision-making, especially in choices made to migrate and move away from exploitative/abusive situations (O'Connell Davidson 2011). Within this debate there is also the issue of finding 'durable solutions' (UNHCR 2003) for children on the move.

The exploitation of children, whether through trafficking or other avenues, is child abuse. This chapter looks at the development of policy and practice in the United Kingdom, investigating why trafficking victims and survivors are treated differently to other abused children, often outwith the existing child protection and safeguarding process. While there may be specific vulnerabilities associated with children who are on the move and exploited, it is not altogether clear if children recruited and moved for the purpose of exploitation are any more vulnerable than other abused children, such that they deserve a place at 'the high table of child suffering' (O'Connell Davidson 2011), requiring their own specific response and support networks. However, when children are in situations of vulnerability risk increases, particularly when these children are seen differently and the support systems designed to care and protect children may be governed by various legislation.

The chapter concludes with a simple proposal for a model of identification and support for child trafficking victims to be located firmly within existing child protection systems, with the added support of a guardian for separated children, in line with international guidelines and good practice (FRA 2014).

Prevalence and scope of child trafficking

There is some consensus that human trafficking is a concern across the United Kingdom, with official statistics indicating 1,746 referrals in 2013 to the UK Human Trafficking Centre, a rise of 47 per cent from 2012. Of these referrals, 450 were for children under the age of 18 years (National Crime Agency 2014). In 2014 there were 2,340 referrals, 671 for children (National Crime Agency 2015). These official statistics indicate that children have been exploited sexually, for labour purposes and domestic servitude, although for nearly a third of children no type of exploitation was recorded. Other studies have suggested that children and young people present with evidence of multiple exploitative situations (Rigby *et al.* 2012b). However, the reality remains that there is little accurate information about the prevalence of child trafficking across the United Kingdom, or elsewhere, (O'Connell Davidson 2011), leading to concerns about moral panics and rushed and poor responses (Cree *et al.* 2012; Spencer and Broad 2012).

International, European and domestic policy responses to human trafficking

Defining and quantifying the phenomenon of human trafficking is a complex, and often controversial, task. The most recent legislative guidelines relevant to the United Kingdom, EU Directive 2011/36/

EU, adopted into national law on 6 April 2013 ('EU Directive 2011') provides a definition based on the Protocol to Prevent, Suppress and Punish Trafficking in Persons, Especially Women and Children (Palermo Protocol), and which has been widely adopted internationally. While this definition remains debateable, along with any clear notion of what constitutes exploitation (O'Connell Davidson 2011), it has aided a focus on the abuse of vulnerable children, who until recently may have fallen outside the child protection system (Bokhari 2008; Rigby 2011).

Urging Member States to adopt a child rights approach, the EU Directive (Articles 13–16) stipulates that the child's best interests should be the primary consideration, and introduces additional provisions specifically directed at child victims of trafficking. These include the appointment of a guardian, an individual assessment of the special circumstances of each child, with obligations to take account of their views, needs and concerns when providing support and assistance, as well as ensuring the protection of child victims in criminal investigations. Perhaps with the exception of a 'guardian', these provisions are those accorded to all children in need of child protection and safeguarding measures, and raises the question of why existing child protection arrangements are not the primary route to protecting and supporting trafficked children.

National Referral Mechanism

Following the ratification of the Council of Europe (2005) Convention, a formal mechanism for identifying and protecting victims of trafficking including children – a National Referral Mechanism (NRM) – was introduced in the United Kingdom in April 2009. Once there is a suspicion, based on specified indicators, that a person may be a victim of trafficking or a child discloses that they have been trafficked, designated agencies – 'first responders' (social workers; police, UK Border Agency, third-sector organisations) – may submit a referral to a 'competent authority' for assessment (Home Office n.d.). The competent authority is either the UK Human Trafficking Centre or, in cases where there are asylum or irregular immigration considerations, the Home Office (UK Visas and Immigration, UKVI). In line with the approach adopted at the international and European level, domestic policy documents and plans have acknowledged the vulnerability of child victims of trafficking and emphasised the significant harm that exploitation causes them (Scottish Government 2009; AWCPP 2011; Department of Education 2011; London SCB 2011; DJNI 2014).

Child-specific guidance recognises the need for embedding responses to child victims of trafficking within general child protection procedures, but falls short of locating decision-making firmly within the safeguarding process. While the introduction of the NRM was welcomed as a positive step towards ensuring that professionals identify and protect victims of trafficking, its relevance and appropriateness to child victims has been questioned (ATMG 2011; London SCB 2011). Although UK Governments have recognised that child trafficking is abuse, and despite calls not to treat child victims as 'mini-adults' (Wallace and Wylie 2011), responses do not always reflect a child-centred approach and are, for non-EU nationals, primarily immigration-focused (ECPAT 2010; ATMG 2011; Pearce 2011; Jones 2012).

If the NRM fails to reflect child trafficking as child abuse, and does not prioritise safeguarding children over any other concerns, including immigration, the compliance of the present identification and support process with a child's best interest and rights is questionable. If the issue of illegal/irregular migration was taken out of the equation for most of the identified children arriving in the United Kingdom, it is likely there would be little debate about the exploitative/abusive nature of their experiences and that it is clearly a child safeguarding and protection issue. In respect of non-EU children specifically, Bovarnick (2010) suggests that whether practitioners are 'child focused' or 'immigration focused' plays a substantial role in the quality of services received by children. This disparity should not exist.

History and development of the NRM

In the months preceding implementation of the NRM in 2009, there was substantial discussion within and between statutory children services, local safeguarding children boards, non-governmental organisations (NGOs), law enforcement agencies and policymakers as to the particular needs of children. These discussions were seen, at the time, as helpful in interpreting what trafficking meant in terms of child protection responses, and afforded the opportunity to share thinking on how to interpret and transpose 'trafficking' as defined within the Palermo Protocol and the Council of Europe Convention (2005) into mainstream child protection definitions, triggers and process.

The outcome of these discussions concluded that if a child is trafficked the actual exploitation of a child could be described as child abuse if it was sexual, physical or emotional abuse, in line with existing UK guidance. It was considered that the acts themselves harmed children irrespective of 'why' they were trafficked (moved, recruited) in the first instance, and the impact on the child will be the same as any other form of child abuse. This was the guiding principle that drove the development of a child trafficking toolkit (London SCB 2009), which aimed to assist children's services and their partners in identifying child victims of trafficking and to respond by following a child protection model of investigation, protection, care and support.

During the development of the toolkit an existing working partnership (focused on child trafficking), between the London Safeguarding Children Board and Association London Government, was extended to a multi-agency law enforcement trafficking task group within the Association of Chief Police Officers. At the time, the taskforce was looking at ways of identifying trafficked children not only as a protection measure, but also to ensure that the United Kingdom was compliant with the identification elements of the international conventions. The partnership developed, in part, because the toolkit contained a child victim identification tool. As with all effective child protection initiatives, a valuable and productive working partnership of shared knowledge and expertise began the process of harmonising a policy, guidance and practice tool, and an implementation strategy, into a single national toolkit pilot project.

The support of the Child Exploitation Online Protection (CEOP) Centre trafficking team was immensely valuable and supportive, again reinforcing the multi-agency approach and establishing a partnership that lasted for a number of years. The UK Home Department (Home Office) and their Organised and Financial Crime Unit were also engaged, feeding into the development of the toolkit and helping to structure a child NRM separate from that of adults, yet linked in policy terms with the human trafficking definition. With the partnerships established and with the work focusing on a child protection-centred NRM toolkit, developments entered the final stages of drafting.

The identification model was based simply around the fact that if a child (be they a UK national or from within or outside the European Union) is suspected of being, or is indeed a victim of trafficking, the organisation best placed to determine this (as a competent authority) would be a trained child protection social worker. This would not only ensure the skills required to speak with a child about an abuse experience were present, but also through that interaction, where there was a suspicion of trafficking or a disclosure, it would trigger an enhanced child protection response, with appropriate guidance (in terms of child trafficking) being provided by the London SCB toolkit.

Other agencies involved would be first responders, and follow the enhanced NRM referral process using a child trafficking multi-agency indicator matrix (London SCB 2009) developed for this purpose, with the matrix to be embedded in a new child NRM referral form and available to all organisations who may come into contact with a trafficked child. This process was also seen as the key to embedding a new definition of 'child trafficking' (as child abuse) into the heart of the child protection system across the United Kingdom. Discussions with the relevant Welsh and Scottish govern-ments and specialist child protection services had been underway for some time, laying the foundations for a harmonised approach both in policy and practice procedures.

This NRM model of identification was agreed across all agen-cies and the relevant forms, tools and guidance drafted, printed and prepared for launch with the NRM on 1 April 2009. In terms of the holistic approaches, this process was seen as providing a sound iden-tification and protection mechanism for children, while enhancing the child protection systems and transposing a little understood and increasing form of internal and transnational child abuse (child traf-ficking) into mainstream practice, utilising the supportive working together to safeguard children partnership approach.

However, in the few weeks before launch it became clear that there had been a reappraisal by the Home Office, Organised and Financial Crime Unit and the UK Human Trafficking Centre (UKHTC). This change of mind produced the current system (pre-implementation of the NRM review process). The NRM process, as structured by the Home Office, made UK Border Agency (UKBA) (now UKVI) personnel the competent authority for non-UK and non-EU children, while the UKHTC were to be the competent authority for UK and EU children.

Discussions at the time made it clear that the UKBA expected most, if not all, cases of child trafficking to come from outside the EU and be accompanied by some sort of asylum claim. It was considered that any decision made outside of the asylum process, which could influ-ence or determine an asylum application, would be unacceptable. For UK and EU children, the driving force was a law enforcement priority and as such the decision would sit with a law enforcement agency, the UKHTC, which at the time was part of the Serious and Organised Crime Agency (SOCA).

Child protection agencies pointed out that as child trafficking was recognised as a form of child abuse, and as such must be approached from a multi-agency child protection perspective as part of the child protection legislative framework, there were inherent and substan-tial risks associated with looking at the child in terms of their immigration situation. Additionally, it was also highlighted that there was a high risk of fragmenting the child protection response, where child trafficking would be seen as an immigration and asylum concern, instead of a high risk child abuse case. It was also not envisaged that a competent authority would disagree with child protection social workers who considered a child to have been trafficked. Ultimately, the child protection argument was lost by the time of implementation of the NRM in 2009.

Impact of the NRM on children

Placing the responsibility for identifying child victims of trafficking with agencies whose primary function is border control (UKVI) and policing (UKHTC, National Crime Agency), potentially creates a conflict of interest and leads to an overly bureaucratic decision-making process, with little regard for its impact on the child (ATMG 2010; ECPAT 2010; London SCB 2011). Similarly, Biaudet (2009) also questions if law enforcement authorities such as the UKHTC are best equipped for the task of identifying child victims and recognising what appropriate support is required.

There is evidence that local authorities in the United Kingdom do not always believe a referral to the NRM is in the child's best interest, and have decided not to refer cases due to concerns about its ability to adequately support and protect children (London SCB 2011). The experience of practitioners also suggests that while a positive conclusive grounds decision may be of little practical benefit to children in terms of an asylum claim (if applicable), a negative one could have an adverse effect on the credibility of their claim, as it is often made by the same case owner (Chandran 2011). The potential negative effect on a child's well-being of a negative decision after sharing their experiences with a number of agencies has also been documented (Rigby *et al.* 2012b).

Recent attempts to review the NRM in the light of such criticism have again failed to locate identification and provision of support for child victims firmly in the existing UK child protection arrangements (Home Office 2014a). New proposals for the establishment of 'boards' to identify victims of trafficking, in line with existing multi-agency safeguarding hubs (Home Office 2014b), continue to sideline the primary child protection agencies and processes – suggesting that trafficked children are trafficking victims first and foremost and children second. Their status as children still seems to be secondary to their status as trafficking victims; a change from migrant first (Crawley 2006), but still categorised by the 'hierarchical' victimisation of trafficking (O'Connell Davidson 2011), not the fact they may be an abused child, primarily in need of support and protection.

Over the last six years, the NRM, as implemented in the United Kingdom, has largely overlooked existing child protection and safe-guarding frameworks, effectively undermining them (ATMG 2011); the new proposals look set to continue this approach. Decisions about whether a child has been exploited through trafficking, raising significant child protection issues, will be made by a central 'expert' panel, whose main remit is neither children nor child protection. It is difficult to imagine any other serious child protection decision-making occurring outside the well-established and existing child protection framework.

A child rights approach to child trafficking requires the issue to be dealt with as an exploitation/abuse issue, and means placing children at the centre of all related identification and support decision-making and listening to them. The child's best interests should be a primary consideration in all actions. These should be determined for each child, giving due consideration to his or her views, in line with the requirements of Article 12 of the UN Convention on the Rights of the Child (OHCHR 1989). The current and proposed NRM argu-ably does not reflect these principles, as it remains primarily a system designed for adults that has been fitted to reflect the needs of chil-dren, without actually doing that. Crucially, the centralised decision makers rarely, if ever, actually speak to the children (see Scottish Parliament 2015). This is apart from the fact that the competent authorities are not trained to interview a child who has been abused (a child protection specialist training), as the risk of re-traumatising and/or contaminating evidence can be substantial.

While the 2014 Home Office proposals involve a multi-agency approach to identifying victims, albeit separate to UKVI and any immigration decisions, it remains somewhat removed from the exist-ing child protection system, and it remains unlikely to constitute pro-fessionals who know the child. It is crucial that trafficked children are not treated differently to any other child in respect of decision-making and inclusion with regard to care and protection.

However, it is also important that due consideration is given to the specific vulnerabilities of trafficked children, especially those who may be unaccompanied (FRA 2014). Even with this caveat, the FRA indicate that as child trafficking victims are likely to have multiple child protection problems, the most effective response will be located in an integrated, systems approach to child protection:

Focusing on selected issues alone, or on particular groups of children, is neither sustainable nor effective. In cases of child victims of trafficking, identification as a child victim or a child at risk of trafficking may occur at different points on a continuum of a child's individual protection needs. (FRA 2014: 17)

The OSCE's Special Representative for Combating Trafficking in Human Beings recommended, based on experience from a number of states, that: 'A multi-agency approach to determining victim status and referral to services, involving child protection professionals and representatives from specialized NGO's providing support to victims' (Biaudet 2009). This multi-agency approach presently exists in the United Kingdom within a well-established child protection system, the question remains why this was side-lined during the development of the NRM and subsequent provision.

Multi-agency child protection in the United Kingdom

UK governments, through their child protection policies (Home Office 2003; Office of the First Minister and Deputy First Minister 2006; Scottish Government 2008), have demonstrated commitment to developing policies promoting the well-being of all children, based on effective multidisciplinary and integrated approaches. Guidance on child protection and trafficking places the primary responsibility of support for child trafficking victims within the child protection framework and delineates the responsibilities of agencies (Home Office 2009; Scottish Government 2009). Due to the complex nature of trafficking and the multiple needs of child victims, which require coordinated responses from a number of agencies (ILO 2006; Asquith and Turner 2008), the guidance urges local safeguarding boards and child protection committees to consider developing inter-agency protocols to support professionals when faced with concerns that a child may be a victim of trafficking. Consequently, it is not clear why the identification of victims of trafficking does not also lie within these systems, so that any decisions are clearly welfare and protection based, in the best interests of the child, involving the child where appropriate, and drawing on the experiences of those professionals working with the children.

O' Connell Davidson (2010) argues the idea that 'trafficking' can be clearly delineated from other violations of human and labour rights is not sustainable. Such an argument may be equally applied to child abuse, such that the exploitation and abuse experienced by child victims of trafficking is similar to that experienced by many victims of child abuse. Factors contributing to any form of child abuse are multiple and the use of 'multiple lenses' (Hynes 2013:

166) to understanding and responding to child trafficking may be more useful than an 'expert' approach. Categorising child victims as a 'special' case for protection and support may serve to view them as victims of trafficking first and foremost, rather than as children in need of protection and support. This may then contribute to the 'othering' of trafficking victims and the identification of 'deserving' and 'undeserving' (O'Connell Davidson 2010) recipients of state intervention.

In terms of child protection in relation to trafficking, the international conventions and European Directives, and their translation into national legislation and policy, may have inadvertently led to this increased neoliberal response where child abuse through trafficking becomes the responsibility of 'expert' agencies. Rogowski (2012) has suggested that child protection in general has moved towards being a socio-legal issue, rather than a medico-social problem; there is a danger that with new legislation across the United Kingdom trafficking continues primarily as a criminal justice responsibility, rather than a human rights response. At the moment, the identification of child trafficking victims remains the role of a centralised government agency (UKHTC/UKVI, competent authority), and emerging legislation across the United Kingdom will still rely on the 'official' identification and conferring of victim status by 'trafficking experts', rather than on a child being in need of protection and support.

By focusing on the movement aspect of child trafficking, and not on the exploitation, responses may be located in the 'expertise' of specialist agencies established for this sole purpose, and, in the case of UKVI, a focus on immigration. This links into the 'securitisation' agenda of securing borders and preventing illegal immigration (Howard and Lalani 2008), with the dominant trafficking agenda of prevention, protection and prosecution (Schloenhardt and Loong 2011; Jones 2012) taking precedence in an immigration-focused lens, rather than the broader imperative of recovery and rehabilitation for abuse victims.

UK problems

There is a counter-argument to this. Child protection agencies, especially local authority services, have often failed to provide appropriate support to separated and trafficked children. There has been much criticism of the local authority response in the United Kingdom, with particular reference to the inability of local authorities to protect children and prevent them from going missing and being 're-trafficked' (Beddoe 2007; Jones 2012). The usual quoted figures of 50–60 per cent of suspected trafficked children in the United Kingdom going missing from local authority care homes (Beddoe 2007) is cited as evidence of the inability of local authorities to protect children. The issues with child protection services struggling to protect children may be a result of the trafficking lens being immigration and law enforcement-focused, rather than child protection.

There is evidence that a child-centred, child protection approach can safeguard children and reduce the number of children and young people going missing from care accommodation. Work undertaken in Glasgow, indicates that 10–15 per cent of suspected trafficked children accommodated by the local authority have subsequently gone missing (Rigby 2011; Rigby et al. 2012b), a figure similar to those missing from the Scottish Guardianship Service (McSween 2013). The Scottish approach, based on the Glasgow Model, which focuses on child protection decision-making and is recognised as best practice (London SCB 2011), may be one reason why the missing figures from Scotland are lower.

A child protection model

While there have been numerous calls for an approach to child trafficking victims that takes account of their particular vulnerabilities, within a child-focused setting (Somerset 2004; Kapoor 2007), there have been few clear models proposed since the initial NRM discussions with the Home Office and other agencies. There have been attempts in Scotland to promote a decision-making, protection and support model based on the experiences of the Glasgow Child Protection Committee, which places the responsibility for identification and decision-making around child trafficking with child protection agencies at a case conference, as part of the existing child protection arrangements (Rigby et al. 2014, see text below). Scottish proposals have identified a solution that is workable, utilises the additional expertise of a guardian, is clearly located within an existing integrated child protection system, and has emerging evidence of its potential effectiveness (Rigby 2009, 2011; Kohli and Crawley 2013; Rigby et al. 2012b).

Proposals for a child centred model (Rigby et al. 2014) envisage that the responsibility for both identification and care of trafficked children rests firmly within the existing safeguarding and child protection systems, and is consistent with everyday child protection practice. Where there is a suspicion or disclosure that a child may have been a victim of trafficking, a referral will be made to social services and police in line with local child protection and safeguarding procedures. Until such a time as all child protection professionals are appropriately trained, there should be at least two nominated, specifically trained child protection leads (social work and police) in each child protection committee/local safeguarding board area, who can screen the initial concerns.

An initial multi-agency child protection case discussion (meeting or virtual) would be convened as soon as possible if the initial screening by the leads (in discussion with other agencies) considered the young person to be a potential victim of trafficking. Contributions to the case discussion would be sought from all professionals who have contact with the young person, including UKVI if there are immigration issues.

The decision from this discussion would in effect be the current 'reasonable grounds' decision, following which a date should be set for a child protection case conference in line with local and national child protection guidance. This initial child protection case conference should include all the relevant agencies working with the young person. The young person and/or carer need not attend the meeting (indeed, it may not be appropriate at this stage if the young person does not know they are a victim of trafficking or there are concerns about the accompanying adults). However, the young person should be given an opportunity to pre-record a statement on video or other form of recording, or have their views heard via the relevant professional.

On the basis of all available evidence the initial child protection case conference should make a multi-agency decision as to whether the child is in need of care and protection as a result of being a victim of trafficking – a 'conclusive grounds' decision. The conference meeting should contain a clear decision outlining the reasons why there is a belief the child has or has not been trafficked, or is at risk. The decision would then be forwarded to UKHTC (and to UKVI where there are immigration and asylum issues).

Under such a model, the multi-agency conference would be the 'competent authority' locating trafficking identification and support in a multi-agency forum of child protection professionals in line with the original vision (OSCE 2004; Biaudet 2009). The process as well as identifying whether a child is a victim of human trafficking or not has the dual, and arguably more important purpose, of assessing each child's particular needs and ensuring access to safe accommodation, education, health, appropriate legal assistance, etc. in line with international and domestic standards.

Rather than relying on a limited number of 'expert' first responders, the new system would enable everyone, including members of the public, to refer cases to child protection authorities in line with any child protection referral. Local authorities, under relevant UK children's legislation and in line with Article 4 of the European Convention on Human Rights, should already be identifying child victims of human trafficking and ensuring that their basic safeguarding and support needs are met. The EU Directive consolidates this duty specifically for trafficking victims, and the proposed model brings trafficking processes in line with any other child protection issue.

The Home Office remain responsible for immigration control and for claims related to international protection. This model does not encroach on their prerogatives with regard to immigration/asylum issues. Rather, it places the child protection interest as the primary decision-making principle, and the immigration authorities are informed that a child is a victim of trafficking, after which the relevant decisions can be made by UKVI regarding asylum and protection status. The model also acknowledges the important central role of UKHTC in centrally recording all trafficking referrals. Most importantly for children, the model places responsibility for decision-making and safeguarding with the authorities who, in any other case of abuse and exploitation, would be the lead agencies in decision-making and providing subsequent support.

The needs of trafficked children are no different from those of other abused children in respect of safety and protection, education, health and legal advice where necessary (Rigby *et al.* 2012b), and similar to other children on the move (O' Connell Davidson 2011). All these groups of children have the potential for 'miserable consequences' (Kohli 2014) if there is a failure to act. Child protection agencies, whose primary duty is the protection of children and who have the experience, training and expertise required to identify and provide care to child victims of abuse and exploitation, are in a better position to ensure that both identification and subsequent interventions are in the child's best interest and meet safeguarding and developmental needs.

The safety and protection of all children is paramount; there should be no complacency, diminishing of responsibility, or hierarchy of responses dependent on immigration status, or route into exploitation and abuse. As indicated above, it is unclear why trafficked children should be treated any differently from other children in need of care and protection, as 'Viewing trafficking of children within the child protection agenda recognises how all children in the UK have access to child protection measures regardless of their legal status or permanent residence' (Hynes 2010: 98). If necessary additional training should be provided to child protection professionals (Beddoe 2007) to take account of additional needs and vulnerabilities for non-UK nationals as a consequence of being alone in a strange country, and not understanding the language and culture.

A multi-agency decision-making procedure led by child protection professionals within the existing integrated child protection system would ensure that practice develops in line with international obligations and best practice (FRA 2014; EU Directive). At all points in the process the child's safety and needs remain paramount, as in any other child protection investigation. Primarily, the model would reflect a child rights approach to child trafficking, enhance the quality of decisions in respect of a child's needs and ensure the primacy of a child's best interest. Crucially, it tasks the decision-making for potential trafficking victims within the same process as any other child where there are safety and well-being concerns.

The model would also be better able to balance the decision-making process and time scales with the recognised difficulty of gathering information from trafficking victims, as it avoids traumatic multiple interviews and, as it is child protection-focused, it allows for a non-time-limited recovery and reflection safeguarding period. It also ensures there is sufficient time to find a durable solution based on a child's needs, rather than any asylum/immigration issue.

Such a model recognises the importance of a guardian, in line with the EU Directive and based on the experiences of the Scottish Guardianship Project (Kohli and Crawley 2013), but firmly locates the guardian in the existing integrated child protection system (FRA 2014). A guardian for separated and trafficked children is important because of the additional vulnerabilities children may face by being alone in a strange country where they may not speak the language (Bokhari 2008). A guardian may be able to support a child through complex legal, immigration and policy processes, and be a consistent person in the child's life in the absence of a parental figure for separated and trafficked children, providing a link between agencies (Crawley 2006). This should not contradict, or usurp the role of child protection agencies.

Conclusion

There have been sufficient concerns raised to indicate that the needs and support for children are not being fully met by the present UK response to trafficking, as responses to child trafficking are not located, first and foremost, in the existing child protection systems. However, there are also concerns that local authorities and child protection workers have not yet been sufficiently trained to identify and support child victims of trafficking (Somerset 2004; Bokhari 2008;

Jones 2012). This does not mean that a new 'trafficking' system is required, as there is little evidence that children's needs will be best met through the 'expert' response of the NRM that operates outside the existing safeguarding systems.

The development of the NRM in the United Kingdom, while initially very much focused on the child protection system, appears by its conclusion and implementation to have been overtaken by political considerations in respect of law enforcement and immigration. This is in variance with UK child protection policy and legislation, which obliges that decisions should be made in the best interests of the child within a child-centred framework. The subsequent six years of practice has indicated substantial problems in meeting the needs of children in terms of protection and support. While the recent developments in the legislative process in the United Kingdom have seen some positive steps towards recognition of the need for the appointment of 'guardians' for child victims of trafficking to support them through the various immigration and welfare systems, the focus on a system of guardians may fail to recognise the multiple child protection needs associated with child victims (FRA 2014).

A model of child protection and trafficking practice in Glasgow since 2009 reflected the initial vision of the London discussions, perhaps it is time to return to these child-centred thoughts in the future UK-wide development of a child rights approach to trafficking.

References

All Wales Child Protection Procedures Review Group (AWCPP) (2011), *All Wales Practice Guidance for Safeguarding Children Who May Have Been Trafficked*, Cardiff: All Wales Child Protection Procedures Review Group, available at: http://www.awcpp.org.uk/wp-content/uploads/2014/03/All-Wales-Practice-Guidance-for-Safeguarding-Children-Who-May-Have-Been-Trafficked.pdf, last accessed 14 April 2015.

Anti-Trafficking Monitoring Group (ATMG) (2011), 'Trafficked Children Briefing Paper', London: Anti-Trafficking Monitoring Group, available at: http://www.antislavery.org/includes/documents/cm_docs/2011/c/children.pdf, last accessed 28 May 2015.

Asquith, S. and E. Turner (2008), *Recovery and Reintegration of Children from the Effects of Sexual Exploitation and Related Trafficking*, Geneva: Oak Foundation.

Beddoe, C. (2007), *Missing Out: A Study of Child Trafficking in the North-West, North-East and West Midlands*, London: End Child Prostitution and Trafficking UK.

Biaudet, E. (2009), 'OSCE Special Representative Encourages UK Government to Improve Identification of Child Victims of Trafficking', available at: http://www.osce.org/cthb/51058, last accessed 28 April 2015.

Bokhari, F. (2008), 'Falling through the gaps: safeguarding children trafficked into the UK', *Children and Society*, 22(3): 201–11.

Bovarnick, S. (2010), 'How do you define a "trafficked child"? A discursive analysis of practitioners' perceptions around child trafficking', *Youth and Policy*, 104: 80–97.

Chandran, P. (2011), 'The identification of victims of trafficking', in P. Chandran (ed.), *Human Trafficking Handbook: Recognising Trafficking and Modern Day Slavery in the UK*, London, LexisNexis, pp. 27–47.

Council of Europe (2005), Convention on Action against Trafficking in Human Beings, Strasbourg: Council of Europe, available at: http:// conventions.coe.int/Treaty/Commun/QueVoulezVous.asp?NT=197& CM=1&CL=ENG, last accessed 28 May 2015.

Crawley, H. (2006), *Child First, Migrant Second: Ensuring that Every Child Matters*, London: Immigration Law Practitioners Association.

Cree, V., G. Clapton and M. Smith (2012), 'The presentation of child trafficking in the UK: an old and new moral panic?', *British Journal of Social Work*, doi: 10.1093/bjsw/bcs120.

Department of Education (2011), *Safeguarding Children Who May Have Been Trafficked*, London: Department of Education, available at: http:// www.education.gov.uk/publications/standard/publicationDetail/Page1/ DFE-00084-2011, last accessed 30 March 2015.

Department of Justice Northern Ireland (DJNI) (2014), *Northern Ireland Human Trafficking Action Plan 2013–14*, Belfast: Department of Justice Northern Ireland, available at: http://www.dojni.gov.uk/search. lsim?sr=0&nh=10&cs=iso-8859-1&sc=doj-cms&sm=0&mt=1&ha=doj-cms&qt=child+trafficking, last accessed 9 April 2015.

End Child Prostitution and Trafficking (ECPAT) (2010), *Child Trafficking in the UK: A Snapshot*, London: End Child Prostitution and Trafficking UK, available at: http://www.ecpat.org.uk, last accessed 28 May 2015.

FRA (2014), *Guardianship for Children Deprived of Parental Care: A Handbook to Reinforce Guardianship Systems to Cater for the Specific Needs of Child Victims of Trafficking*, Luxembourg: European Union Agency for Fundamental Rights.

Home Affairs Committee (2009), *The Trade in Human Beings: Human Trafficking in the UK*, Sixth Report of Session 2008–9, London: House of Commons, available at: http://www.publications.parliament.uk/pa/ cm200809/cmselect/cmhaff/23/23i.pdf, last accessed 3 April 2015.

Home Office (2003), *Every Child Matters*, London: Home Office, available at: www.education.gov.uk/consultations/downloadableDocs/Every ChildMatters.pdf, last accessed 30 March 2015.

Home Office (2009), Update to the UK Action Plan on Tacking Human Trafficking, London: Home Office, available at: http://www.ungift. org/doc/knowledgehub/resourcecentre/Governments/Update_to_the_ UK_Action_Plan_on_Tackling_Human_Trafficking_en_2009.pdf, last accessed 12 June 2015.

Home Office (2011), *Human Trafficking: The Government's Strategy*, London: Home Office, available at: http://www.homeoffice.gov.uk/publications/crime/human-trafficking-strategy?view=Binary, last accessed 29 April 2015.

Home Office (2014a), *Review of the National Referral Mechanism for Victims of Human Trafficking*, London: Home Office.

Home Office (2014b), *Multi-Agency Working and Information Sharing Project: Final Report*, London: Home Office.

Home Office (n.d.), *National Referral Mechanism: Guidance for Child First Responders*, London: Home Office, available at: http://www.gov.uk/government/uploads/system/uploads/attachment_data/file/244697/NRM_First_Responder_Guidance.pdf, last accessed 28 April 2015.

Howard N. and M. Lalani (2008), 'The politics of human trafficking', *St Andrews International Review*, 4(1): 5–15.

Hynes, P. (2010), 'Understanding the "vulnerabilities", "resilience" and processes of the trafficking of children and young people into, within and out of the UK', *Youth and Policy*, 104: 97–118.

Hynes, P. (2013), 'Trafficking of children and young people: community knowledge and understanding', in M. Melrose and J. Pearce (eds), *Critical Perspectives on Child Sexual Exploitation and Related Trafficking*, Basingstoke: Palgrave, pp. 153–66.

International Labour Organisation (ILO) (2006), *Rehabilitation of the Victims of Child Trafficking: A Multidisciplinary Approach*, Bangkok: ILO, available at: http://www.humantrafficking.org/uploads/publications/20070626_124732_ilocpcr06_rehab_of_th_victims_octama.pdf, last accessed 24 April 2015.

Jones, J. (2012), 'Human trafficking in the UK: a focus on children', *Child and Family Law Quarterly*, 24(1): 77–94.

Kapoor, A. (2007), *A Scoping Project on Child Trafficking in the UK*, London: Child Exploitation and Online Protection.

Kohli, R. S. (2014), 'Protecting asylum-seeking children on the move', *Revue Européenne des Migrations Internationales*, 30(1): 83–104.

Kohli, R. and H. Crawley (2013), *She Endures With Me: An Evaluation of the Scottish Guardianship Service Pilot*, University of Aberystwyth/University of Bedfordshire.

London Safeguarding Children Board (London SCB) (2009), *London Safeguarding Trafficked Children Toolkit*, London: London Councils, available at: http://www.londonscb.gov.uk, last accessed 30 March 2015.

London Safeguarding Children Board (London SCB) (2011), *Final Monitoring Report, Local Authority Pilots of the London Safeguarding Trafficked Children Guidance and Toolkit*, London: London Councils, available at: http://www.londonscb.gov.uk/trafficking, last accessed 14 April 2015.

McSween, C. (2013), Evidence presented to the Modern Slavery Bill Joint Committee, House of Commons, London, available at: http://www.publications.parliament.uk/pa/jt201314/jtselect/jtslavery/166/16606.htm#n169, last accessed 30 March 2015.

National Crime Agency (2014), *National Referral Mechanism Statistics 2013*, London: National Crime Agency, available at: http://www.national crimeagency.gov.uk/publications/139-national-referral-mechanism-sta tistics-2013/file, last accessed 28 April 2015.

National Crime Agency (2015), *National Referral Mechanism Statistics – End of Year Summary 2014*, London: National Crime Agency, available at: http://www.nationalcrimeagency.gov.uk/publications/national-referral-mechanism-statistics/502-national-referral-mechanism-statistics-end-of-year-summary-2014/file, last accessed 28 April 2015.

O'Connell Davidson, J. (2010), 'New slavery, old binaries: human trafficking and the borders of "freedom"', *Global Networks*, 10(2): 244–61.

O'Connell Davidson, J. (2011), 'Moving children? Child trafficking, child migration, and child rights', *Critical Social Policy*, 31: 454.

Office of the First Minister and Deputy First Minister (2006), 'Our Children and Young People – Our Pledge: A Ten-Year Strategy for Children and Young People in Northern Ireland 2006–2016', available at: http://www.delni.gov.uk/ten-year-strategy_1_.pdf, last accessed 12 June 2015.

OHCHR (1989), Convention on the Rights of the Child, Office of High Commissioner for Human Rights, Geneva, available at: www.ohchr.org/en/professionalinterest/pages/crc.aspx, last accessed 28 April 2015.

Organisation for Security Co-operation Europe (OSCE) (2004), *National Referral Mechanisms: Joining Efforts to Protect the Rights of Trafficked Persons – A Practical Handbook*, Warsaw: Organisation for Security Co-operation Europe, Office for Democratic Institutions and Human Rights.

Pearce, J. (2011), 'Working with trafficked children and young people: complexities in practice', *British Journal of Social Work* , 30 March 2011, doi:10.1093/bjsw/bcr029, 1–18.

Rigby, P. (2009), *Child Trafficking in Glasgow: Report of a Case File Analysis of Unaccompanied Asylum Seeking Children*, Glasgow: Glasgow Child Protection Committee, available at: http://www.glasgowchildpro tection.org.uk, last accessed 30 March 2015.

Rigby, P. (2011), 'Separated and trafficked children: the challenges for child protection professionals', *Child Abuse Review*, 20(5): 324–40.

Rigby, P., M. Malloch and N. Hamilton-Smith (2012a), *Child Trafficking and Care Provision: Towards Better Survivor Care*, available at: http://www.sccjr.ac.uk/pubs/A-Report-on-Child-Trafficking-and-Care-Pro vision-Towards-Better-Survivor-Care/354, last accessed 30 March 2015.

Rigby, P., S. Murie and M. Ball (2012b), *Child Trafficking in Glasgow: The Journey So Far*, Glasgow: Glasgow Child Protection Committee, available at: http://www.glasgow.gov.uk/CHttpHandler.ashx?id=14223&p=0, last accessed 30 March 2015.

Rigby, P., K. Thomson, C. Macsween and C. Tudor (2014), *The Identification and Support of Child Victims of Trafficking in Scotland: A Child Protection Model*, Edinburgh: Scottish Parliament, available at: http://www.scottish.parliament.uk/S4_JusticeCommittee/Meeting%20 Papers/Papers20150310.pdf, last accessed 7 April 2015.

Rogowski, S. (2012), 'Social work with children and families: challenges and possibilities in the neo-liberal world', *British Journal of Social Work*, 42(5): 921–40.

Schloenhardt, A. and M. Loong (2011), 'Return and reintegration of human trafficking victims from Australia', *International Journal of Refugee Law*, 23(2): 143–73.

Scottish Government (2008), *A Guide to Getting It Right for Every Child*, Edinburgh: Scottish Government, available at: http://www.scotland.gov. uk/Publications/2008/09/22091734/9, last accessed 12 June 2015.

Scottish Government (2009), *Safeguarding Children in Scotland Who May Have Been Trafficked*, Edinburgh: Scottish Government, available at: http://www.scotland.gov.uk/Publications/2009/02/18092546/0,   last accessed 30 March 2015.

Scottish Parliament (2010), *Inquiry into Migration and Trafficking*, Equal Opportunities Committee, Edinburgh: Scottish Parliament, available at: http://archive.scottish.parliament.uk/s3/committees/equal/reports-10/ eor10-05-00.htm, last accessed 30 March 2015.

Scottish Parliament (2015), Response from the UK Human Trafficking Centre to questions raised during the Committee's evidence session on the Bill, on 17 March 2015, Edinburgh: Scottish Parliament, available at: http://www.scottish.parliament.uk/S4_JusticeCommittee/Meeting%20 Papers/Papers20150331.pdf, last accessed 14 April 2015.

Somerset, C. (2004), *Cause for Concern*, London: End Child Prostitution and Trafficking UK.

Spencer, J. and R. Broad (2012), 'The "groundhog day" of the human trafficking for sexual exploitation debate: new directions in criminological understanding', *European Journal of Criminology Policy and Research*, 18: 269–81.

UNHCR (2003), *Framework for Durable Solutions for Refugees and Persons of Concern*, Geneva: United Nations High Commissioner for Refugees, available at: http://www.unhcr.org/3f1408764.html, last accessed 28 April 2015.

United Nations (2000), Protocol to Prevent, Suppress and Punish Trafficking in Persons, Especially Women and Children, Supplementing the United Nations Convention against Transnational Organized Crime (Palermo Protocol), available at: http://www.uncjin.org/Documents/Conventions/ dcatoc/final_documents_2/convention_%20traff_eng.pdf.

Wallace, M. M. and K. Wylie (2011), 'Child trafficking: a Scottish perspective', *Commonwealth Judicial Journal*, 19: 1.

6 Responding to Victims of Human Trafficking: The Good, the Bad and the Ugly

Jim Laird

One of the key models of care and support for victims of human trafficking is the need for comprehensive and coordinated services. In this chapter I will share my experiences in dealing with over 200 victims of trafficking, identifying that this coordination has been far from the case in practice.

As Manager of the Refugee and Asylum Seeker Consortium in Scotland, I dealt with a number of human trafficking victims. Following this, I was appointed Trafficking Services Team Leader in Scotland for Migrant Help. The Trafficking Awareness Raising Alliance (TARA) and Migrant Help are the two agencies in Scotland funded by the Scottish Government to accommodate and support victims of human trafficking. TARA are funded to support female victims of sexual exploitation, and Migrant Help receives financial support to assist male and female victims of labour exploitation, male and female victims of domestic servitude, and male victims of sexual exploitation.

All the cases referred to in this chapter, and the operations mentioned, took place between 2009 and 2012. I am aware practice and procedures are continually developing, however, documenting some of the issues will highlight problems than can arise without good collaboration. The majority of cases with which I was involved related to labour exploitation. These comprised various types of exploitation, including cockle picking, selling DVDs and CDs in bars, distributing collection bags for clothing. In addition, there was the more common fruit and vegetable picking, labouring, etc. However, there were also a sizeable number of domestic servitude and sexual exploitation cases, including female victims. I also dealt with organ transplant and forced marriage victims.

In my considerable experience, the approach to the recovery of victims has been haphazard and frequently lacked any organisation, with participants from various agencies being unclear as to their role and to the overall objectives of the 'operation'. Often there are competing priorities among the agencies involved and a lack of any strategic overview.

This chapter will look at models of good practice, giving specific examples, examine interventions that have been less than successful, and look at areas where promising actions were hindered by poor strategic coordination. It will conclude by looking at how things can be improved in future. Some improvements have already been made, and the establishment of a Scotland-wide human trafficking unit, as part of Police Scotland, holds the promise of improved practices. In looking at a range of 'operations' here names have been changed to protect the guilty, as well as some innocents!

The Council of Europe Group of Experts on Action against Trafficking in Human Beings (GRETA) holds the long-standing view that a human rights-based approach is required by states to combat trafficking in human beings. This would require the establishment of a comprehensive framework for the prevention of trafficking in human beings, the protection of trafficked persons as victims of a serious human rights violation, and the effective investigation and prosecution of traffickers. This would involve ensuring that all victims of trafficking are properly identified, and measures put in place to empower trafficked persons by ensuring their rights to adequate protection, assistance and redress. This would include recovery and rehabilitation in a participatory and non-discriminatory framework, irrespective of their immigration status.

The human rights-based approach to action against trafficking in human beings entails, among other things, transparency and accountability on the part of the state through the adoption of a national policy and action plans for combating trafficking in human beings and *the coordination of the efforts of all relevant actors*. The United Kingdom's Human Trafficking Strategy for 2011–15 refers to trafficking in human beings as an 'abuse of basic rights' (UK Government 2011).

All the official material published on human trafficking in the United Kingdom stresses the importance of working together and the primacy of protecting victims of human trafficking. Unfortunately, words, policies and strategies fail to translate into action, and frequently victims are not properly supported and certainly not supported for long enough. Some of this is due to government policies and occasionally the failure of support and other agencies, but there have been many instances of victim support bodies not providing adequate advice, guidance and assistance.

Many of the raids and operations detailed here involved large groups of victims. However, there have also been many failings where only one or two victims have been identified and services have not been fully and properly coordinated.

One of the biggest human trafficking operations in Scotland began on a very small scale, but soon escalated into the biggest in the country to date. It started off with a couple of people turning up at a local police station to complain about the way they had been treated since arriving in the United Kingdom. Further investigation led to many more people being identified and ultimately over seventy people were interviewed. Unfortunately, many of them decided against cooperating with the investigation and declined to enter the National Referral Mechanism (NRM).

The NRM is the process by which people who may have been trafficked are referred, assessed and supported in the United Kingdom. The process was established in 2009 following the signing of the Council of Europe Convention on Action Against Trafficking in Human Beings (2005) by the UK Government. There have been numerous criticisms of the NRM process, not least that individuals have to sign the dedicated form to acknowledge that they are a victim before they can receive any assistance. The government has recently carried out a review of the NRM system and recommendations have been made.

The victims had all been persuaded to come to the United Kingdom to work and improve their lives by a range of deceptions. These included the use of advertising, websites, social media and visits to their locale from people posing as successful employees who had earned considerable amounts while employed in the United Kingdom. The victims ranged from well-qualified students to ordinary workers, both skilled and unskilled, and even included the mayor of a town that the traffickers had visited.

There were no officers who had any experience of human trafficking or in dealing with victims of this crime at the police station attended by the initial victims. After a couple of days spent looking for information and support agencies, contact was made with the Scottish Crime and Drugs Enforcement Agency Human Trafficking Coordinator. Following this, referrals were made to Migrant Help. The victims were picked up from the hotel, which had been arranged by the police, and put into safe accommodation that had been procured specifically for these victims.

The number of victims who came to the attention of the police over the next few days and weeks overwhelmed the officers who had been assigned to deal with these cases, and it soon became obvious that additional resources would be required. A small team was established to work on the investigation, which considerably improved the timescales involved in progressing things. This also helped to avoid what I had termed 'Taggart syndrome'. This is where police have been involved in investigating serious human trafficking offences, but are then moved away to work on other crimes, usually because 'there's been a murder'. This is a reference to the phrase used regularly in the police-related television series 'Taggart' where, invariably, other investigations take a back seat to the regular killings taking place in Glasgow. Crime briefings were always being interrupted by a senior officer coming into the room and proclaiming 'there's been a murder'!

The volume of cases was such that there were times when the police did not have sufficient resources to pick up victims from their accommodation provided by the traffickers. On occasion Migrant Help was asked to substitute. This, obviously, presented significant dangers; however, the risk to the victims was felt to be even more serious and the request was agreed to. In one instance, when picking up three victims from the accommodation, two of the traffickers turned up.

During the investigation it became apparent that there were a number of other crimes being perpetrated in addition to human trafficking. These included benefit fraud, identity theft, money laundering, as well as serious assault. One of the interesting aspects of this operation was the links between Eastern European crime syndicates and local Asian crime gangs. The Eastern European group provided the victims and the enforcers, and the Asians provided the accommodation and the transport.

It was only approaching the very end of the operation that the first multi-agency meeting took place. At the meeting, the Crown Office and Procurator Fiscal Service announced there was sufficient evidence to proceed with a prosecution, but that it would not be for human trafficking offences. The charges would be for fraud and deception and aggravated assault. There was some annoyance amongst agencies that after all their work no trafficking offences were being taken forward, particularly in the light of the very low number of such prosecutions that have taken place in Scotland. There had only been one successful prosecution in Scotland at that time. The resulting court case saw the alleged traffickers receive sentences averaging four years, but not for human trafficking. The prosecution of the case and the way it proceeded, in particular the handling of witnesses, also served to highlight the shortcomings in the way cases going to court were handled in Scotland.

In another large-scale operation, the lack of coordination and awareness of police and other structures in Scotland proved problematic. In a case involving trafficking victims picking shellfish from beaches on a Scottish island, one section of the police had received intelligence about people trafficking activity. They decided that they would take the lead in the operation and contacted the local police force for support on the ground. The police Human Trafficking Coordinator was left out of the loop and only found out about the operation third-hand. The support organisation, which was required to be on site to provide practical support and, more importantly, accommodation, were contacted only at the last minute as an afterthought. Another local-based third-sector agency became involved, roles were confused, organisational relationships were damaged and the whole exercise proved far more costly, in a fiscal sense, than was actually required.

The lack of forward planning, contact with appropriate service providers, and general absence of knowledge of structures and operational procedures in Scotland caused major difficulties for all concerned, not least the trafficking victims themselves. The outcome was a successful prosecution, but, again, not on human trafficking grounds. Gangmaster offences were used to prosecute and the outcome was community service, no custodial sentences were applied.

The Gangmasters Licensing Authority (GLA) is a non-departmental government body that was set up to protect workers from exploitation. Employment agencies, labour providers or gangmasters working in the agriculture, horticulture, shellfish gathering or any associated processing and packaging sector need a GLA licence to operate. Labour providers are assessed to check that they meet the GLA licensing standards, which cover health and safety, accommodation, pay, transport and training. The GLA check that these providers are fit to hold a licence and that tax, National Insurance and VAT regulations are met. A labour provider must have a GLA licence to work in the regulated sectors and it is a criminal offence to supply workers without a licence or to use an unlicensed labour provider.

The first successful prosecution for human trafficking in Scotland was a good example of how proper planning and good multi-agency working can achieve the desired, oft stated, aims; that is, protecting and supporting victims, and achieving a successful outcome in terms of convictions for traffickers. Close cooperation between a number of police forces across the United Kingdom, multi-agency meetings involving all the key players, including the UK Border Agency (UKBA), support organisations, HMRC and others, as well as good communication, all led to a successful conclusion. Clear leadership, a strategic overview and joined-up working all contributed to ensuring a first prosecution in Scotland. Unfortunately, lessons were not always learned and other operations fell into the same previous, unsuccessful, ways of working. These will be considered shortly.

This particular operation involved victims of sexual exploitation and included women trafficked from South America and the Far East through Europe and into the United Kingdom, as well as pre-op transsexual individuals from Scotland who were trafficked internally throughout the United Kingdom, including Scotland.

Although it was the first successful prosecution, only two of the four people on trial were actually convicted. The trial was also cut short as two of the four changed their pleas from not guilty to guilty. This led to them being given shorter sentences. Although this was beneficial to the victims, in that they did not have to go through the ordeal of giving evidence, the lack of a full trial meant that we could not get all the detail about how the trafficking operation was set up and conducted.

It is important to stress that a lack of joint working and cooperation frequently contributed to individuals who had been identified as trafficking victims failing to be properly supported. In addition, there can be less likelihood that any prosecution, far less a successful one, takes place. This can result in victims failing to receive appropriate support and protection. In one case, I received a call from a police force to say that a woman from the Far East had come in to a local station and identified herself as a victim of human trafficking. They asked for someone to come and collect her and put her in to safe accommodation. This, in spite of the fact that no one had interviewed her or taken a statement from her. I explained that, as we were particularly busy at that time, we did not have anyone available to pick her up. I also informed the caller that normal procedure would be for the police to interview the victim and then to call us to arrange for accommodation. Following this, the police would drop the victim off to us. I also pointed out that this was part of their duty of care towards the victim.

The unfortunate outcome of this case was that, despite repeated calls to the police station and conversations with the desk sergeant, the woman just got up and walked out of the police station. This was a number of hours after the initial phone call. No one had spoken to the woman during all that time, no one had noticed her leaving the station, and there was no interest in trying to ascertain what had happened to the woman. What became of the woman and what fate befell her remains unknown.

Other cases involving individuals who have been trafficked have identified other areas of concern over the support of victims. There have been a number of instances where people have found themselves kept in police cells, ostensibly for their own protection. Little or no training and no cascading of information regarding support arrangements for victims has been the norm. Victims of human trafficking, who have not committed any crime, being incarcerated, for no matter how short a period of time and even, allegedly, for their own protection, is unacceptable.

One particular instance of inappropriate care of victims took place following a UKBA operation. Four women who were suspected of being trafficked into the United Kingdom were picked up by officers from the UKBA. No coordination with any other agencies took place before the raid, so there was no police involvement and no assistance from victim support organisations. The operation took place on a weekend. I took a phone call from a police officer the following week informing me that the victims had been detained in the Immigration Detention Centre as they had entered the country illegally. I contacted the Immigration Detention Centre to arrange to see the victims and ascertain their circumstances and offer support. I was informed that they had already been returned to their country of origin. Is it little wonder that people are so suspicious of an asylum system whereby the investigator of their immigration status is also the same person who makes the decision on whether someone has been trafficked or not?

One of the best examples of a well-planned, properly coordinated operation actually resulted in no victims being identified. The operation was led by Lothian and Borders Police and involved raids on a number of premises in Edinburgh, all of which were suspected of holding victims of human trafficking. The initial meeting included the principal players who should have been involved in any planning meeting concerning human trafficking. The Scottish Crime and Drug Enforcement Agency Human Trafficking Unit, the Police, UKBA and the support organisation were all present. Chatham House rules, obviously, applied.

Full disclosure of the intelligence received about the potential victims was given. This allowed a full and frank discussion about what could be expected during the operation. It also allowed the victim support organisation to consider what arrangements would be required to be put in place to allow full and proper support to be provided.

It was agreed that the best way to proceed would be to establish a number of sub-groups to look at specific issues. One was set up solely to look at how any recovered victims would be supported. The others would consider the roles of the police and UKBA, and examine how and where the perpetrators would be interviewed and, if necessary, detained. Regular planning meetings took place and by the time of the raid every participant fully understood their roles and responsibilities.

Following the operation, a meeting reviewing the processes involved and their success, or otherwise, took place. No victims were recovered, so there was no opportunity to look at support arrangements to see if they worked or not. However, important lessons were learned, particularly in the pre-planning and coordination arrangements.

Final thoughts

There are many other past examples of how poor planning and preparation has led to poor performance, particularly in the care and support of victims, and, as indicated, some more positive practice. The case studies shared here are examples of the way things were actually conducted on the ground. Recent reports from the National Crime Agency (2014) and the Home Office (2014) emphasise the importance of victim support. New tougher legislation across the United Kingdom also promotes the same. However, these developments will mean nothing unless they are translated into action and lessons learned from the past.

Much more has to be done to put victim care at the centre of the responses of all key players involved in human trafficking. It should not just be left to the organisations funded to support victims to prioritise victim care and support. Nor should these groups be seen as the conscience of all of those involved.

Much of what has been written by way of policies and outlined in legislation would be more than adequate to provide a platform for supporting and caring for victims. However, in my experience, few of these policies and procedures seem to translate into action and improved practice. Infrequent training and seminars, occasional distribution of appropriate information, and little or no publicity will never translate the rhetoric into consistent support and care of victims.

Putting into practice many of the stated objectives of anti-trafficking policy in the United Kingdom would go a long way towards protecting victims and should lead to more successful prosecutions. The 'reflection period' of forty-five days as part of the NRM process is not long enough to properly support victims following their recovery. The recommended period contained in the Explanatory Notes to the Council of Europe's Convention (Council of Europe n.d.) is thirty days, and no doubt the UK Government would argue that their scheme is more generous. However, I have yet to meet any victim who has not required support of varying kinds beyond a forty-five-day period. In addition, I have never met any other professional working in the field who believes that forty-five days is adequate. In one case with which I am still involved, the legal process has taken almost five years to date and we still have not been to trial yet.

To end on a positive note, there are a number of developments that have the potential to change the way victims are protected and should lead to more prosecutions. The case studies provided in this chapter are obviously from the (recent) past, and I am hopeful that we can learn from mistakes by acknowledging some of the problems I have encountered and build on the identified issues.

The establishment of a dedicated National Human Trafficking Unit (NHTU) by Police Scotland should lead to a more consistent approach in the recovery of victims and the prosecution of traffickers. Previously, out of the eight police forces in Scotland only one, Strathclyde, had a dedicated unit. The Scottish Crime and Drugs Enforcement Agency also had a small unit, but many forces were unaware of its existence.

The NHTU was established to ensure 'an effective, coordinated and victim-focused response' to human trafficking, and to act as a single point of contact for law enforcement agencies and statutory and non-statutory agencies. Fourteen Human Trafficking 'champions' have been created in each of the policing divisions, which Police Scotland state will 'embed best practice and ensure a consistently high level of investigation and victim care' (Police Scotland 2015). The early signs are certainly promising, but it is too soon to properly evaluate the unit's effectiveness.

The second opportunity to achieve a meaningful response to victim support for trafficking victims in Scotland is the introduction in the Scottish Parliament of the Human Trafficking and Exploitation (Scotland) Act. This ground-breaking piece of legislation seeks to 'consolidate and strengthen the existing criminal law against human trafficking and exploitation and enhance the status of and support for its victims' (Scottish Parliament 2014: 3). The Act is in six parts, and Part 2 (Protection of Victims) includes provision on prosecutorial instructions for the prosecution of victims and for the support and assistance to which adult victims are entitled.

Obviously, the devil will be in the detail, but there seems to be a genuine groundswell of opinion that the final clauses in the Act will be robust enough to finally ensure a fully joined-up approach to supporting victims. The hope is that the time frame for supporting victims will, at last, be realistic and reflect the period that victims need.

References

Council of Europe (n.d.), *Explanatory Note to the Council of Europe's Convention on Human Trafficking*, Strasbourg: Council of Europe, available at: http://www.conventions.coe.int/treaty/en/reports/html/197.htm, last accessed 30 March 2015.

Home Office (2014), *Review of the National Referral Mechanism for Victims of Human Trafficking*, London: Home Office, available at: http://socialwelfare.bl.uk/subject-areas/services-activity/criminaljustice/homeoffice/170470Review_of_the_National_Referral_Mechanism_for_victims_of_human_trafficking.pdf, last accessed 30 March 2015.

National Crime Agency (2014), *NCA Strategic Assessment: The Nature and Scale of Human Trafficking in 2013*, London: National Crime Agency, available at: http://www.nationalcrimeagency.gov.uk/publications/399-nca-strategic-assessment-the-nature-and-scale-of-human-trafficking-in-2013/file, last accessed 30 March 2015.

Police Scotland (2015), Justice Committee Human Trafficking and Exploitation (Scotland) Bill, Written Submission, available at: http://www.scottish.parliament.uk/S4_JusticeCommittee/Inquiries/HTE45PoliceScotland.pdf, last accessed 30 March 2015.

Scottish Parliament (2014), *Human Trafficking and Exploitation (Scotland) Bill: Explanatory Notes (and other accompanying documents)*, Edinburgh: Scottish Parliament, Session 4, available at: http://www.scottish.parliament.uk/S4_Bills/Human%20Trafficking%20Bill/b57s4-introd-en.pdf, last accessed 30 March 2015.

UK Government (2011), *Human Trafficking: The Government's Strategy*, London: Home Office.

7 Does It Happen Here?

Sheila Murie and Liz Owens

The issue of child trafficking is one that Glasgow City Council has been grappling with since 2006–7, when, along with partner agencies, concerns first started to be raised about unaccompanied and separated children arriving in the city. These concerns centred around the nature of their journeys and their stories of exploitation and abuse, prior to, during their journeys and on arrival in the city. During our first encounter with the concept of child trafficking we asked the question 'does it happen here?' We were expecting the answer to be 'no', but clearly this was not the case. This was the start of a long journey for child protection professionals in Glasgow. Both in coming to terms with the fact it was happening in the city, and having to respond and react to serious cases of child abuse without a national commitment to the established child protection framework as the most suitable multi-agency forum for identifying and supporting child trafficking victims.

As members of the local authority social work department we sit within the centre strategic and policy team, with a specific child protection remit. In brief, our role and function is to promote and support best practice in child protection policy and practice. This is done via policy and practice development, training and case consultation. We work in partnership with managers and practitioners from our own agency, as well as collaborating with partner agencies represented within Glasgow Child Protection Committee. We are also involved in collaborative work with academic institutions and the Scottish Government, and in relation to trafficking specifically we work closely with the Home Office (UK Visa and Immigration) and the UK Human Trafficking Centre.

In order to support the development of best practice responding to research and new trends in the area of child protection, it is vital that we keep up to date with current research and developments both nationally and internationally. Our commitment and experience of child trafficking has developed considerably since 2006. At the outset, although vaguely aware of child trafficking, our experience was limited and we forged a working partnership with the London Safeguarding Children's Board (LSCB), recognising their experience in this field. In partnership with LSCB we developed a risk assessment tool for child trafficking. We then began, with their support, to transfer their experience and learning into a Glasgow and Scottish context. It should be noted that in these early stages we were reliant on UK-wide policy and procedures, but, importantly, also reliant on years of practice, management and policy experience of working with vulnerable and abused children.

In Glasgow we drew on our experience and absorbed the new knowledge and learning, and further developed and amended our existing child protection procedures creating specific guidance for child trafficking (Glasgow CPC 2009, 2014). We also engaged in local research, which enabled us to commit to the development of the evidence-based inter-agency policy and procedures. The learning from the research and case review audits enabled us to challenge errors made in both single and multi-agency practice in a much more informed and detailed way. We believe our most crucial decision at the outset, informed by the research and practice experience, was to locate child trafficking firmly in the existing child protection framework. While this is widely recognised now as best practice (although perhaps not in implementation as decision-making regarding identification still rests outside the child protection system), it attracted criticism outside of Glasgow. However, Glasgow Child Protection Committee has always been fully supportive of this approach.

A variety of working groups were established, the main one being a trafficking sub-group of the Child Protection Committee. Key partners included, police, health, education, voluntary sector agencies and the Home Office. This forum enabled the learning to continue to develop and be shared across all agencies. We were continually examining the details of the referrals, nationality, journeys and the types of exploitation, in addition to any social and biographical details we could collate. The working group is not designed to fix individual case difficulties, such as when policy and procedures have not been followed; however, there have been a number of occasions where we have used this forum to review and address practice deficits. This has been problematic at times as, in the absence of clear national guidance and strategy, we have been learning on a case-by-case basis.

From 2008 substantial activity has taken place in raising awareness of child trafficking both within the social work setting and across partner agencies. This has included single agency training and practice development sessions, as well as multi-agency briefings across the city. As child protection is everyone's responsibility, it is essential across all agencies that workers are alert to the indicators of child trafficking. Although targeted training goes some way to raise awareness, the ability to translate this into practice is often more of a challenge. More recently the team and key partners have been heavily involved in the Scottish developments relating to the National Referral Mechanism (NRM) and ongoing work with the Scottish Government following the Scottish trafficking summit and the debate around the human trafficking legislation.

As a strategic team developing our own knowledge of practice within this area we continually face challenges in driving practice improvement in both our own organisation and on a multi-agency basis. From the outset positive and productive relationships were established with specialist and dedicated staff within all organisations, however, any changes to personnel diluted the effectiveness of the joint work and led to a 'begin again syndrome'. While the child protection team within social work has remained consistent, and has developed substantial experience in working with trafficking cases, we have found that staff changes in partner organisations has resulted in slow strategic progress and the repeating of discussions that we were having six years ago. This has resulted in practice development also being stalled and delayed.

The slow development across agencies has also been replicated within our own organisation, as the relatively rapid research and policy response across Glasgow has not always been replicated in practice. Specifically in relation to residential and fieldwork services we encountered difficulties and inconsistencies in the identification of trafficked children. There was, and remains in some cases, a reluctance to acknowledge trafficking as an issue in Scotland. Where there was a commitment to address the issues workers struggled to identify indicators of trafficking along with the risks associated with the safe care of the young people. One of the major challenges was, and remains to date, changing the views of professionals that children are no longer at risk, and their trafficking journey and exploitation ended, when we found and accommodated them.

One of the ways the team sought to support improvements in practice was to be informed and involved in every trafficking referral, providing advice, guidance and support, attending meetings and taking responsibility for facilitating the NRM referral. Local and national guidance (Glasgow CPC 2009, 2014; Scottish Government

2013), developed from the research and practice experience, indicates that all child trafficking referrals should come via social work child protection in conjunction with police colleagues before referral to the NRM. Since 2008, the child protection team have been made aware of, and have been involved in assessments and screening of over 200 trafficking referrals, although not all have been referred to the NRM as many are historical. This has allowed us to have an overview of the picture in Glasgow and identify trends. This in turn enables us to refresh guidance and workers' knowledge based on the collective experience.

While mistakes have been made, the awareness of trafficking across Glasgow has increased, as has an holistic child protection response. However, we remain concerned that all suspicions of trafficking are not approached through the agreed child protection procedures. We are also not complacent about the challenges of raising awareness of child trafficking amongst all professionals and the need to revisit training in the light of developing knowledge and legislation. Constant staff changes in all organisations suggest that while updating of knowledge is vital for those previously trained, there is also a continued requirement to repeat basic training and awareness sessions. Keeping child trafficking on the agenda after the new Scottish legislation is enacted will be difficult; it would be easier if it were an integrated part of the child protection system, not an add-on.

On occasion, to promote changes in practice and enhance the support provided to children, we were required to be assertive in our approach with colleagues, challenging their assessment, assumptions and often decision-making. Although this can still be the case, it is to a lesser degree as knowledge and experience has developed, it is vital this experience is not lost as staff changes occur. A result of this assertive approach has been the recognition that a comprehensive child's assessment and plan, based on the 'Getting it right for every child principles' (Scottish Government 2015), coupled with a specific child trafficking assessment is most likely to identify and manage risks. However, ensuring everybody adopts this integrated approach has been problematic.

Our learning developed as our experience grew; our first identified young people were part of the unaccompanied asylum population and as such immigration was an issue. We were focused on trying to understand their journey and what the implications were for these children and young people. We needed to understand what their needs were; were they something specific and different from UK and European children? As time and practice developed, with improvements in identification and workers' awareness, our experience of child trafficking victims became more varied, and we quickly identified similar needs across all children who had been trafficked, exploited or abused. We have identified specific issues with some of the trafficked children group, but believe on the whole that their need for protection, safety, education and health is the same as for all children. Some of the specific issues include:

- young children who appear in a family who have allegedly travelled to join them, this often raises questions over DNA testing and who pays for it;
- fathers presenting with young babies and the whereabouts of mothers are unknown;
- Chinese children who go missing are allegedly returned home to extended families with no ability to confirm travel details etc.;
- groups of young people from the same country who are found in cannabis cultivations or nail bars;
- pregnant women who present late in their pregnancy and often go missing again shortly after the birth of the child;
- a more recent trend that has been identified is trafficked victims already being linked with a solicitor at the time of identification, this obviously raises questions;
- internal trafficking and sexual exploitation.

In Glasgow, despite opposition from some of the 'expert' agencies, we made a conscious decision to locate child trafficking within our child protection procedures and processes; this approach has now been adopted as national guidance in Scotland. However, challenges have been many. While the police were always receptive to social work as the lead child protection agency and we have worked closely together from the outset, the UK-wide consensus has to date viewed trafficking as an immigration or criminal issue with less focus on the protection of vulnerable children.

While the Home Office (UK Visas and Immigration) have to come to the table when it is child trafficking, attendance at child protection meetings as a matter of course has been a new role for them. A role that at times may not be in harmony with child protection and best interests of the child when immigration is the main focus. Some of the difficulties have been in relation to the decision-making process for immigration and how that can conflict with the decision for trafficking.

We have found this to be a particularly difficult time for children. When they get a negative decision, it can reinforce to them that they have not been believed, which is often what the traffickers will have threatened them with. We have witnessed the deterioration in a child's presentation and demeanour following negative decisions of the competent authority, despite a child protection case conference, attended by professionals they know and trust, believing them and making a referral to the NRM.

As our experience has developed over the last six years we have been less concerned about a negative NRM decision. We have been clear that safeguarding children, and our belief in the primacy of the child protection process and duty of care to the child remains the priority. We are presently involved in the current debate around the NRM review (Home Office 2014), where our belief, based on experience and practice, is that the decision regarding trafficking should not sit with the Home Office, UKHTC or any expert panel, but should sit within the child protection process.

In a Glasgow context, there is a view that outcomes for children are identified as being positive. Although this is still early in the process, to date, we believe we do not have the same numbers of young people going missing from care that other authorities experience. We consider that this has been a result of the child-centred, child protection approach that we adopted from the outset. However, we are not complacent and recognise that longitudinal research, and increased scrutiny of our database, is required to allow us to say with conviction whether this remains the same longer term. We are concerned that in general responses to child trafficking are not underpinned by a clear evidence base, something that we would like to see addressed in Scotland at least, following the forthcoming legislation and guidance.

When considering what we could have done differently we have reflected particularly on the use of the child protection register. We initially chose not to use this for older young people and to use local procedures that mirrored the child protection process, for teenagers. However, with the updated national child protection procedures (Scottish Government 2014) there is now the opportunity to record these children on the child protection register, similar to any other child at risk of significant harm. This is something we will consider, and again reflects our acknowledgement of the need to constantly improve our policies and practice.

The use of the Children's Hearing, a specifically Scottish system that provides support for all children with care and protection and offending-related needs, is something of a controversial debate. In our opinion the referral of unaccompanied young people does not happen for two reasons: (1) children arriving at 16 are not considered as children in terms of a referral to a Children's Hearing; and (2) a 'no order principle' indicates they are voluntarily agreeing to comply with their protection plans and compulsory measures are not required. If we decide to use the child protection process differently this may resolve the issue of referrals to the Hearing system. However, the age issue remains a problem, especially when there are concerns about 16- and 17-year-old trafficked children falling through the net.

More recently, following work over the last three years, there has been a concerted effort to locate the sexual exploitation of UK children within the broader trafficking discourse. There is now little disagreement that the trafficking and exploitation of non-UK nationals is an issue in Glasgow; following a number of recent initiatives there are also substantial concerns about the sexual exploitation of children in the city. The bringing together of these issues, as an overall child protection concern is proving problematic. While the broad approach of the local Child Protection Committee has consistently been to locate any exploitation and abuse of children in a child protection framework, this has often met with some resistance as the call for 'specialist' or 'expert' services is made.

Overall, from a practitioner's perspective, and from a commitment to the safeguarding and protection of all children, it has been disconcerting that those professionals with substantial experience of child protection and trafficking have consistently been side-lined as trafficking became a media and political issue over the last couple of years. Our experience in Glasgow has suggested that the needs of trafficked children mirror those of most children who have been abused and exploited, and that many of the problems associated with their identification and protection are a result of the focus on immigration and asylum. As experienced professionals this has been, and remains, frustrating. This frustration is deepened when children are lost amongst the debates about human trafficking which focus attention on adults. A focus on children has, in our experience, never been a priority in the human trafficking discourse. This was exemplified in Scotland when the first draft of the Human Trafficking Bill as introduced largely overlooked children, in the hope that the child protection system would be the vehicle for support and protection, even though this system has been largely ignored by policymakers in the past as the ideal framework for identification and safeguarding.

Glasgow has made tremendous progress over the last ten years in its multi-agency response to child trafficking. While we have made mistakes and are continually learning, it is difficult to witness the protracted debates happening nationally that we had nearly ten years ago. It is hard to see why trafficked children are not afforded the same rights to a child-centred, safeguarding and protection process as all other children. Our experiences suggest that while there may be additional concerns regarding risks and protection plans (including rehabilitation), a child's need to be safe, healthy, included and educated does not differ depending on country of origin, immigration status or route into abuse and exploitation. We fear there remains much work to do before parity of response and support is achieved.

References

Glasgow CPC (2009), *Inter Agency Guidance for Child Trafficking*, Glasgow: Child Protection Committee.

Glasgow CPC (2014), *Inter Agency Guidance for Child Trafficking: Child Trafficking Assessment National Referral Mechanism*, Glasgow: Child Protection Committee, available at: https://www.glasgowchildprotection. org.uk/CHttpHandler.ashx?id=12917&p=0, last accessed 24 April 2015.

Home Office (2014), *Review of the National Referral Mechanism for Victims of Human Trafficking*, London: Home Office, available at: http:// socialwelfare.bl.uk/subject-areas/services-activity/criminaljustice/homeof fice/170470Review_of_the_National_Referral_Mechanism_for_victims_ of_human_trafficking.pdf, last accessed 24 April 2015.

Scottish Government (2013), *Inter-Agency Guidance for Child Trafficking: Child Trafficking Assessment National Referral Mechanism*, Edinburgh: Scottish Government, available at: http://www.gov.scot/Resource/0043/ 00437636.pdf, last accessed 24 April 2015.

Scottish Government (2014), *National Guidance for Child Protection in Scotland*, Edinburgh: Scottish Government, available at: http://www.gov. scot/Resource/0045/00450733.pdf, last accessed 24 April 2015.

Scottish Government (2015), *Wellbeing: Getting it Right for Every Child*, Edinburgh: Scottish Government, available at: http://www.gov.scot/ Topics/People/Young-People/gettingitright, last accessed 24 April 2015.

8 Promoting Psychological Recovery in Victims of Human Trafficking

Sharon Doherty and Rachel Morley

Introduction

Trafficking has been described as 'a multi-stage process of cumulative harm' (Zimmerman *et al.* 2011: 327) that occurs at the severe end of a 'continuum of exploitation' (Skrivankova 2010: 19). Trafficking can involve victims being subjected to extreme violence and abuse, psychological manipulation, coercion and control over extended periods of time. This abuse has been described, in some cases, as akin to torture (OSCE 2013) and the psychological effects can be severe.

In the face of such suffering, there is an imperative to act to restore the human rights, health and well-being of victims. This is enshrined in the Council of Europe Convention on Action Against Trafficking (2005) and articulated in EU Directive 2011/36/EU (2011). This Directive, which stipulates that victims of trafficking should receive assistance towards 'their physical, psychological and social recovery' (p. 6) was transposed into UK law in April 2013.

This chapter will focus on the psychological effects of being trafficked for exploitation and explain how psychological therapy can contribute to the psychological recovery of victims. It describes the approach to working psychologically with adult and adolescent victims of trafficking used by the COMPASS Team (NHS Greater Glasgow and Clyde Psychological Trauma Service), as well as some of the challenges associated with this work. In this chapter, those who have experienced being trafficked will be referred to as 'victims of trafficking' to convey the serious harm that trafficking can do. However, the authors have also learned from their clients about the strength, determination and resilience that it takes to be a 'survivor of trafficking'.

Although the focus of this chapter is psychological therapy, it is recognised that, for psychological recovery to be possible, a multi-agency response, providing protection from traffickers, safe housing, physical healthcare, psychosocial support, interpreting, legal representation, and a welcoming and hospitable host community is also needed (Macy and Johns 2012).

Glasgow service context

The authors offer insights into responding to the psychological needs of victims of trafficking that are based on their experience of working therapeutically with victims of all forms of trafficking for sexual exploitation, forced labour and domestic servitude. This work has taken place within the COMPASS Team, an all-age NHS mental health service for victims of complex trauma who are seeking asylum in Glasgow and, more recently, in the context of innovative partnership work between the COMPASS Team and the Trafficking Awareness Raising Alliance (TARA) Service (Community Safety Glasgow). The TARA Service is a specialist front-line support service for women who have been trafficked for sexual exploitation. This partnership is currently funded by the Scottish Government and involves a consultant clinical psychologist being co-located with the service. By promoting a close working relationship between post-trafficking support and psychological services, this service model allows the mental health needs of trafficked women to be identified, assessed and responded to at an early point following their entry into post-trafficking support. Psychological understanding is also available to inform multi-agency care and support plans, as well as National Referral Mechanism (NRM) and asylum decisions.

Trafficking as a process of cumulative trauma

To understand the psychological impact of human trafficking, it is important to appreciate the cumulative nature of the abuse and harm experienced by victims. Children targeted by traffickers are often vulnerable through prior experiences of sexual or physical abuse or neglect (Abas *et al.* 2013). Early death of parents may leave children with no one to advocate for them, protect them or provide for them financially. Children may already be living on the street. Families living in dire poverty may be persuaded by false promises of money or education to give up their children. Those trafficked in adulthood may be exploited as they try to escape poverty, forced marriage, female genital mutilation or other forms of hardships and abuse.

Traffickers operate in areas where they can trade in human beings with impunity. They often use a combination of physical and sexual violence and psychological abuse to gain power and control over their victims and to maintain secrecy. They shame and humiliate victims, and use a variety of techniques to make victims feel complicit in, or to blame for, what is happening. In parts of Nigeria, traffickers often use the culturally deep-rooted fear of the power of ju-ju, voodoo or black magic to coerce and maintain control over victims (ECPAT 2008). Ritual oath ceremonies may take place over many hours, are often cruel, painful and degrading, and involve suggestion about the power of ju-ju to harm the victim or others close to them if the oath is broken. Victims who escape traffickers to tell of their experiences can often experience a paralysing sense of being cursed.

Victims of trafficking are physically removed from community, family and friends. This means that the trauma of being trafficked is not buffered by access to any social support. Trafficked children often have no access to the protective factors of education, play, predictable routines or the support of reliable adults. It is not surprising, in the context of this cumulative trauma and neglect, that the capacity of the individual to cope can be overwhelmed, and result in significant mental health difficulties.

Understanding psychological distress in victims of trafficking

Research into the mental health consequences of human trafficking is at a relatively early stage. In the main, research has documented the impact of human trafficking on mental and physical health, and has been based on the experiences of women and girls who have been trafficked for the purpose of sexual exploitation, and who are in receipt of post-trafficking support services. Research into the impact of forced labour and domestic servitude on mental health has received more limited attention.

Existing studies indicate that women who have been trafficked for sexual exploitation, and who are in contact with post-trafficking support services, display symptoms of post-traumatic stress disorder (PTSD), depression and anxiety (Cwikel *et al.* 2004; Tsutsumi *et al.* 2008; Zimmerman *et al.* 2008; Hossain *et al.* 2010; Ostrovschi *et al.* 2011), as well as high levels of 'hostility' and 'aggression' (Zimmerman *et al.* 2008; Deb *et al.* 2011). High levels of symptomatology are consistently reported and there is evidence that distress persists over time (Zimmerman *et al.* 2008; Hossain *et al.* 2010; Ostrovschi *et al.* 2011). A range of physical symptoms, including fatigue, headaches, dizziness, poor memory, poor appetite, back and pelvic pain, have also been documented (Zimmerman *et al.* 2008; Oram *et al.* 2012). In addition, there is evidence that longer time spent in the trafficking situation is associated with higher levels of depression and anxiety symptoms (Hossain *et al.* 2010), and that distress is predicted by a history of child sexual/emotional abuse as well as by number of unmet needs in the post-trafficking environment (Abas *et al.* 2013). High levels of social support in the post-trafficking environment have been found to predict lower levels of mental disorder (Abas *et al.* 2013).

Although victims of exploitation for forced labour are commonly subject to 'threats . . . physical and psychological abuse, intimidation and isolation as well as dangerous working conditions' (Geddes *et al.* 2013), the impact of this type of exploitation on mental health has received limited attention and more research is clearly needed. Those studies which do exist (Tsutsumi *et al.* 2008; Turner-Moss *et al.* 2013) nonetheless report that victims of labour exploitation experience clinically significant levels of anxiety and depression symptoms.

Existing studies have begun to define the nature and extent of the effects of human trafficking on the mental health of victims. They are limited, however, in the main by their reliance on questionnaire measures of psychological functioning, which may not capture the range, complexity, severity or functional impact of the mental health difficulties experienced by victims of trafficking. Research based on victims of other forms of repeated and prolonged interpersonal trauma indicates that this type of trauma can result in victims developing a complex range of mental health difficulties (Cloitre *et al.* 2009). Studies using structured clinical interviewing are therefore needed to more fully describe the mental health difficulties of victims of trafficking for all forms of exploitation.

Complex PTSD

The term 'complex PTSD' has been developed by the International Society for Traumatic Stress Studies (ISTSS 2012) to provide a framework and description of the effects that cumulative interpersonal trauma can have on the mental health of victims. Complex PTSD is defined as:

> the result of exposure to repeated or prolonged instances of multiple forms of interpersonal trauma, often occurring under circumstances

where escape is not possible due to physical, psychological, matura-
tional, family/environmental or social constraints. Such traumatic stress-
ors include childhood physical and sexual abuse, recruitment into armed
conflict as a child, being a victim of domestic violence, sex trafficking or
slave trade; experiencing torture, and exposure to genocide campaigns or
other forms of organised violence. (p. 4)

Being trafficked for exploitation constitutes a prolonged and interpersonal trauma where escape is not possible. Complex PTSD comprises
the core symptoms of PTSD (re-experiencing, numbing/avoidance
and hyper-arousal), as well as a broader range of difficulties affecting emotional regulation; the capacity to form and maintain relationships; attention and consciousness; and beliefs about the self,
the world and others. Somatic distress and disorganisation is also
often present. In our clinical experience, not all victims of trafficking
present with all types of difficulties characteristic of complex PTSD.
We have nonetheless found this framework to be a useful way of
capturing and describing the range of mental health difficulties that
victims of trafficking can experience.

Best practice guidelines for complex PTSD

The ISTSS has developed best practice guidelines for treating
complex PTSD in adults that are based on consensus expert opinion
and a review of the empirical literature (Cloitre *et al.* 2011). These
guidelines recommend taking a phase-based, sequenced approach to
therapy using a range of types of intervention 'tailored to the most
prominent symptoms' (p. 3). An emerging consensus for working
with children and young people who are experiencing complex
traumatic stress also supports the use of a phase-based therapeutic
approach (Leenarts *et al.* 2013).

The ISTSS guidelines specify that:

[The first stage of treatment (Phase 1) should] focus on ensuring the individual's safety, reducing symptoms, and increasing important emotional,
social and psychological competencies. Phase 2 focuses on processing
the unresolved aspects of the individual's memories of traumatic experiences. This phase emphasises the review and re-appraisal of traumatic
memories, so that they are integrated into an adaptive representation of
self, relationships and the world. Phase 3, the final phase of treatment,
involves consolidation of treatment gains to facilitate the transition from
the end of the treatment to greater engagement in relationships, work or
education, and community life. (p. 5)

The ISTSS guidelines emphasise 'not only the reduction of psychiatric symptoms, but equally, improvement in key functional capacities for self-regulation and strengthening of psychosocial and environmental resources' (p. 5).

The following section describes phase-based psychological intervention for victims of trafficking. This section is not intended to provide a detailed description of psychological therapy for complex PTSD per se (for this, see ISTSS guidelines; Courtois and Ford 2013; Ford and Courtois 2013) or a comprehensive description of therapy for victims of trafficking. It aims, instead, to show some ways in which psychological therapy can contribute towards restoring the rights, integrity and emotional well-being of those who are trafficked.

Psychological assessment, formulation and treatment planning

Psychological therapy is underpinned by psychological assessment, which leads to a formulation (that is, a shared sense-making) of the factors maintaining a client's current difficulties. This formulation should be jointly shared, culturally meaningful, make clear the links between past experiences and current difficulties, and inform a treatment plan. Making sense of trauma symptoms in this way can help to relieve the client's anxiety that they are permanently damaged by their experiences or 'going crazy'. Identifying treatment goals can instil hope that recovery can be possible.

Consideration is also given to the need for psychiatric assessment or medication (for example, in response to suicide risk or depression). Clients can benefit from medication, in conjunction with psychological therapy, to treat depression, severe anxiety and nightmares, sleep difficulties and paranoid feelings. A psychiatric in-patient stay, or input from crisis services may be necessary if mental health difficulties are severe and there is a significant risk of suicide or self-harm.

Phase I interventions: establishing safety

Being safe and protected from traffickers and further harm

In therapy, attention should be paid to the real ongoing risks faced by victims of trafficking. Risks should be responded to by multi-agency child and adult protection plans and, where appropriate, by support from the police.

Clinical psychologists can support victims to manage the stress of navigating the NRM/asylum system by acknowledging how hard this can be, monitoring mental health risks, and helping with stress management. Where appropriate, psychologists can liaise with lawyers and advocate directly with UK Visas and Immigration (UKVI). Psychologists can also contribute psychological reports documenting the impact of trafficking on the mental health of victims to inform NRM and asylum decisions, and providing information on psychological factors that may make it difficult for victims to give a coherent and well-structured account of their experiences. Psychologists can also contribute advice on ways to interview in legal contexts to reduce the risk of re-traumatisation.

Safe and supportive relationships

As victims of trafficking can find social contact very difficult to tolerate because they fear and mistrust others, it is particularly important to take time to develop trust in the therapeutic relationship. Victims of trafficking can then be helped to develop a gentle routine, to orientate to where they are living, to understand local systems, and learn the language and other skills that will help them assimilate into the host society. Efforts should be made to help the client to establish and build social networks, whether through religious organisations, school, college, community classes or volunteering.

Where young victims of trafficking are living in children's homes or with supported carers, it can be helpful to work with care-givers to help them understand the needs and difficulties of the young person. Work of this nature can increase the strength and supportiveness of the care-giving relationship.

Where victims struggle with social contact because they are afraid that others will ask them about their lives, their history and their family, it can be helpful to support clients to develop and role-play a version of their life story that they feel they can comfortably tell others. Assessing and addressing risk factors for re-victimisation, and helping the client to reflect on what qualities make good, as well as unequal and unhelpful, relationships is also important.

Safe health

Where victims suffer with physical illness, it is important that they are supported to access and understand healthcare systems and to make informed decisions about the treatment options available to them. Therapy can also help victims to understand and adjust to the meaning of medical diagnoses. Victims who find it hard to prioritise their own self-care needs, can, through therapy, be helped to improve their self-care, sleep and diet.

Emotional safety

A range of psychological strategies can be used to improve coping and reduce distress, fear and panic linked to intrusive post-traumatic memories and nightmares. These include providing normalising explanations of why intrusive memories and nightmares develop after trauma, trigger identification to increase a sense of control and predictability over intrusive memories, and grounding techniques, mindfulness exercises, breathing and relaxation exercises and other self-soothing techniques.

Where nightmares are understood as portentous and indicating that further trauma is anticipated, it can be helpful to discuss the meaning of nightmares and to offer alternative possible explanations. Nightmares can be planned for and responses prepared in advance (for example, using comforting photographs, objects, books and nightmare scripts that can be placed near the bed).

It can be useful to share understanding that self-harm and reliance on substances may have been useful coping/survival strategies in the past which may no longer be so helpful, and to identify alternatives. Triggers to self-harming should be identified and a safety plan agreed at an early point in contact. Similarly, suicide risk should be assessed and a multi-agency plan put in place to help manage this risk.

Where dissociation is a prominent response to distress, triggers to dissociation can be identified and other means of regulating emotions developed (for example, see Boon *et al.* 2011). Victims suffering with low mood and depression linked to multiple losses and current hardships can be supported through psychological and occupational therapy to access psychosocial support and advocacy, and to identify and engage in pleasurable or meaningful activities.

Where low mood is linked to the loss of family members, or friends or of previously valued roles, relationships, jobs, community and culture, it can be important to provide opportunities for the victim to speak about this, and to grieve for what has been lost. It can also be helpful to explore ways in which meaningful connections can be made between people's previous and present lives.

Where distress is linked to shame, a focus on developing self-compassion and the use of compassion-focused approaches can be helpful (Gilbert 2010). Where pain is linked to a trauma memory, it may resolve with trauma-processing therapy. Where pain is linked to physical injury, medical interventions may need to be sought.

Cognitive behavioural and mindfulness strategies can also be helpful interventions for chronic pain.

Scars inflicted on trafficking victims can serve as a constant reminder of past trauma. Medical procedures can be sought to remove or mask scars, and clients can be helped to use make-up to hide scars. For those who have been forced to take a ritual voodoo oath, distress may be linked to the memory of taking the oath and/or to the fear of the consequences of breaking/having broken the oath. Since talking about the fact of the oath might in itself be distressing for the client, it is important to actively seek the client's permission before entering into a discussion around this subject. Therapy should be sensitively directed at helping victims to believe that they can be free from the power of the traffickers to hurt and harm them.

Where victims of trafficking are so traumatised that they struggle to speak even about how they feel, non-verbal approaches such as art therapy can be helpful in contributing to an increased sense of emotional safety.

Safe sense of identity

Individuals can be helped, for example, through narrative therapy, to develop a safer sense of identity that is not defined by their being a victim or by the identity conclusions imposed on them by abusers (for example, that they are worthless, complicit in or to blame for what happened). Through therapy, a safer sense of identity can be discovered by building a shared understanding of what is important to the person, and how the person responded to, resisted and survived the abuse (Yuen 2007).

Phase 1 group interventions

Group therapy approaches can help to decrease isolation, self-blame and stigma and to increase social support and hopefulness. Two Phase 1 groups developed at COMPASS are described briefly below.

Establishing safety: a trauma-coping skills group

A ten-week Phase 1 group treatment programme for women who have been trafficked for sexual exploitation has been piloted at Compass @ TARA, and is presently undergoing evaluation. The programme aims to increase understanding of trauma symptoms, increase capacity for emotional regulation and self-care, reduce symptomatic distress, foster an awareness of human rights and the law, and enhance social connections. The programme has a cognitive behaviour therapy (CBT) orientation, adapted to accommodate cultural differences, and incorporates mindfulness training and practice. This group is currently under evaluation. However, qualitative analysis of client feedback indicates that the group content and format is helpful to clients. Early analysis of psychometric data also indicates that attendance at the group is associated with improved mood and a reduction in post-traumatic stress symptoms.

Sharing stories of survival: a resilience-building group for young people

The 'tree of life' approach was developed in South Africa (Ncube 2006) and has been used to inform a group therapy programme for young people referred to the COMPASS team (Morley *et al.* 2013). The tree of life is a pictorial approach that enables young people to draw out what is important to them in their lives (their cultural heritage, present context, skills and knowledge, hopes for the future, gifts they have received from others). Young people are enabled to jointly consider the traumas they have experienced from a position of a safer sense of their own identity (see White 2005, on second-story development), and to consider the responses that have helped them to survive. This approach can be described as 'thickening stories of resilience' (Ungar 2005) and is an opportunity to honour young people's achievements in surviving what they have been though.

Phase 2 interventions: processing and making sense of trauma

If clients continue to experience distress linked to post-traumatic symptoms such as flashbacks or nightmares, it can be appropriate to offer trauma-processing therapy. Clients should be in a situation of relative stability, have developed the ability to manage distressing feelings without dissociating or using self-harm, and wish to undertake this therapy.

Trauma-processing therapy helps with the transfer of trauma memories into autobiographical memory, and, as a result, victims can experience a reduction in flashbacks and nightmares, reduced physiological arousal and an increased sense of safety. Trauma-processing treatment enables the victim to identify and re-appraise trauma-related beliefs in a way that does justice to their experiences of abuse, challenges guilt and self-blame, and helps them to understand and honour what they did to survive.

Assessment and preparation for this phase of work should be

carried out according to established PTSD treatment frameworks, for example, for trauma-focused CBT, eye movement desensitisation and reprocessing or narrative exposure therapy.

Phase 3 interventions: reconnection

The third phase of therapy consolidates the gains made in the previous phases and emphasises building relationships and future planning. It may be necessary to help young people compensate for the missed developmental opportunities and deprivation associated with trafficking. Therapeutic intervention during this phase can also be individual- or group-based. COMPASS has, for example, developed a partnership with the National Forestry Commission to offer 'Branching Out', a group programme that uses woodland and outdoor activities and forestry skills to increase well-being and connectedness with others. Collaboration between COMPASS and the Ignite Youth Theatre Company has helped young people develop their English, their assertiveness and their confidence whilst integrating with other young people from Glasgow. This phase may also include further work on parenting and sexual relationships and can involve helping victims trace missing family members. For all survivors, however, this stage is about envisaging a future and taking steps to make this vision a possibility.

Promoting psychological recovery: therapeutic outcomes

Therapeutic outcomes are evaluated at COMPASS using a combination of clinical assessment, psychometric data and service user feedback. Compass also has a thriving user involvement group that contributes to evaluating service delivery and to service planning. Based on this information, we have found evidence of psychological recovery for many victims of trafficking. We have witnessed young victims of trafficking, who initially had very severe mental health difficulties, go on to develop community connections, and to thrive and excel at college. We have witnessed very traumatised adults become free of trauma symptoms and go on to establish relationships and make significant contributions to their communities through volunteering and work. We have also borne witness to the ongoing distress experienced by some victims due to an enduring fear of traffickers, uncertain asylum status and fear of deportation. For some, guilt and loneliness linked to the loss of children and family, due to trafficking, particularly where it is not known whether family members are alive or dead, has been impossibly hard to bear. For others, recovery has been significantly impeded by chronic medical conditions or by the belief that life has been permanently and irretrievably damaged.

Further research is now needed to understand the factors that support and impede the psychological recovery of victims of trafficking, and to inform the systems and services designed to meet the needs of those who are trafficked for exploitation.

Conclusion

Promoting psychological recovery for victims of trafficking is challenging. The severity of the traumas and losses suffered, and the lengths to which traffickers go to psychologically control and demean victims can have profound effects on the mental health of victims. The UK asylum and immigration context can also be challenging, because there is often a tension between the welfare and protection needs of victims and the perceived need for the immigration system to protect its borders, to discourage trafficking and to reduce 'pull' factors for illegal immigration. For victims of trafficking, navigating the stresses of the NRM and the asylum system and having an uncertain future can compound anxiety and depression and exacerbate trauma symptoms.

Globally, dedicated psychological service provision for victims of trafficking is still at an early stage. Quantitative studies detailing therapeutic outcomes for victims of trafficking have yet to be published. Further research is needed involving survivors of all ages in speaking about what is helpful for them. At this stage, however, practice-based evidence, gained from direct clinical experience of providing therapy to victims of trafficking, suggests that psychological therapy, based on good practice guidelines for complex PTSD, can make a significant contribution to the psychological recovery of victims of trafficking. There are clear indications that, where survivors are protected from traffickers, supported by statutory and third sector agencies, provided with healthcare, welcomed by a host community, given a secure future and offered psychological therapy, psychological recovery from the effects of human trafficking is possible.

References

Abas, M., N. V. Ostrovschi, M. Prince, V. I. Gorceag, C. Trigub and S. Oram (2013), 'Risk factors for mental disorders in women survivors of human trafficking: a historical cohort study', *BMC Psychiatry*, 13: 204.

Boon, S., K. Steele and O. van der Hart (2011), *Coping with Trauma-related Dissociation. Skills Training for Patients and Therapists*, New York: W. W. Norton.

Cloitre, M., B. C. Stolbach, J. L. Herman, B. van der Kolk, R. Pynoos, J. Wang and E. Petkova (2009), 'A developmental approach to complex PTSD: childhood and adulthood cumulative trauma as predictors of symptom complexity', *Journal of Traumatic Stress*, 22: 339–408.

Cloitre, M., C. A. Courtois, A. Charuvastra, R. Carapezza, B. C. Stolbach and B. L. Green (2011), 'Treatment of complex PTSD: results of the ISTSS expert clinician survey on best practices', *Journal of Traumatic Stress*, 24(6): 615–27.

Council of Europe Convention on Action Against Trafficking in Human Beings (2005), Council of Europe Treaty Series No. 197, available at: http://conventions.coe.int/Treaty/Commun/QueVoulezVous.asp?NT=197& CM=7&DF=02/02/2015&CL=ENG, last accessed 1 June 2015.

Courtois, C. A. and J. D. Ford (2013), *Treatment of Complex Trauma, a Sequence Relationship-based Approach*, New York: Guildford Press.

Cwikel, J., B. Chudakov, M. Paikin, K. Agmon and R. Belmaker (2004), 'Trafficked female sex workers awaiting deportation: comparison with brothel workers', *Archives of Women's Mental Health*, 7(4): 243–9.

Deb, S., A. Mukherjee and B. Matthews (2011), 'Aggression in sexually abused trafficked girls and the efficacy of intervention', *Journal of Interpersonal Violence*, 26(4): 745–68.

End Child Prostitution and Trafficking (ECPAT) (2008), *Vulnerability and Control of African Child Victims of Trafficking: UK Experience*, ECPAT UK Discussion Paper, London: ECPAT UK, available at: http://www.ecpat.org.uk/sites/default/files/ritual_abuse_dp.pdf, last accessed 29 November 2014.

EU Directive (2011), Directive 2011/36/EU of the European Parliament and of the Council of 5 April 2011 on Preventing and Combating Trafficking in Human Beings and Protecting its Victims, and Replacing Council Framework Decision 2002/629/JHA, Official Journal of the European Union.

Ford J. D. and C. Courtois (2013), *Treating Complex Traumatic Stress Disorders in Children and Adolescents: Scientific Foundations and Therapeutic Models*, New York: Guildford Press.

Geddes, A., G. Craig and S. Scott (2013), *Forced Labour in the UK*, Joseph Rowntree Programme Paper, June, available at: http://www.jrf.org.uk/sites/files/jrf/Forced%20Labour%20in%20the%20UK%20FINAL%20prog%20paper.pdf, last accessed 19 November 2014.

Gilbert, P. (2010), *Compassion-focused Therapy: The CBT Distinctive Features Series*, London: Routledge.

Hossain, M., C. Zimmerman, M. Abas, M. Light and C. Watts (2010), 'The relationship of trauma to mental disorders among trafficked and sexually exploited girls and women', *American Journal of Public Health*, 100(12): 2442–9.

International Society for Traumatic Stress Studies (ISTSS) (2012), *Consensus Treatment Guidelines for Complex PTSD in Adults*, Deerfield, IL: International Society for Traumatic Stress Studies, available at: http://www.istss.org/AM/Template.cfm?Section=ISTSS_Complex_PTSD_Treatment_Guidelines&Template=%2FCM%2FContentDisplay.cfm&ContentID=5185, last accessed 29 May 2015.

Leenarts, L. E., J. Diehle, T. A. Doreleijers, E. P. Jansma and R. J. Lindauer (2013), 'Evidence-based treatments for children with trauma-related psychopathology as a result of childhood maltreatment: a systematic review', *European Child and Adolescent Psychiatry*, 22(5): 269–83.

Macy, R. J. and N. Johns (2012), 'Aftercare services for international sex trafficking survivors: informing US service and program development in an emerging practice area', *Trauma Violence and Abuse*, 12(2): 87–98.

Morley, R., L. Barrie and R. Frost (2013), 'Storying skills of survival: a narrative group for young women who are unaccompanied and seeking asylum', *British Psychological Society Clinical Psychology Forum*, No. 244, April.

Ncube, N. (2006), 'The Tree of Life Project: using narrative ideas in work with vulnerable children in South Africa', *International Journal of Narrative Therapy and Community Work*, 1: 3–16.

Oram, S., N. V. Ostrovschi, V. I. Gorceag, M. A. Hotineneau, L. Gorceag, C. Trigub and M. Abas (2012a), 'Physical health symptoms reported by trafficked women receiving post-trafficking support in Moldova: prevalence, severity and associated factors', *BMC Women's Health*, 12: 20, available at: http://www.biomedcentral.com/1472-6874/12/20, last accessed 29 May 2015.

Organization for Security and Co-operation in Europe (OSCE) (2013), *Trafficking in Human Beings Amounts to Torture and Other Forms of Ill-treatment*, Office of the Special Representative and Co-coordinator for Combating Trafficking in Human Beings, available at: http://www.osce.org/cthb/103085?download=true, last accessed 29 May 2015.

Ostrovschi, N. V., M. J. Prince, C. Zimmerman, M. A. Hotineau, L. T. Gorceag, V. I. Gorceag, C. Flach and M. A. Abas (2011), 'Women in post-trafficking services in Moldova: diagnostic interviews to assess returning women's mental health', *BMC Public Health*, 11: 232, available at: http://www.biomedcentral.com/1471-2458/11/232, last accessed 29 May 2015.

Skrivankova, K. (2010), *Between Decent Work and Forced Labour: Examining the Continuum of Exploitation*, Joseph Rowntree Foundation, available at: http://www.jrf.org.uk/work/workarea/contemporary-slavery, last accessed 29 May 2015.

Tsutsumi, A., T. Izutsu, A. K. Poudyal, S. Kato and E. Marui (2008), 'Mental health of female survivors of human trafficking in Nepal', *Social Science and Medicine*, 66: 1841–7.

Turner-Moss, E., C. Zimmerman, L. M. Howard and S. Oram (2013), 'Labour exploitation and health: a case series of men and women seeking post-trafficking services', *Journal of Immigrant and Minority Health*, doi: 10.1007/s10903-013-9832-6.

Ungar, M. (2005), 'A thicker description of resilience', *International Journal of Narrative Therapy and Community Work*, 2005(3/4): 89–96.

White M. (2005), 'Children, trauma and subordinate storyline development', *International Journal of Narrative Therapy and Community Work*, 2005(3/4): 10–22.

Yuen, A. (2007), 'Discovering children's responses to trauma; a response-based narrative practice', *International Journal of Narrative Therapy and Community Work*, 2007(4): 3–18.

Zimmerman, C., M. Hossain, K. Yun, V. Gajdadziev, N. Guzun, M. Tchomarova, R. A. Ciarrocchi, A. Johansson, A. Kefurtova, S. Scodanibbio, M. N. Motus, B. Roche, L. Morison and C. Watts (2008), 'The health of trafficked women: a survey of women entering post-trafficking services in Europe', *American Journal of Public Health*, 98(1): 55–9.

Zimmerman, C., M. Hossain and C. Watts (2011), 'Human trafficking and health: a conceptual model to inform policy, intervention and research', *Social Science and Medicine*, 73: 327–35.

9 'We Cannot Collect Comprehensive Information on All of These Changes': The Challenges of Monitoring and Evaluating Reintegration Efforts for Separated Children

Claire Cody

Introduction

Every year across the world many children become separated from their families. Some children may run away or leave home in search of a better life. Some may be abandoned or placed in alternative forms of care. Others will be separated by disasters or war. And some will be taken away from their families by others. Suffering from a lack of care and attention, and more likely to be exposed to risky behaviours and activities, the circumstances of separation are widely acknowledged to leave these children more vulnerable (Williamson and Greenberg 2010; Maholmes *et al.* 2012). The perceived vulnerability of these children has made them a preferred 'target group' for many child protection agencies around the world. Organisations have focused their work towards various sub-groups of separated children, including children associated with the fighting forces – and specifically former child soldiers; street-connected children; child labourers; children in institutions; unaccompanied asylum-seeking children; and child migrants. Some of these children may be at more risk of being exploited and trafficked, and 'trafficked children' themselves have become a distinct sub-group for organisations supporting separated children.

The reintegration of separated children has attracted greater attention and resources from international organisations and child protection agencies in recent years. Despite the amplified focus on this area of work, rigorous evaluations of these endeavours are rare and it is not always clear what lessons are being learned (Jordans *et al.* 2012). Previous evaluations have had a tendency to focus explicitly on the programme objectives, and whether or not they were achieved. There has, however, been little insight into whether the activities benefitted the child, or how and why the initiative in question made a positive impact. So we may learn whether a programme achieved what it set out to do (reunify x number of children with their families, for example), but we gain no insight into how reintegration was supported, or what worked (or did not work), and how these factors affected the overall well-being of the child and family.

This chapter considers why the monitoring and evaluation of reintegration activities is so challenging; and why listening to children's and young people's views on, and experiences of, reintegration following separation and exploitation is so critical. The chapter provides background to the work undertaken with separated children and the development of reintegration efforts. It outlines the difficulties in monitoring and evaluating reintegration programmes and determining what 'success' looks like. And it describes a project that attempts to improve monitoring and evaluation in this area of work. The results of a consultation process with children and young people are also shared. Finally, it discusses some conclusions and future directions that may help to develop our understanding of reintegration work – with trafficked children in particular.

Background: supporting separated children

Identifying and calculating the number of children outside of family care is not easy (Pullum *et al.* 2012; Stark *et al.* 2014). It can be very difficult to gather an accurate picture for those who are growing up outside the confines of a family. Children may not be registered at birth, may not be 'counted' in household surveys, or may be 'hidden away' in institutions, places of work or battlefields. In addition, the mobile nature of some children and young people – particularly migrant and street-connected children – can make it difficult to quantify the magnitude of the issue globally. This lack of reliable information can make it challenging for governments to plan comprehensive responses and deliver well-resourced reintegration efforts.

The knowledge base surrounding the reintegration experiences of separated children has developed unevenly. Beginning in the 1990s, the international community started to document experiences and learning from the disarmament, demobilisation and reintegration (DRR) programmes that targeted ex-combatants, including former child soldiers. A strong body of knowledge surrounding the reintegration experiences for this group of young people developed and continues to deepen, expand and evolve (Akello *et al.*

2006; Boothby *et al.* 2006; Burman and McKay 2007; Kohrt 2007; Cortes and Buchanan 2007;Williamson 2006; Betancourt *et al.* 2008; Betancourt *et al.* 2010; McKay *et al.* 2010; Jordans *et al.* 2012).

As funding priorities have shifted towards other sub-groups of children (such as trafficked children) in the early twenty-first century, questions regarding how best to support their recovery and reintegration have again emerged (Asquith and Turner 2008). Trafficked children, due to their exploitation, may have distinct and complex physical and psychological recovery needs. However, the process of reintegrating trafficked children back into families and communities may be similar to work with other groups of children.

Unfortunately, the focus on specific groups of children has to some degree led to knowledge blockages between organisations supporting the reintegration process. The labelling and categorising of 'children in need' into groups is endemic within the development sector (Moncrieffe 2006: 38). The consequence of this tunnel vision is that discrete pockets of knowledge develop in isolation. Such distinctions also tend to be disingenuous in many cases, as children do not always fit neatly into the labelled boxes professionals create. A child identified and categorised as a street-connected child may in fact have started his or her journey as a migrant or may be running from domestic violence and abuse and may, due to his or her circumstances, be involved in exploitative work and/or 'transactional sex'. This has been echoed by Boothby *et al.* who note that:

> interventions targeting vulnerable children, many of whom are outside of family care for various reasons, are often similar, yet programs tend to focus on addressing the needs of children according to their category of vulnerability rather than building sustainable child protection systems that effectively address the needs of all vulnerable children. (2012: 745)

Reunification and reintegration

Traditionally many separated children who were identified by welfare services may have been cared for in institutions, centres and orphanages. Today, with the acknowledgement that the best place for a child to grow up is within a nurturing family environment, the ultimate goal for most welfare agencies is to reunify separated children with their families, or, if this is not possible, place children into alternative family-based environments. In either scenario, supporting their reintegration back into the wider community is an equally important endeavour.

International legislation clearly states that growing up in a family environment is the best place for a child (United Nations 1989, preamble):

> the family, as the fundamental group of society and the natural environment for the growth and well-being of all its members and particularly children, should be afforded the necessary protection and assistance so that it can fully assume its responsibilities within the community.

It is in the child's best interests to be reunified with family members when possible and safe to do so. In cases where the child has no family, is unwilling to be reunited with family, or where the family is not deemed safe or able to care for the child, the child may be integrated into extended family or into a new family or community.

States have ultimate responsibility for ensuring that children are reintegrated and cared for. Article 39 of the United Nations Convention on the Rights of the Child notes that:

> States Parties shall take all appropriate measures to promote physical and psychological recovery and social reintegration of a child victim of: any form of neglect, exploitation, or abuse; torture or any other form of cruel, inhuman or degrading treatment or punishment; or armed conflicts. Such recovery and reintegration shall take place in an environment which fosters the health, self-respect and dignity of the child. (United Nations 1989)

However, in many contexts reintegration work is 'subcontracted out' to non-governmental organisations (NGOs) and other agencies that directly assist children and young people. This particularly appears to be the case for victims of trafficking. When this happens there may be specific rules, time limits and exclusion policies that restrict what support can be offered. Similarly, in contexts where government agencies do not have the resources to contract out this work, NGOs and international agencies may acquire funding from donors to support reintegration efforts. Again, time-limited programmes and projects mean that in reality it is often local community-based organisations who are involved in longer-term reintegration efforts (Wedge 2013).

Where children do have a family that is able to care for the child, it is often not as easy as simply reuniting children with family members. A greater duration and level of assistance may be required for children who have been separated for a length of time, or who have become separated due to difficulties within the home (such as the death of a parent, abuse, violence or conflict), or whose time away has been marred by sexual abuse, exploitation, addiction or violence. This enhanced assistance may include help to access basic services such as health and education; support to gain new skills, knowledge and behaviours; legal assistance; psychosocial support; and family mediation and economic strengthening of the household. Such activities often fall under the umbrella term that is described and framed here as 'reintegration work'. Of course, not all children are assisted in their reintegration and it is thought that many children return and reintegrate without the support of organisations.

The term reintegration can be defined as:

> The process that involves the reunification of children and young people with family members (or into an alternative permanent family-based setting) and results in a healthy, happy child who is safe, accepted, respected and has the same opportunities as other children in their community. (Cody 2013a: 9)

Reintegration is not a one-off occurrence, but involves a process of adjustment. Reimer *et al.* (2007) have described reintegration as a three-stage process involving a phase of pre-reintegration, reintegration and post-reintegration. These periods of time cover the initial steps taken in the run-up to either reunification with the family or integration (such as family tracing and assessments) and continue right up to follow-up visits once the child has left the care of a service provider. Others have also emphasised that reintegration should not be seen as a 'programme', as it requires the involvement of multiple stakeholders and bodies. It is not simply a stand-alone initiative delivered by one organisation (Anthony *et al.* 2010).

Common themes in reintegration work

The research that does exist around reintegration, which is briefly explored below, indicates that different 'groups' of children (for instance, trafficked children, street-connected children and former child soldiers) often share a number of similar experiences and challenges when it comes to being reunited with families and reintegrated into communities.

Children who return after a period of separation do not just return to the family unit, they return to a community. Shigekane (2007: 132) notes that 'a community's response to trafficking is as important to a survivor's successful integration as is the availability of meaningful services and support'. How the family and community view, respond and support the child will affect how easily the child is able to adjust. When young people who have been separated return home, family and community members may know or assume that these children have been involved in what may be perceived as immoral or illegal activities. This may include involvement in the sex industry, violence, killing and other criminal activities. Such perceptions often mean that children are stigmatised or demonised when returning home (Feeny 2005; Burman and McKay 2007; Betancourt *et al.* 2008; Betancourt *et al.* 2010; Ray *et al.* 2011; Cody 2013b; Guntzberger 2013).

Where separated children (including trafficked children) are unable to return home, they may also encounter shared experiences with other groups who are integrating into a new setting, such as unaccompanied asylum-seeking children. Research with unaccompanied asylum-seeking and refugee children has identified a range of challenges, including social isolation and loneliness, which can be exacerbated by the inability to speak the language; lack of support systems, connectedness and a sense of belonging; homesickness; and in some cases a sense of limbo as their legal status is reviewed and determined (Kohli and Mather 2003; Hek 2005; Kohli 2011; Thomas and Devaney 2011).

Professionals working to facilitate reintegration have also noted many similar challenges in supporting children and families through the reintegration process. This includes the fact that so-called 'groups' of children are rarely homogeneous. Every child has distinct experiences, personal characteristics, family circumstances, support networks and coping strategies which make it impossible to prescribe a standardised approach to reintegration. There is no one-size-fits-all solution and no recipe for reintegration.

Reintegration activities carried out with the best of intentions have, in some circumstances, led to a number of negative, unintended consequences or 'collateral damage', the term used by one organisation criticising interventions driven by anti-trafficking providers (GAATW 2007). One concern has been that the targeting of specific groups of children can actually heighten stigma and increase risks for children and their families (Wessells 2006; Boothby *et al.* 2012). In some circumstances, targeting can also lead to jealously if certain children and young people are offered free education and training or if support is provided to some families and not others. This can lead to envy in a community where the rest of the population is also struggling to support their children and cover the costs of their education. It has been reported that such programming can create a dangerous and paradoxical view in the community that child survivors of rape or trafficking and their families are 'lucky' in some way (Simcox and Marshall 2011).

The use of alternative care has been another area of contention in reintegration work. Although emergency accommodation and alternative care options are an important part of recovery and reintegration, reports suggest that in some contexts children are staying for far too long in what essentially are institutions (Cody 2013c). Parents may believe that their child is 'better off' staying in a residential shelter where they will have access to food, shelter and education. Reports from Cambodia suggest that social workers believe that girls who have been raped or trafficked should stay longer in centres so they can access vocational training and education (Simcox and Marshall 2011). This clearly is a concern as such developments may promote and prolong family separation in contexts where resources and opportunities are limited in the areas where children have come from.

A traditional failing in reintegration work has been to focus work primarily towards either boys or girls without applying a gendered lens to reintegration efforts (Tefferi 2003). For children associated with the fighting forces, it has been well documented that girls were very much neglected in the Disarmament, Demobilisation and Reintegration (DDR) programmes that were put in place to support the reintegration of young people following conflict (Williamson 2006). Girls' roles were perceived as peripheral and their needs were not catered for (McKay and Mazurana 2004). In other situations, the needs of boys have also tended to overshadow the needs of girls, for example, in work focusing on gang-affected young people (Firmin 2011) and street-connected youth (Guntzberger 2013). On the other hand, work focusing on sexual abuse and sexual exploitation repeatedly fails to notice, understand or cater for boys and young men (Pawlak and Barker 2012; Brayley *et al.* 2014).

With these and other commonalities, it appears that there is some value in breaking down the partitions that have developed around reintegration thinking and practice for these specific 'categories' of children. Recent developments, such as the US Government Evidence Summit on Protecting Children Outside of Family Care in 2011 (US Government International Assistance for Children in Adversity 2011) and the development of the Interagency Group on Reintegration in 2013 (see Wedge 2013), indicate that there is a desire for such cross-sector learning.

Background to the monitoring and evaluating reintegration project

The need to share learning across reintegration efforts, paired with the lack of understanding of 'what works' when it comes to facilitating the reintegration of separated children, (specifically trafficked children) led to the establishment of a new monitoring and evaluating (M&E) reintegration project. Following an inception workshop in 2012, hosted by the University of the Highlands and Islands (UHI) Centre for Rural Childhood, Perth College and Home, The Child Recovery and Reintegration Network (which was hosted at the Centre), an inter-agency steering group was formed to support the project which included representatives from international organisations such as EveryChild, the International Organization for Migration (IOM), Save the Children UK and UNICEF, together with organisations directly supporting children in their reintegration including Retrak and Mkombozi.

Once approval was gained from the UHI Research Ethics Committee, a number of data collection activities were undertaken. First, literature on the reintegration experiences of children affected by varying forms of adversity, along with handbooks, manuals and articles related to monitoring and evaluation were identified and reviewed. Secondly, an online survey was developed for professionals with experience of working in the reintegration field. Finally, a consultation with children and young people with various experiences of separation, and who had been assisted by organisations, was designed and undertaken.

Survey respondents

The online survey remained active for five weeks. It explored the views held by the participants who had taken part in the UHI Centre inception workshop in relation to the challenges of M&E and asked if these views were supported by workers in the field. It also looked at what M&E data was currently being collected and how organisations were gathering this information. Finally, it sought to understand what 'changes' organisations sought to understand when assessing reintegration and to gather views regarding different methods and approaches.

Fifty-one individuals based in twenty-one countries responded to the survey. The majority (55 per cent) worked for NGOs. Other respondents were independent consultants or worked for universities, governments, funders or community-based organisations. Altogether, the respondents had experience of reintegration work with children and young people in forty different countries. When provided with a list of different groups of children (for example, children who had been trafficked for sex, labour or other purposes; children living and working on the streets; children in residential care settings) and asked 'which "groups" of children and young people do you work with', seven individuals reported working with just one 'group' of children. Most respondents, however, indicated that they had worked/were working with three to four 'groups' of children (Cody 2013d).

Barriers to monitoring and evaluating

When presented with a pre-developed list of challenges and asked 'in your experience what are some of the key barriers to monitoring and evaluating reintegration programmes?', the most frequent responses were: the short-term project cycles (NGOs often develop projects to fit within 2–3-year donor funding cycles); children move on/disappear so are hard to follow-up once they leave the programme; difficult to develop relevant meaningful indicators; lack of resources to plan and carry out M&E activities; the complexity of reintegration programmes; staff not sufficiently trained in M&E; hard to determine what 'success' is; lack of baseline data so difficult to measure change over time; lack of toolkits and guides to help organisations know how to monitor and evaluate; and difficult to know how to involve children in M&E activities (Cody 2013d).

Although some of the barriers identified come down to resource deficits, such as short funding cycles and scarce resources for M&E in general, other challenges relate specifically to the complexity of reintegration work. For example, following up with children who have returned home can be challenging. Many children are likely to end up returning to a different area, or state within a country or even to a different country. As one staff member working at Retrak, an organisation supporting street-connected children in Ethiopia and Uganda, reported: 'providing adequate follow-up support is a challenge since children are reintegrated all over both countries, often at a large distance from Retrak's centres' (Retrak 2012: 2). A respondent to the survey noted that one challenge was 'the geographic dispersion of reunited children, often in remote rural areas, and an increasing caseload with a limited number of personnel to make follow-up visits' (Cody 2013d: 9).

The time and economic costs involved in this work often mean that it is not feasible to carry out face-to-face follow up visits to assess how the child and family are adjusting. For example, practitioners in Cambodia have highlighted the outlay of fuel needed to visit remote areas where children are typically returned (Cody 2012). In addition, there are the ethical implications of undertaking follow-up visits: is it possible that visits can do more harm than good? Regularly visiting a child may increase stigma and gossip, and lead to the perception that the family are unable to care and provide for their own children. This quote from a case study in Uganda indicates that this may very well be an issue on the ground: 'They [the community] also openly resented the special attention Apiyo received from her counsellors, which in turn made the girl decide to bar any follow-up activities by the World Vision (WV) counsellors' (Akello *et al.* 2006: 231).

Despite these barriers and tensions to following up, conclusions from a recent review exploring the protection of children outside of family care reiterate the importance of this work: 'long-term tracking enables more careful study of the interaction of multiple influences on children, gives strong clues about better approaches to protecting children and supporting their resilience and can indicate the long-term impact of interventions' (Ager *et al.* 2012: 735).

In addition to the complexity of follow up work, the contributions of particular activities or aspects of support can also be difficult to deconstruct; organisations typically provide a holistic package of support. Reintegration work also often involves working not only with the child, but also working with the parents or carers, siblings and extended family. This work can help the family to prepare and build a safe, stable, supporting and secure household for the returning child. Initiatives may also seek to change the knowledge, attitudes and behaviours of community members so that they are more welcoming, sensitive, accepting and respectful to returning children. At the same time, efforts may be made to enable the community to protect these young people and others from future danger. Organisations may also be working towards higher level changes, influencing policy and legislation at the local, state or national level. Or working regionally or internationally, to learn and share information on how to better care for and work with children and young people during the reintegration process. This means organisations do more than collect information on one activity or with one group.

The multiplicity of activities that organisations feel they have to be involved in to effectively support reintegration was reflected in the answers to the following survey question: 'What are the particular changes you hope to see based on your programming?' The most frequent responses being changes in the child's safety and protection, education, health status, life skills, and confidence and self-esteem. Respondents also stated that they worked to change the communities' acceptance of and attitudes and behaviours towards the child, the child's involvement in activities in the community and the child's relationship with family or carers. In addition, a number of respondents also selected changes in the implementation of existing laws and policies, and changes in the community systems and structures to make environments more welcoming and inclusive for returning children (Cody 2013d).

In addition to the pre-defined categories provided, respondents also described other changes. These included: 'space for child decision-making and agency'; 'coordination and cooperation between government and non-government agencies in reintegration planning, preparation and follow-up'; 'children remaining in a household over time, with the above being achieved at an acceptable level'; and 'less pathologising of people in difficult situations' (Cody 2013d: 10–11). Together the responses demonstrate why, for many, trying to understand and assess whether and which reintegration activities are 'successful' is not a straightforward task.

The consultation with children and young people

In addition to the survey with practitioners, the project undertook a consultation with children and young people who had been supported in their reintegration by organisations. The aim of the consultation was to understand children's views on two main areas: what children and young people felt were the most significant changes that had happened to them from their involvement in a reintegration programme; and what indicators, in their opinion, showed that a child had 'successfully reintegrated'.

Organisations supporting children to reintegrate were identified and approached to ask if they would be interested in taking part. From those that were interested, a number were selected and took part in the consultations. The selection process was based on a number of factors, such as the geographical location of the organisation, the background of the children they supported, and the type of support they offered to try to gain a diverse sample of children and young people in different settings with various experiences.

The author, along with an experienced child participation consultant, worked together with nine partner organisations that were based in seven countries: Challenging Heights in Ghana; Pendekezo Letu in Kenya; UYDEL in Uganda; Retrak in Uganda; Shalom Centre in Tanzania; Retrak in Ethiopia; Atina in Serbia; and Tjeter Vizion and Different and Equal, both in Albania. The activities were piloted by the organisation Retrak in Ethiopia and Uganda. Following the pilot, all the partner organisations received virtual training and in-depth guidelines, including an ethical protocol developed by the consultant on how to safely carry out the consultation with children and young people (Veitch 2013b).

The children and young people who took part in the consultation

Staff members from the partner organisations facilitated the consultations with children and young people that they had previously supported, or were still supporting in their reintegration journey. The majority of children and young people involved were perceived to have been reintegrated ($n = 87$) and had moved on from shelter homes and centres and were living back with families, in foster families, with friends or independently. Two young people were in the process of accessing support to prepare for their 'reintegration' into a stable, permanent setting.

When asked to provide a brief description of the children's and young people's background, it was clear that partner organisations themselves struggled in coming up with one discrete label to describe the young people's previous vulnerabilities. This process in itself revealed the overlaps in experience. Children were not just affected by one form of vulnerability, and partner organisations were not just working with one homogeneous group. Instead, one organisation, for example, explained the young women they were consulting with had all left school early and, as a group, had been affected by sexual exploitation, sexual abuse, labour exploitation and trafficking.

Thirty-five boys were involved in the consultation: seven boys from Ethiopia, who had lived and worked on the streets (13–17 years); eleven boys from Uganda, with similar experiences (14–18 years); ten boys from Ghana, who had been trafficked into the fishing industry (12–14 years); and seven boys from Albania, who had backgrounds of violence, abuse, abandonment and trafficking (10–14 years).

The fifty-four girls and young women involved included: ten young women from Uganda, who had been sexually exploited and had experienced other forms of adversity, such as labour exploitation and abuse (19–22 years); fifteen girls from Kenya with backgrounds of domestic work and/or scavenging (10–13 years); ten girls from Tanzania with experiences of sexual exploitation and street connection (11–14 years); nine girls from Serbia (15–20 years), who had been trafficked for the purposes of sexual exploitation; and ten girls from Albania (19–20 years), who had been trafficked for sexual or labour exploitation.

The consultation did not claim to represent the differential experiences of all children supported; that is, either by the partner organisation, or of children and young people more generally in those settings or circumstances. The partner organisations, based on their knowledge of the child or young person and whether it was safe and appropriate for them to be involved, selected the sample to invite to take part in the workshop. It is likely that the children and young people who took part had positive experiences with the organisation, which may explain their willingness to come back and take part in the consultation. Again, this may not have been the case for other children and young people who had been supported. Notwithstanding these potential biases, the consultation process led to some interesting and important insights into how children and young people experienced the reintegration process and how they determined 'success'.

The 'most significant changes' for young people

To elicit responses to the question 'what do children and young people feel are the most significant changes that have happened to them since engaging with the programme?' children and young people were invited to use a method known as 'river of life'. Children and young people were asked to draw or write 'their story' starting from when they first came into contact with the partner organisation. Along this journey they were asked to draw or refer to relevant events or changes that they felt had come about due to their contact with the partner organisation or due to other experiences unconnected to the support they received from the organisation.

Through the images and words they created, they were able to tell their reintegration stories identifying key people, events and changes. A number of children talked about their experiences of initially coming to the centre or shelter and how this was an unnerving experience for them. They also talked about how their basic needs were met by the partner organisations, and how they had been provided with food, medical treatment and shelter. 'The most important things I got in my two months stay in Retrak were medical treatment, shower service, food and night shelter' (Konso, 17 years old, Ethiopia).[1]

For young women – specifically those who had been trafficked – being somewhere safe and secure was mentioned as a significant change in their stories. 'In the beginning I felt like everything is unfamiliar to me and later I cannot describe it, I finally had people around me, I was safe' (Milja, 20 years old, Serbia). In addition to their basic needs being met, they reflected on what else they had gained and learned from the staff and their time spent in shelters. This included opportunities and experiences that built their confidence and self-esteem, allowed them to attend school, trust again, and build relationships with friends and family. 'I am now in school and it has helped me a lot, I can now write and read' (One Lovely, 12 years old, Ghana).

Children and young people also spoke about how they had learned about rights and responsibilities, developed values, life skills and positive behaviours. 'I think twice before I act and I have become reflective person; I can take decisions for myself' (Kleja, 19 years old, Albania).

On moving on, some young people spoke about being nervous about leaving behind friendships, supportive adults, and the relative safety and security of the shelter or transit centre. However, many felt like they had been well prepared for going back to families – expressing that the partner organisation had helped them to rebuild relationships with family members:

> Reunion with my sister after many years changed my life; meeting with my mother; conversation with psychologist helped me to express my feelings; finding a foster family made me happy and I felt loved for the first time in my life. (Emanuela, 20 years old, Albania)

In some cases the organisation had also helped the family by making improvements to the family home or helping a parent secure vocational training or work. 'When I came back home our house had light and water wasn't coming in, my aunt was now selling clothes, she now gets money' (Carolina, 14 years old, Kenya).

For the older young people, securing their own income was also significant. As Romeo, 18 years old from Uganda said: 'I am now doing a course in building and concrete practice and have hope that with these skills I will get a job and be able to support myself.' It was clear that although many of the children and young people were doing well, some had faced a number of challenges in their lives after leaving the shelter in terms of building relationships, finding a permanent place to live and securing an income:

> Life was not easy when I left the centre after the training. It was hard for me to find other friends and even more hard to find a job. It took me a month to find a job, so I worked at home where I was staying with my elder sister. After working for the entire month, I decided to talk to my elder sister if she could assist me to start a small salon. I convinced her to give me some money to start my own salon but this did not materialise because she passed on. (Pretty, 20 years old, Uganda)

Indicators of 'successful reintegration'

The second key question that the consultation aimed to address was 'what "indicators" or "signs" show us that a child has "successfully reintegrated" and, out of these, which indicators are most important for children and young people?' Following discussions that explored how to define the concept of 'successful reintegration' with the different groups of children and young people, the groups were asked to imagine what a 'successfully reintegrated' child may look like and to brainstorm and create a list of indicators or 'signs' that might demonstrate this success.

Following this initial activity, the group were asked to rank the indicators along a line with what they felt the most important indicator was at one end and the least important indicator at the other. The young people were asked to rank the indicators by discussing with each other where they felt each indicator should be placed and why. These activities were based on and adapted from similar activities that had been undertaken with groups of children and young people in various international settings to understand the concepts of 'well-being' and reintegration (Crivello et al. 2009; Stark et al. 2009).

Through analysing the information that came out of these exercises, it was clear that children and young people across the different consultations felt that one of the most important indicators of successful reintegration should be whether a child's basic needs were met. Indicators that were mentioned by the groups included things like 'has good shelter', 'has access to water', 'has access to medical care' and 'feeds well'.

The children and young people were able to give clear reasons as to why these basic needs were of primary importance. 'Child can get treatment when sick because if they are in good health it will make them study well and live a healthy life. You cannot go to school without being in good health' (boys at Retrak in Uganda; Veitch 2013a: 3).

Young people also gave equal importance to the area of emotional support, safety and their relationship with their family and the community. Children and young people spoke about different aspects such as: 'feels safe', 'has a safe house', 'acceptance', 'has good relationship with family and community', 'good relationship with familiar people and friends', 'friends', 'being respectful and also respected', 'being able to associate with other people in the community', 'respected by people in the community' and 'when a child is shown love and valued within the family and the community'.

Following these areas of importance, children also described how certain internal strengths, skills and behaviours could indicate successful reintegration. This included things such as 'being confident', 'children believe in themselves and abilities', 'avoiding peer pressure', 'children will not go back to previous situations', 'emotionally and psychologically stable', 'communication skills', 'has gained new problem-solving and decision-making skills', 'self-awareness', 'self-control', 'happy and smiling', 'is adaptable in different new environment' and 'independence'.

Children and young people also identified indicators related to educational and employment status along with knowledge of child rights. Indicators included things such as 'the children are in school or skills training', 'goes to school', 'having vocational skills', 're-enters the school system or follows a professional course', 'has a sustainable income', 'has a sustainable job place', 'getting my own money from my sweat', 'support family but not exploited', 'documents and rights', 'community is aware of children's rights' and 'know our basic children's rights'. The children and young people's views in some ways mirrored what practitioners had indicated, that as reintegration is in essence about achieving overall well-being, there are far too many aspects to consider and measure in isolation.

The indicators developed by children and young people in many ways mirrored the 'changes' that practitioners identified in the survey; changes or improvements in a child's safety and protection, education, life skills, confidence and self-esteem, relationship with family or carers; and the communities' acceptance of and attitudes and behaviours towards a returning child. By ranking the indicators, children and young people were able to show what they felt were the most important areas to consider when ascertaining whether reintegration had been successful.

Given the complex nature and multiple facets of reintegration work, such exercises can be important and helpful, providing critical knowledge and understanding to organisations working in different communities. The exercise also demonstrated again the different stakeholders that need to be considered in reintegration work, not only the individual children, but the family, peers and the wider community.

Conclusions and future directions

This chapter aimed to consider why evaluating reintegration work and sharing learning between organisations working with different 'groups' of separated children, including trafficked children, is so challenging. Through exploring the siloed approach to work with separated children, together with the nature of reintegration work and the experiences of practitioners involved, an abundance of barriers and difficulties clearly emerge. The chapter has also contributed new voices to our understanding of the important elements of reintegration, as understood by assisted children and young people.

What is clear from both the experiences of practitioners and children and young people, is that those working to support reintegration must go beyond the numbers. Reporting that 'twenty-three children were successfully reintegrated' means very little. As a respondent to the survey expressed: 'it would be already useful to go beyond the simple notion of reintegration as the physical transfer from a situation A to B, but looking at well-being of people in their context' (Cody 2013d: 24). It is clear from the literature, views and voices of those involved in this work that reintegration is not simply about reunification. Reintegration work essentially involves all aspects of well-being, and due to this there is not one magic 'indicator' that can capture the range and complexity of reintegration and help us to conclude whether or not reintegration has been 'successful'. As the same respondent noted in the survey: 'there is a need to capture as much as possible process indicators instead of insisting on the numbers of children reunified as the only indicator for success since reintegration is process-based' (Cody 2013d: 24). This is something that organisations supporting trafficked children need to be mindful of as reunification in itself is unlikely to prevent re-victimisation and re-trafficking in the future.

The data from the survey and consultation not only offer food for thought on the areas where organisations could consider collecting information to assess whether a child has successfully reintegrated, but the consultation also demonstrates that children are, as has been recognised by others, 'experts in their own lives' (Langstead 1994, as cited in Crivello et al. 2009). Children and young people should not only be consulted, but meaningfully involved in the planning, design and implementation of monitoring and evaluation processes. The children and young people involved in this consultation, who ranged from the ages of 10 to 22 years old, were all able to discuss what support and changes they felt were important to them, and were able to articulate, based on their own experiences, what successful reintegration looked like in their communities. Such a participatory process could therefore be the first step in developing appropriate, socially and culturally grounded indicators of successful reintegration.

This is a particularly important point when it comes to trafficked children. Trafficked children are often deemed to be 'too vulnerable' to participate in consultations, planning and research. Authors, reflecting on this point in relation to sexually exploited children, note that there are specific tensions between protection and participation, 'this tension is rooted in the two seemingly contradictory positions on young people – that they are either "victims" or agents of change', they cannot be both (Warrington 2013: 112). Such conclusions resonate and explain why trafficked children's voices and views are often so hard to find in the literature. This project demonstrated that trafficked children and young people have a lot to say about the support they need. Although, of course, such work needs to be well planned and ethically sound, children must be given the spaces and opportunities to share their wishes, experiences and knowledge when it comes to reintegration.

Another interesting finding from the project is that much of the basic information that was identified as useful during data collection could be collected in case management forms and processes. This information could not only be used to monitor and plan appropriate support for the young person, but could also, if appropriate consent was acquired, provide a rich source of data for monitoring and evaluation purposes. This would minimise the burden of additional data gathering for both the child and organisation. For example, if standard follow-up questions were developed and workers were trained appropriately and were able to record accurately, then information on the child's education, relationships and so on could provide essential evidence on how the child had integrated.

Of course, there are a number of potential problems and questions that may arise from involving internal staff in this type of data collection, for example, does this create blurred boundaries between research and assistance? And what level of rigour and independence can be expected if data is collected by support workers? (Surtees and Craggs 2010). However, if organisations or welfare agencies are not able to fund robust external evaluations from the start, then using data from the case management system may be the next best thing in terms of trying to understand experiences of reintegration and being able to reflect on and respond to that learning.

The findings from the M&E reintegration project have helped shape the development of a number of tools and papers for organisations supporting reintegration (see www.childrecovery.info for more information). The consultation also provided insights into the types of simple participatory tools and methods that could be used to explore reintegration with children and young people (for full details, see Veitch 2013a). The hope is that in the future more organisations working with separated and trafficked children will start working closely together and will start listening to children and young people, shaping activities to support 'successful reintegration' as defined by young people rather than by adult professionals and funders.

Acknowledgements

The author would like to thank all the children and young people and partner organisations who took part in the consultation process. Thanks are also due to Helen Veitch who developed the consultation guidelines and reported on the findings. Key inputs and insights provided throughout the process by the inter-agency steering group are also greatly appreciated.

Note

1. All names are pseudonyms selected by the children and young people.

References

Ager, A., C Zimmerman, K. Unlu, R. Rinehart, B. Nyberg, C. Zeanah, J. Hunleth, I. Basiaens, A. Weldy, G. Bachman, A. B. Blum and K. Strottman (2012), 'What strategies are appropriate for monitoring children outside of family care and evaluating the impact of the programs intended to serve them?' *Child Abuse and Neglect*, 36: 732–42.

Akello, G., A. Richters and R. Reis (2006), 'Reintegration of former child soldiers in northern Uganda: coming to terms with children's agency and accountability', *Intervention*, 4(3): 229–43.

Anthony, E., M. Samples, D. de Kervor, S. Ituarte, C. Lee and M. Austin (2010), 'Coming back home: the reintegration of formerly incarcerated youth with service implications', *Children and Youth Services Review*, 32: 1271–7.

Asquith, S. and E. Turner (2008), *Recovery and Reintegration of Children from the Effects of Sexual Exploitation and Related Trafficking*, Geneva: Oak Foundation.

Betancourt, T., I. Borisova, J. Rubin-Smith, T. Gingerich, T. Williams and J. Agnew-Blais (2008), *Psychosocial Adjustment and Social Reintegration of Children Associated with Armed Forces and Armed Groups: The State of the Field and Future Directions*, report prepared for Psychology Beyond Borders, Texas: Psychology Beyond Borders.

Betancourt, T., I. Borisova, T. Williams, R. Brennan, T. Whitfield, M. de la Soudiere, J. Williamson and S. Gilma (2010), 'Sierra Leone's former child soldiers: a follow-up study of psychosocial adjustment and community reintegration', *Child Development*, 81(4): 1077–95.

Boothby, N., J. Crawford and J. Halperin (2006), 'Mozambique child soldier life outcome study: lessons learned in rehabilitation and reintegration efforts', *Global Public Health*, 1(1): 87–107.

Boothby, N., R. Balster, P. Goldman, M. Wessells and C. Zeanah (2012),

'Coordinated and evidence-based policy and practice for protecting children outside of family care', *Child Abuse & Neglect*, 36: 743–51.

Brayley, H., E. Cockbain and K. Gibson (2014), *Rapid Evidence Assessment – The Sexual Exploitation of Boys and Young Men*, London: University College London.

Burman, M. and S. McKay (2007), 'Marginalization of girl mothers during reintegration from armed groups in Sierra Leone', *International Nursing Review*, 54: 316–23.

Cody, C. (2012), *Reintegration of Victims of Trafficking: 'Towards' Good Practice in Cambodia*, Phnom Penh: The National Committee to Lead Suppression of Human Trafficking, Smuggling, Labour, and Sexual Exploitation.

Cody, C. (2013a), 'M&E and Reintegration Toolkit', unpublished paper, UHI, Centre for Rural Childhood.

Cody, C. (2013b), 'What Do we Know About … Returning Home: One Option for Children Affected by Sexual Exploitation and Related Trafficking?' Working Paper, Perth Home: The Child Recovery and Reintegration Network, available at: http://www.childrecovery.info, last accessed 2 June 2015.

Cody, C. (2013c), 'What Do We Know About … Safe Accommodation and Alternative Care for Children Affected by Sexual Exploitation and Related Trafficking?' Working Paper, Perth Home: The Child Recovery and Reintegration Network, available at: http://www.childrecovery.info, last accessed 2 June 2015.

Cody, C. (2013d), 'Findings from the Survey "Monitoring and Evaluating Reintegration Programmes for Children"', Perth Home: The Child Recovery and Reintegration Network, available at: http://www.child recovery.info, last accessed 2 June 2015.

Cortes, L. and M. Buchanan (2007), 'The experience of Columbian child soldiers from a resilience perspective', *International Journal for the Advancement of Counselling*, 29: 43–55.

Crivello, G., M. Woodhead and L. Campfield (2009), 'How can children tell us about their well-being? Exploring the potential of participatory research approaches with Young Lives', *Social Indicators Research*, 90(1): 51–72.

Feeny, T. (2005), *In Best or Vested interests? An Exploration of the Concept and Practice of Family Reunification for Street Children*, London: The Consortium for Street Children.

Firmin, C. (2011), *This Is It, This Is My life: Female Voice in Violence on the Impact of Serious Youth Violence and Criminal Gangs on Women and Girls Across the Country*, London: ROTA.

Global Alliance Against Traffic in Women (GAATW) (2007), *Collateral Damage: The Impact of Anti-trafficking Measures on Human Rights Around the World*, Bangkok: GAATW.

Guntzberger, M. (2013), *Research on Factors Surrounding the Family Reintegration of Street Girls in Kinshasa, DRC: The Search for Long-term and Durable Solutions in the Light of 'Multiple Stigmatisations'*,

Family for Every Child and War Child, available at: http://www.warchild. org.uk/sites/default/files/War-Child-Kinshasa-Final-Report-July-2013. pdf, last accessed 14 June 2015.

Hek, R. (2005), *The Experiences and Needs of Refugee and Asylum-seeking Children in the UK: A Literature Review*, National Evaluation of the Children's Fund, University of Birmingham: Department for Education and Skills.

Jordans, M., I. Komproe, W. Tol, A. Ndayisaba, T. Nisabwe and B. Kohrt (2012), 'Reintegration of child soldiers in Burundi: a tracer study', *BMC Public Health*, 12: 905–1007.

Kohli, R. (2011), 'Working to ensure safety, belonging and success for unaccompanied asylum-seeking children', *Child Abuse Review*, 20: 311–23.

Kohli, R. and R. Mather (2003), 'Promoting psychosocial well-being in unaccompanied asylum-seeking people in the United Kingdom', *Child and Family Social Work*, 8(3): 201–12.

Kohrt, B. (2007), *Recommendations to Promote Psychosocial Well-being of Children Associated with Armed Forces and Armed Groups (CAAFAG) in Nepal*, Kathmandu, Nepal: TPO Nepal.

Maholmes, V., J. Fluke, R. Rinehart and C. Huebner (2012), 'Protecting children outside of family care in low and middle income countries: what does the evidence say?' *Child Abuse & Neglect*, 36: 685–8.

McKay. S and D. Mazurana (2004), *Where are Girls? Girls in Fighting Forces in Northern Uganda, Sierra Leone and Mozambique: Their Lives During and After War*, Montreal: Rights & Democracy.

McKay, S., A. Veale, M. Worthern and M. Wessells (2010), *Community-based Reintegration of War-affected Young Mothers: Participatory Action Research (PAR) in Liberia, Sierra Leone and Northern Uganda*, available at: http://www.uwyo.edu/girlmotherspar/_files/pubs-final-report.pdf, last accessed 14 June 2015.

Moncrieffe, J. (2006), 'The power of stigma: encounters with "street children" and "restavecs" in Haiti', *IDS Bulletin*, 37(6): 34–46.

Pawlak, P. and G. Barker (2012), *Hidden Violence Preventing and Responding to Sexual Exploitation and Sexual Abuse of Adolescent Boys: Case Studies and Directions for Action*, MenCare, available at: http:// www.men-care.org/data/Hidden%20Violence%20-%20Preventing%20 and%20responding%20to%20sexual%20exploitation%20%20 and%20sexual%20abuse%20of%20adolescent%20boys.pdf, last accessed 14 June 2015.

Pullum, T., C. Cappa, J. Orlando, M. Dank, S. Gunn, M. Mendenhall and K. Riordan (2012), 'Systems and strategies for identifying and enumerating children outside of family care', *Child Abuse & Neglect*, 36: 701–10.

Ray, P., C. Davey and P. Nolan (2011), *Still on the Street – Still Short of Rights. Analysis of Policy and Programmes Related to Street Involved Children*, London: Plan International and the Consortium for Street Children.

Reimer, J. K., E. Langeler, S. Sophea and S. Montha (2007), *The Road Home: Toward a Model of 'Reintegration' and Considerations for*

Alternative Care for Trafficked Children for Sexual Exploitation in Cambodia, Phnom Penh: Hagar/World Vision Cambodia.

Retrak (2012), *Sustainable Reintegration of Orphans and Vulnerable Children into Family and Community Life in Uganda and Ethiopia*, Summary Report December 2008–November 2011, available at: http://www.streetchildrenresources.org/wp-content/uploads/gravity_forms/1-0 7fc61ac163e50acc82d83eee9ebb5c2/2013/01/Retrak-PEPFAR-Summary-Report.pdf, last accessed 2 June 2015.

Shigekane, R. (2007), 'Rehabilitation and community integration of trafficking survivors in the United States', *Human Rights Quarterly*, 29: 112–36.

Simcox, A. and K. Marshall (2011), *Case Study Evaluation*, World Hope International, New Steps Reintegration Pilot Project, Phnom Penh: World Hope International.

Stark, L., A. Ager, M. Wessells and N. Boothby (2009), 'Developing culturally relevant indicators with armed groups', *Intervention*, 7: 4–16.

Stark, L., B. Rubenstein, K. Muldoon and L. Roberts (2014), *Guidelines for Implementing a National Strategy to Determine the Magnitude and Distribution of Children Outside of Family Care*, Washington, DC: Center for Excellence on Children in Adversity.

Surtees, R. and S. Craggs (2010), *Beneath the Surface. Methodological Issues in Research and Data Collection with Assisted Trafficking Victims*, Geneva: IOM and NEXUS Institute.

Tefferi, H. (2003), *Reintegration and Gender*, Stockholm: Save the Children Sweden.

Thomas, N. and J. Devaney (2011), 'Editorial: safeguarding refugee and asylum-seeking children', *Child Abuse Review*, 20: 307–10.

United Nations (1989), United Nations Convention on the Rights of the Child (UNCRC), Geneva: United Nations.

US Government International Assistance for Children in Adversity (2011), *US Government Evidence Summit on Protecting Children Outside of Family Care*, available at: http://www.childreninadversity.gov/news-information/in-the-press-events/news---full-view/u.s.-government-evidence-summit-on-protecting-children-outside-of-family-care, last accessed 19 February 2015.

Veitch, H. (2013a), '"Feeling and Being a Part of Something Better": Children and Young People's Perspectives on Reintegration', Perth Home: The Child Recovery and Reintegration Network, available at: http://www.childrecovery.info, last accessed 2 June 2015

Veitch, H. (2013b), *Guidelines for Organisations Facilitating Consultations with Children*, Centre for Rural Childhood, Perth Home: The Child Recovery and Reintegration Network, available at: http://www.childrecovery.info, last accessed 2 June 2015.

Warrington, C. (2013), 'Partners in care? Sexually exploited young people's inclusion and exclusion from decision making', in M. Melrose and J. Pearce (eds), *Critical Perspectives on Child Sexual Exploitation and Related Trafficking*, Basingstoke: Palgrave Macmillan, pp. 110–24.

Wedge, J. (2013), *Reaching for Home: Global Learning on Family*

Reintegration in Low and Lower-middle Income Countries, Inter-agency Group of Reintegration, available at: http://www.familyforeverychild.org/sites/default/files/resources/Reaching%20for%20home_0.pdf, last accessed 14 June 2015.

Wessells, M. (2006), *Child Soldiers: From Violence to Protection*, Cambridge, MA: Harvard University Press.

Williamson, J. (2006), 'The disarmament, demobilization and reintegration of child soldiers: social and psychological transformation in Sierra Leone', *Intervention*, 4(3): 185–205.

Williamson, J. and A. Greenberg (2010), 'Families, Not Orphanages', Better Care Network Working Paper, UNICEF, New York: Better Care Network.

10 Policing Forced Marriages Among Pakistanis in the United Kingdom

Stefano Bonino

Ongoing revelations emerging from the Independent Inquiry into Child Sexual Exploitation in Rotherham (Jay 2014) have dealt another blow to the already tense relationship between the British state and its ethnic minorities, and have taken the Pakistani community to centre stage in public debates. The Inquiry highlighted rape, trafficking, abduction, violence and intimidation of over a thousand children – predominantly white girls – by a number of (mostly) Pakistani heritage men which took place between 1997 and 2013. Over ten years after the 2001 riots and the Report of the Independent Review Team into Community Cohesion (Cantle 2001) accused ethnic minority communities, especially Pakistanis, of living parallel lives and threatening social cohesion, the Rotherham case is set to further undermine ethnic and community relations.

Following this scandal, forced marriages continue to be a national problem associated with British Pakistanis. Unlike arranged marriages, in which the individual is free to agree or disagree with the partner selected by his or her family, forced marriages are premised upon coercion, deception and lack of consent. This is not only an issue for the Pakistani community; both nationally and globally it involves people with links to other south Asian and African countries (Forced Marriage Unit 2014; UNICEF 2014). Yet almost half of all cases of forced marriages in the United Kingdom involve Pakistanis, approximately four times more than Indians and Bangladeshis (Forced Marriage Unit 2014). Given the prominence of this issue within British Pakistani communities, this chapter will restrict its focus to their specific experiences of forced marriages.

Arguably, one should not criticise minority communities without attempting to understand the nuances and complexities of cultural practices and without considering that such practices also fall within broader, not necessarily ethnocultural-specific, issues of gender discrimination, social justice and human rights. At the same time, when focusing on hotly debated 'cultural practices', such as forced marriages or female genital mutilation (Nussbaum 1999), which are forced upon non-consensual children and are often illegal, one should know that we are entering a political minefield. Yet this should not deter researchers and practitioners from empirically assessing the issue, as this chapter aims to do. Forced marriages are a cultural practice prevalent within certain communities; regardless of their cultural permissibility, they breach international human rights standards, contravene British law, and often defy Islamic and south Asian laws too.

Most importantly, many forced marriages involving British Pakistanis are a result of human trafficking as (predominantly female) children are taken to or from Pakistan without either knowing that they are going to be married or having agreed to be married. The exploitation of these children can involve 'domestic and sexual servitude, physical and psychological violence and often severe restrictions on their movement' (ECPAT 2008). British Pakistanis who are taken abroad often return to the United Kingdom, where their spouse can subsequently obtain citizenship. However, the whole process of forced marriage is premised upon a lack of consent and free and informed choice. Among a number of international tools, the 1989 Convention on the Rights of the Child, which has been ratified by all UN members except the United States and Somalia, prioritises the best interests of the child in all actions concerning children (here defined as anyone below the age of 18) and de facto makes it a human right to be free to consent or refuse to marry. Although forced marriages defy basic human rights, the practice is still popular in Pakistan and, as a result, also among some Pakistani families living in the United Kingdom (Shaw 2001; Gangoli et al. 2006). National and international legislators are yet to agree an effective legal model to combat forced marriages. The police and victims of forced marriages have also found it hard to deal with a problem that has its roots in complex patriarchal cultural practices located in Pakistan, but that has taken a transnational dimension with the settlement and development of Pakistani communities in the United Kingdom.

Locating marriage at the intersection with Pakistani mores and customs

Research conducted by Shaw (2001) demonstrates that many British-born, second- and third-generation Pakistanis marry relatives, predominantly cousins. This follows an ethnocultural trend typical of south and western Asian, North African and Middle Eastern regions of the world where consanguineous marriages account for between 20 per cent and 55 per cent of all marriages. While the low number of consanguineous marriages is declining throughout the West, Shaw found that the rate for British Pakistanis is on the rise. Many of these Pakistanis are the children of migrants from central Punjab, in particular the prosperous areas of Faisalabad and Sahiwal, and from northern Punjab, especially the less prosperous areas of Mirpur, Attock and Jhelum. In the United Kingdom, Mirpuris constitute a large component of the Pakistani community in Bradford and Birmingham, where they are usually employed as factory workers, while Faisalabadis are more prevalent in Manchester and Glasgow, where they normally work as entrepreneurs. In Shaw's study of British Pakistanis in Oxford, 71 per cent of her respondents contracted marriages with spouses from Pakistan; 87 per cent of the seventy recorded marriages took place within the *biraderi* (extended kinship structure) or *zat* (caste). Most marriages reported in Shaw's study were 'conventionally arranged marriages' (about 85 per cent), while 'arranged love marriages' accounted for about 10 per cent and love/elope (about 3 per cent) were less common.

The role that women play within traditional Pakistani communities is important to consider. Research shows that a significant number of Muslims,[1] who are predominantly of Pakistani origin or heritage, consider sexual relationships before marriage to be unacceptable, if not forbidden (*haraam*) under Islamic principles (Pilgrim 2012). This predominantly affects women, who have traditionally been conceived as the main carriers of family honour (Kabir 2010) within Pakistani communities. Confining female sexual relationships with men to marriage achieves the goal of maintaining the honour of the whole family, and keeping the extended kinship system (*biraderi*) intact. To put it in Werbner's words:

> The politics of marriage [is] embedded in customary notions of honour and shame, which surround the right to control the sexuality and reproductive powers of young people, particularly younger women's bodies, specifically by men and more generally by an older generation of migrants. (Werbner 2012: 108)

Therefore, transnational marriages serve as a tool of social control that preserves the family's honour. Furthermore, they achieve an additional goal as they both reinforce cultural bonds with Pakistan and support another member of the *biraderi* financially (Bolognani 2007). The *biraderi* has a hierarchical structure and is often coloured by the politics of tribe and caste. Certainly, it enhances its members' sociocultural belonging to an extended network of kinship (Wardak 2000). Importantly, it plays a crucial role in both social control and transmitting norms (Bolognani 2009). At times the *biraderi* may act as a symbolic transplant of rural Pakistani life, in which:

> People could not just marry whoever they wanted to. If they did, then over time tribal lands would be broken up by the rules of inheritance, and the economic base of the tribe, or *biraderi* (brotherhood), would be destroyed. This was one reason why children in rural Pakistan were often treated as the property of their elders and encouraged, or forced, to marry within the *biraderi*. (Kabir 2010: 43)

Transnational marriages are mostly a feature of the older generation of Pakistanis who want to see their sons and daughters married to someone from their village and/or clan. However, in line with Shaw's findings, Lewis (2007) found that first-cousin marriages among younger British Pakistanis, which are contracted to reaffirm *biraderi* loyalties, have increased. While some certainly exhibit orthodox views, following the trends of a religious group – the Muslim one – which displays more conservative social attitudes than other Britons (Lewis and Kashyap 2013), young British Pakistanis' attitudes towards this practice are at least ambivalent. In fact, Lewis further reflects on the 'battle [that] is taking place between *biradari* diehards and those who believe it has no place in modern British society', and in which 'the youth are the casualties' (Lewis 2007: 46). Lastly, this issue is often located at the intersection of ethnicity, culture and religion, and some academics (for example, Macey 1999) consider arranged marriages as an extension of a patriarchal society that promotes the oppression of women.

Forced marriages in the United Kingdom: data, legislation and international obstacles

Many cases of forced marriage are not reported to the police. The available official statistics collected by the Forced Marriage Unit (2014) recorded 1,302 cases of (possible) forced marriage throughout the United Kingdom in 2013. This includes people (a) going through a forced marriage, (b) having already been forced to marry and (c) at risk of future forced marriage. The gender distribution, in cases that are reported, is heavily tilted towards women (82 per cent) compared with men (18 per cent), and includes very young people; in fact, 15 per cent of all reported cases involved victims below 16 (age of consent), while 25 per cent involved victims aged 16–17. A further 33 per cent of reported cases involved victims aged 18–21, with the remaining 25 per cent involving victims aged over 22. In terms of geographical distribution, the four most targeted regions, according to the Forced Marriage Unit (2014) were London (24.9 per cent), the West Midlands (13.6 per cent), the southeast (9.9 per cent) and the northwest (9.3 per cent). Of the seventy-four countries involved, Pakistan alone accounted for 555 (that is, 42.7 per cent) of all cases, followed by India (10.9 per cent, 142 cases) and Bangladesh (9.8 per cent; 127 cases).

These three main south Asian countries together account for more than 60 per cent of all reported cases of (possible) forced marriages in the United Kingdom. Such a number is reflected globally (UNICEF 2014). Although Niger has the highest prevalence of child marriage,[2] over 40 per cent of all child brides are south Asian, and about 25 per cent are married before the age of 15, with Bangladesh recording the highest rate. Across the world, more than 700 million women have been married before reaching the age of 18, while about 250 million are married before their fifteenth birthday (UNICEF 2014). Still a cultural aspect of predominantly less developed countries, the practice of child marriage is usually correlated with poverty, living in a rural area (UNICEF 2014) and discriminatory gender practices (Human Rights Council 2014). Despite some disagreement among scholars (Rao and Presenti 2012), the broader practice of human trafficking and the concept of sexual and domestic exploitation are tightly linked to economic disadvantage and gender inequality (Phinney 2001; US Department of State 2011), thus forced marriages are influenced by dimensions other than culture alone.

While marriages other than 'love-based' take different forms, arranged marriages and forced marriages are the most known and discussed. The difference between the two revolves around consent, which is lacking in cases of forced marriage. To use the official words of the Forced Marriage Unit:

> A forced marriage is where one or both people do not (or in cases of people with learning disabilities, cannot) consent to the marriage and pressure or abuse is used. It is an appalling and indefensible practice and is illegal in Great Britain. It is recognised as a form of violence against women and men, domestic/child abuse and a serious abuse of human

rights . . . The pressure put on people to marry against their will can be physical (including threats, actual physical violence and sexual violence) or emotional and psychological (for example, when someone is made to feel like they're bringing shame on their family). Financial abuse (taking your wages or not giving you any money) can also be a factor. (Forced Marriage Unit 2013b)

Whether consent has been granted out of personal choice or out of coercion is very difficult to measure and, therefore, some cases might be hard to assess. When such problems in defining consent are coupled with the difficulty in establishing coercion, the distinction between arranged marriage and forced marriage can become very blurred. In the author's previous work (Bonino 2014), this was exemplified in the case of a Scottish-born Pakistani woman who was sent to her parents' home village abroad (where she had never lived) as soon as she completed her high school studies. There, she married a cousin whom she had never met before. Now in her mid-thirties, she recounted how she had to reluctantly consent to her parents' decision and was allowed to return to Scotland only after she had given birth to a child. On returning to Scotland, she sponsored her husband to live in the United Kingdom and to obtain British citizenship. After obtaining this, her husband subsequently deserted her. Unfortunately, there is evidence of a number of other, similar cases among British Pakistanis (Carroll 1998).

International tools such as the 2000 Protocol to Prevent, Suppress and Punish Trafficking in Persons, Especially Women and Children (supplementing the United Nations Convention against Transnational Organized Crime), which was ratified by the United Kingdom but not by Pakistan, brings many of the practices around British Pakistani forced marriage under the definition of trafficking for the purpose of exploitation, especially when involving people who are taken to/ from Pakistan through coercion, deception, pressure, and so on, for example, to enter relationships of domestic and/or sexual servitude. Article 3, (subparagraph (a)) states that:

'Trafficking in persons' shall mean the recruitment, transportation, transfer, harbouring or receipt of persons, by means of the threat or use of force or other forms of coercion, of abduction, of fraud, of deception, of the abuse of power or of a position of vulnerability or of the giving or receiving of payments or benefits to achieve the consent of a person having control over another person, for the purpose of exploitation. Exploitation shall include, at a minimum, the exploitation of the prostitution of others or other forms of sexual exploitation, forced labour or services, slavery or practices similar to slavery, servitude or the removal of organs.

Subparagraph (b) makes consent irrelevant once the above-mentioned means are proved. Furthermore, subparagraph (c) removes the burden to prove that such means have been used when children (that is, persons under the age of 18) are trafficked. The UN Office on Drugs and Crime (UNODC 2009) clarifies the terms of reference applying to the three main forms of exploitation: (1) sexual exploitation; (2) trafficking for non-commercial sexual purposes (including forced or servile marriage); and (3) labour trafficking (including domestic servitude).

Under UK legislation forcing someone to marry is a criminal offence falling within the remit of the Anti-social Behaviour, Crime and Policing Act 2014[3] and carrying a penalty of up to seven years in prison (in Scotland this may also include a fine). Marriage is extensively considered as 'any religious or civil ceremony of marriage (whether or not legally binding)' (Article 4, s. 121; also Article 4, s. 122). The legislation also criminalises the act of taking someone overseas to force him or her to marry, regardless of whether the marriage takes place.[4] Moreover, it makes it a criminal offence to breach a Forced Marriage Protection Order, that is, a legal document issued by courts under the Forced Marriage (Civil Protection) Act 2007 to prevent people from being married against their consent. This crime carries a penalty of up to five years in prison and/or a fine.

From a policing perspective, while this new legislation can help to make clear the terms of forced marriage, there exist cultural issues that cannot be addressed by law alone. As noted previously, retaining control over their children's marriage is a way in which some Pakistani parents can ensure the survival of kinship bonds and tribal continuity. Refusal to be married can incur social costs that, in certain cases, may include being repudiated by one's family. Therefore, it would not be surprising if some Pakistani children prefer to reluctantly proceed with the marriage rather than lose their families. For those cases in which a forced marriage is resisted, there are provisions in the Children Act 1989 aimed at families that are uncooperative with statutory bodies. In particular, section 44 allows courts to deliberate on applications made by a wide range of actors (social workers, police, neighbours, etc.) to grant local authorities the parental responsibility for children who are likely to suffer significant harm for up to eight days.

Pakistani girls may also appeal to classical Islamic law (jurisprudence of Shia Islam and the Hanafi School within Sunni Islam), which states that a girl who has reached majority (post-pubescent age) 'cannot be contracted in marriage by her father or any other relative without her consent expressed at the time the contract is entered into' (Carroll 1998). As Carroll notes, establishing what constitutes the 'age of majority' is tricky. The Majority Act of 1875, which is valid across south Asia and sets the age of majority at 18, does not apply to marriage. To this end, one has to turn to the intricacies of Muslim personal law. In Pakistan, the Child Marriage Restraint Act 1929 (No. XIX) defines the minimum age for marriage as 16 for girls and 18 for boys and criminalises contraventions of this. However, the situation is rather complex as the practice of forced marriage is still very common, and 'while the question of whether a marriage is a "child marriage" thereby inviting criminal sanctions, is determined by reference to the Child Marriage Restraint Act. The question of whether the marriage itself is valid is determined, in the case of Muslims, by reference to the uncodified Muslim law' (Carroll 1998). The Convention on Consent to Marriage, Minimum Age for Marriage and Registration for Marriages could clarify this issue by clearly stating that marriages need to be consensual; however, Pakistan has not signed this treaty (United Nations 1962) and, therefore, the issue is dealt with by its 'chaotic' legal system discussed above.

In the United Kingdom, the Matrimonial Causes Act 1973 (s. 11) declares a marriage to be void when either partner is under the age of 16. Despite the challenges of enforcing the law due to the complex nature of transnational marriages, which fall under different jurisdictions, there is leeway around (a) consent and (b) age of majority under Islamic, Pakistani and UK laws in rendering a forced marriage void. Nevertheless, the real priority is about how best to prevent forced marriages in the first place.

The challenges in policing forced marriages

The previously discussed Anti-social Behaviour, Crime and Policing Act 2014 and the related criminalisation of forced marriages have been criticised for deterring women from reporting to the police and, more broadly, employing the legal system (Wilson 2014). It could be argued that, similarly to the Domestic Violence, Crime and Victims Act 2004, the police-led nature of anti-forced marriage interventions, as opposed to grassroots support to (predominantly) women, could be perceived as yet another state tool deployed to criminalise, surveil and racially profile minority groups/communities. Wilson (2014) argues that support organisations such as Newham Asian Women's Project in London,[5] which deals with about 1,500 cases every year, can attest to women's unwillingness to report cases of forced marriage due to perceived heavy-handedness of the police response. Furthermore, contacting the police would in turn involve the Multi-

Agency Assessment Conference (MARAC). MARAC includes agencies such as the police, housing providers, children's services and health services and deals with domestic abuse; however, some women who have been supported by Newham Asian Women's Project think that MARAC disempowers, rather than helps, them (Wilson 2014).

Many people forced into a marriage are unlikely to report the issue to the police thereby incriminating their parents or family members, running the risk of driving the practice underground rather than accessing the tools offered by the current legislation. Claims of lack of protection, and safeguarding, of victims and witnesses of forced marriages is another factor allegedly impeding collaboration with the police in a context where grassroots organisations advocate for a stronger partnership between Black, Asian, Minority Ethnic and Refugee (BAMER) women's voluntary sector (Ashiana Network 2012) and statutory agencies. Lastly, victims may also be uneasy about engaging with the police given the difficulties of withdrawing allegations due to the possibility of either being charged with wasting police time or perjury[6] (Wilson 2014) or, more seriously, having the Crown Prosecution Service proceed with the prosecution without the victim's consent should there be strong evidence that such a course of action would be in the public interest (Forced Marriage Unit 2013a).

These views have been challenged in various ways (Kazi 2014), in the first place by noting that the British criminalisation of forced marriages complies with Article 37 of the Istanbul Convention on violence against women and domestic violence. Furthermore, research shows an increase in reports of cases of forced marriage since the government announced its plans to criminalise the practice in 2012 (Proudman 2011). Similarly, when marital rape was criminalised, reporting to the police significantly increased (Burman *et al.* 2009). Moreover, victims can, and are often willing to, make use of the legislation as a bargaining tool with their parents to find ways not to be forced to marry (Proudman 2011). Lastly, some argue that the effort of the criminal justice system through the police and the Crown Prosecution Service to uphold justice and pursue offenders, even without the victim's consent, should take priority over protecting the honour of a family and/or a community (Kazi 2014).

One of the main challenges faced by law enforcement agencies in policing forced marriages is the hard-to-reach nature of the groups among which it predominantly takes place (Chantler *et al.* 2009). When individuals lack information about their rights or when they are deceived by their parents, victims may not even be aware that the practice to which they are subject constitutes a forced marriage. As with other forms of (especially sexual) abuse and exploitation, victims face enormous emotional and psychological difficulties in speaking out, for example, for fear of being shamed and losing face with members of their community. As a consequence, reports to the police and possibly even other agencies, such as social services and voluntary organisations, tend to be low. In turn, this impacts negatively on victims who may not receive support, also distorting recorded national figures on forced marriage and failing to deter people from abstaining from such practice, given that perpetrators often face no legal and social consequences for their unlawful actions.

Law enforcement agencies also have to deal with potential denial that forced marriages are a problem within Pakistani communities and the related uncooperativeness of some of their members. In particular, local Muslim leaders and representatives may downplay the prevalence of practices within their local communities which may otherwise be perceived as abusive. In Gangoli *et al.*'s (2006) research, a mosque representative who was interviewed maintained that forced marriages and domestic violence (about which he claimed not to have heard a single case) were not an issue in his community. Furthermore, he advocated for non-intervention in personal matters, lamenting existing legislation as being an attack on Muslims and stating that children would never go against their parents. Clearly one respondent is hardly sufficient to generalise to a whole population. Yet the reluctance to involve the police and the criminal justice system more widely in cases of domestic violence has been highlighted previously among Muslim communities (BBC One 2013). Such issues are not specific to Muslim and Pakistani populations alone, however, they *also* characterise such populations. Broadly speaking, the fact that younger Pakistanis find it difficult to question some of the older generation's cultural practices and negotiate age- and power-based community structures (Hemmings and Khalifa 2013) might well explain why certain forms of abuse may appear to be tolerated and perpetuated. In this sense, two cultural changes need to take place. The first relates to the broader, not Pakistani-specific, objectification of children for the achievement of parents' goals (whatever these are) and the degradation of women in their unequal positioning within family and community structures. The second specifically relates to Pakistani communities (and other groups in which forced marriages are prevalent) and requires younger generations to openly challenge practices which are unlawful, morally objectionable and culturally inexcusable.

Lastly, one should consider the possibility that the police might find it difficult to deal with such a politically sensitive area, in which issues of culture and race come to the foreground. While it is important not to exoticise forced marriages and related honour-based practices, and to avoid blaming culture only when such practices happen within minority communities (Volpp 2000), it is also crucial that agencies are able to work towards reducing crime that the evidence suggests is prevalent among British south Asians, specifically Pakistanis (Forced Marriage Unit 2014). While public confidence in the police has been undermined by the consequences of the Stephen Lawrence Inquiry and the more recent exaggerated responses to the threat of terrorism (Bonino 2012, 2013), the police need to strive for a visibly fairer, stronger participatory, community-oriented and trust-based approach in dealing with sensitive issues involving vulnerable populations. This requires a more open cooperation with grassroots organisations that support victims of forced marriages and that may function as intermediaries between the police and victims. Moreover, where possible, law enforcement agencies should strengthen links with key members of the community, including younger generations, who may assist in establishing safe forums for direct connection between the police and victims of forced marriages. This may help assess the problem informally, build trust and slowly improve relationships between minority communities and law enforcement agencies with a view to reach a solution that, having taken all elements into consideration, is in the best interest of the victim. Finally, the police need to improve their overall handling of cases of domestic abuse, which have been compromised by a range of factors at both management and front-line levels, from poor attitudes towards, and lack of skills in dealing with, victims to a failure to tackle the crime in the first place (HMIC 2014).

Policing transnational forced marriages

The previous section highlighted a number of domestic challenges to the policing of forced marriages, including the complexities of enforcing anti-forced marriage legislation, the ways in which the police (are perceived to) handle cases, the formal involvement of the criminal justice system, victims' unwillingness to cause trouble to their families, pressures to downplay the abuse and exploitation, potential complacency among certain community members, and cultural elements that may both promote this unlawful practice and make it hard for law enforcement agencies to take action. Moreover, the transnational element of this practice further problematises the work of the police. Given that most forced marriages take place outside the United Kingdom, human trafficking, deception and abduction are potential features and narrow 'the window of time when intervention is possible' (Voulgari 2012: 17). The likelihood that the victim is unaware that they are being taken abroad to be married, as opposed to visit family or on holiday as he or she may be made to believe, dramatically affects the potential for authorities to be aware that a crime is imminent and to prevent it. When the victim is abroad, his or her passport and travel documents are likely to be taken by their family and, as discussed earlier, different legislation, criminal procedure and sociocultural customs may not be particularly helpful in assisting the victim before or after the marriage takes place.

Therefore, the police and other law enforcement agencies face the dilemma of adopting a reactive approach – that is, acting only when the crime is reported – or a preventative approach. If the former approach is often unfeasible for the reasons just mentioned, the latter approach is problematic on several grounds. Obviously, policing borders so that people 'at-risk' are stopped before travelling would incur public and political outrage and only further feelings of ethnoracial targeting by the criminal justice system. Also, how would people 'at-risk' of being trafficked for the purpose of forced marriage be identified in the first place? Who would carry out such a risk assessment and through what means? Arguably, such a solution would not stand pragmatic and ethical scrutiny.

A more feasible solution lies with an increase in trust-based partnerships between the police and communities so that mutual information is shared with the aim of acting in the best interest of actual and potential victims, and with a view to minimising the social, cultural and psychological costs that reporting a forced marriage may have on such victims. To this end, members of the community, and not necessarily victims themselves, should be encouraged to cooperate with the police and report known cases of impending forced marriage, so that interventions can be put in place well before a victim disappears abroad. If the recent experience of dealing with minority (often Muslim) communities in a post-9/11 age of stigmatisation teaches something, it is that top-down approaches to crime prevention often fail to meet with the approval and the understanding of these communities. Instead, bottom-up, community-led approaches may be more easily accepted and taken up by minority groups, especially by those more progressive British-born members who distance themselves from some ethnocultural practices and who are supportive of a liberal multicultural project that positively integrates diversity within Britain's social, political and legal boundaries.

Conclusion

As a practice not necessarily Pakistani-specific, yet prevalent among Pakistani communities in the United Kingdom, forced marriage entails the abuse and the exploitation, often as a result of human trafficking, of boys and (more often) girls who are denied the freedom to lead the lives that they wish. Still heavily entrenched in tribal customs originating in Pakistan and transplanted in Britain, yet also influenced by gender inequality and economic disadvantage typical of sexual and domestic exploitation, such practices are unlawful. Whether in pragmatic terms the criminalisation of forced marriage has been a good move is yet to be assessed. Arguably, international legislation and, especially, south Asian, Pakistani and Islamic law have not been harmonised to ensure that this issue is dealt with in a coherent fashion across the transnational spectrum. Certainly, there is a risk that the issue of forced marriage may be taken up by those who wish to advocate for anti-immigration policies and to promote the idea of a failed British multicultural project. However, there may be an opportunity to rectify the wrongdoing that victims of forced marriages are subject to without entailing and furthering perceptions and experiences of ethnocultural targeting.

To this end, this chapter has demonstrated that the policing of forced marriages is fraught with problems, the most significant ones being the tense relationships between police and minorities and the unwillingness of victims to report the crime due to distrust in the wider criminal justice system and the social, cultural and emotional risks associated with incriminating family members. Furthermore, the transnational element of forced marriages, which de facto makes them an act of human trafficking entailing domestic and/or sexual exploitation, limits the scope of police prevention, particularly in a context in which victims may be deceived as to the nature of their travel. Grassroots organisations may also face similar limitations in dealing directly with victims, or mediating through the police, when marriages happen abroad. The fact that victims under the age of 16 can have their marriage voided under UK legislation is reassuring, yet not necessarily the best course of action. Despite their fairness and effectiveness having been questioned (sometimes with good reasons), the police and, more broadly, the criminal justice system remain the actors with the strongest financial and institutional resources to deal with the abuses of forced marriage. However, grassroots organisations and support from community members are indispensable, especially for prevention, and the police need to foster stronger trust-based partnerships with such actors in order to create a safe place for victims of forced marriage. As recently highlighted by the collective failure of the police, the local authority and social care to address the seriousness of child sexual exploitation in Rotherham (Jay 2014), there is an urgent need to strengthen multi-agency capacities and build trust in policing activities in order to effectively communicate to, and improve relations with, ethnic communities.

Notes

1. In Lewis and Kashyap's (2013) survey, 68 per cent of British Muslims agreed that 'premarital sex is always wrong', while only 10 per cent of Britons of other religions and 2 per cent of 'religious nones' (those of no religion) gave the same response to the question.
2. This is normally considered as marriage before the age of 18 and as 'forced' marriage given that children are unable to consent (Chantler *et al.* 2009)
3. There are some minor legal differences between England and Wales (s. 121) and Scotland (s. 122), for example, with regard to one's mental capacity to consent to marriage, as this issue is regulated by different legislation (Mental Capacity Act 2005 in England and Wales; and Mental Health (Care and Treatment) (Scotland) Act 2003).
4. Often, psychological and physical violence, as well as close monitoring of their movements, ensure that potential victims of forced marriage may not ask for help. Removal of passports also prevents them from returning to the United Kingdom.
5. Other organisations are Southall Black Sisters, Ashiana Network and Henna Foundation.
6. However, this is a problem that may affect all victims across the criminal justice system.

References

Ashiana Network (2012), Forced Marriage Consultation, March 2012, available at: http://www.ashiana.org.uk/attachments/article/5/Ashiana%20Network%20Response%20to%20Forced%20Marriage%20Consultation%202012.pdf , last accessed 2 September 2014.

BBC One (2013), *Secrets of Britain's Sharia Councils*, aired 8 April 2013.

Bolognani, M. (2007), 'The myth of return: dismissal, survival or revival? A Bradford example of transnationalism as a political instrument', *Journal of Ethnic and Migration Studies*, 33(1): 59–76.

Bolognani, M. (2009), *Crime and Muslim Britain: Race, Culture and the Politics of Criminology Among British Pakistanis*, London: Tauris.

Bonino, S. (2012), 'Policing strategies against Islamic terrorism in the UK after 9/11: the socio-political realities for British Muslims', *Journal of Muslim Minority Affairs*, 32(1): 5–31.

Bonino, S. (2013), '*Prevent*-ing Muslimness in Britain: the normalisation of exceptional measures to combat terrorism', *Journal of Muslim Minority Affairs*, 33(3): 385–400.

Bonino, S. (2014), 'Negotiated Muslimness in Post-9/11 Scotland: Integrations, Discriminations and Adaptations of a Heterogeneous Community of Faith', unpublished PhD thesis, University of Edinburgh.

Burman, M., J. Lovett and L. Kelly (2009), *Different Systems, Similar Outcomes? Tracking Attrition in Reporting Rape Cases in Eleven Countries*, London: Child and Woman Abuse Studies Unit.

Cantle, T. (2001), *Community Cohesion: A Report of the Independent Review Team*, London: Home Office.

Carroll, L. (1998), *Dossier 20: Arranged Marriages: Law, Custom and the Muslim Girl in the U.K.*, London: Women Living Under Muslim Laws.

Chantler, K., G. Gangoli and M. Hester (2009), 'Forced marriage in the UK: religious, cultural, economic or state violence?', *Critical Social Policy*, 29(4): 587–612.

End Child Prostitution, Pornography and the Trafficking of Children (ECPAT) (2008), *Child Trafficking for Forced Marriage*, London: ECPAT.

Forced Marriage Unit (2013a), *Forced Marriage: A Survivors Handbook*, London: Home Office and Foreign & Commonwealth Office.

Forced Marriage Unit (2013b), *What is a Forced Marriage?*, London: Home Office and Foreign & Commonwealth Office.

Forced Marriage Unit (2014), *Statistics January to December 2013*, London: Home Office and Foreign & Commonwealth Office.

Gangoli, G., A. Razak and M. McCarry (2006), *Forced Marriage and Domestic Violence Among South Asian Communities in North East England*, Bristol: University of Bristol.

Hemmings, J. and S. Khalifa (2013). *'I Carry the Name of my Parents': Young People's Reflections on FGM and Forced Marriage*, Bristol: Create Youth Network.

HM Inspectorate of Constabulary (HMIC) (2014), *Everyone's Business: Improving the Police Response to Domestic Abuse*, London: HMIC.

Human Rights Council (2014), *Human Rights Council Holds Panel Discussion on Preventing and Eliminating Child, Early and Forced Marriage*, 23 June 2014, available at: http://www.ohchr.org/EN/NewsEvents/Pages/DisplayNews.aspx?NewsID=14760&LangID=E, last accessed 30 August 2014.

Jay, A. (2014), *Independent Inquiry Into Child Sexual Exploitation in Rotherham: 1997–2013*, Rotherham: Rotherham Metropolitan Borough Council.

Kabir, N. (2010), *Young British Muslims: Identity, Culture, Politics and the Media*, Edinburgh: Edinburgh University Press.

Kazi, T. (2014), 'Let's criminalise forced marriage: secular and Islamic perspectives', *Open Democracy*, 20 January 2014, available at: https://www.opendemocracy.net/5050/tehmina-kazi/let's-criminalise-forced-marriage-secular-and-islamic-perspective, last accessed 28 August 2014.

Lewis, P. (2007), *Young, British and Muslim*, London: Continuum.

Lewis, V. and R. Kashyap (2013), 'Are Muslims a distinctive minority? An empirical analysis of religiosity, social attitudes, and Islam', *Journal for the Scientific Study of Religion*, 52(3): 617–26.

Macey, M. (1999), 'Class, gender and religious influences on changing patterns of Pakistani Muslim male violence in Bradford', *Ethnic and Racial Studies*, 22(5): 845–66.

Nussbaum, M. (1999), *Sex and Social Justice*, Oxford: Oxford University Press.

Phinney, A. (2001), *Trafficking of Women and Children for Sexual Exploitation in the Americas*, Washington: Inter American Commission of Women (Organisation of American States) and Women, Health and Development Program (Pan American Health Organisation).

Pilgrim, A. (2012), 'Sexuality politics in Islam', in M. Farrar, S. Robinson, Y. Valli and P. Wetherly (eds), *Islam in the West: Key Issues in Multiculturalism*, Basingstoke: Palgrave Macmillan, pp. 121–37.

Proudman, C. (2011), *Forced and Arranged Marriage Among South Asian Women in England and Wales: Critically Examining the Social and Legal Ramifications of Criminalisation*, London: LAP Lambert.

Rao, S. and C. Presenti (2012), 'Understanding human trafficking origin: a cross-country empirical analysis', *Feminist Economics*, 18(2): 231–63.

Shaw, A. (2001), 'Kinship, cultural preference and immigration: consanguineous marriage among British Pakistanis', *Journal of the Royal Anthropological Institute*, 7(2): 315–34.

United Nations (UN) (1962), Convention on Consent to Marriage, Minimum Age for Marriage and Registration of Marriages, Treaty Series 521, p. 231, available at: https://treaties.un.org/pages/ViewDetails.aspx?src=TREATY&mtdsg_no=XVI-3&chapter=16&lang=en, last accessed 2 March 2015.

UN Children's Fund (UNICEF) (2014), *Ending Child Marriage: Progress and Prospects*, New York: UNICEF.

UN Office on Drugs and Crime (UNODC) (2009), *Combating Trafficking in Persons: A Handbook for Parliamentarians*, Vienna: UNODC.

US Department of State (2011), *Trafficking in Persons Report 2011*, Washington, DC: US Department of State.

Volpp, L. (2000), 'Blaming culture for bad behavior', *Yale Journal of the Law and the Humanities*, 1(1): 89–116.

Voulgari, A. (2012), *Women and Forced Marriage in Scotland*, Edinburgh: Sahelía.

Wardak, A. (2000), *Social Control and Deviance: A South Asian Community in Scotland*, Aldershot: Ashgate.

Werbner, P. (2012), 'Veiled interventions in pure space: honour, shame and embodied struggles among Muslims in Britain and France', in M. Farrar, S. Robinson, Y. Valli and P. Wetherly (eds), *Islam in the West: Key Issues in Multiculturalism*, Basingstoke: Palgrave Macmillan, pp. 103–20.

Wilson, A. (2014), 'Criminalising forced marriage in the UK: why it will not help women', *Open Democracy*, 13 January 2013, available at: https://www.opendemocracy.net/5050/amrit-wilson/criminalising-forced-marriage-in-uk-why-it-will-not-help-women, last accessed 28 August 2014.

11 Criminalising Victims of Human Trafficking: State Responses and Punitive Practices

Margaret Malloch

Introduction

Despite the existence of national and international legislation (see earlier chapters), underpinned by practice guidelines and commitments, victims and survivors of human trafficking continue to be subject to prosecution and punishment by nation states that either fail to identify, recognise or acknowledge their status as victims of exploitation. Many individuals appear to be detained as 'illegal migrants' rather than treated as victims (or survivors) of crime. As with all areas of human trafficking, the extent to which this occurs is impossible to determine. However, despite a clear gap in evidence, there is a growing awareness of this problem. Indeed, it has been suggested that there are more victims of human trafficking detained in Scottish prisons than convicted traffickers (House of Lords 2014); while RACE in Europe (2013: 16) highlight significant concerns that while prosecution and conviction rates for trafficking crimes in the United Kingdom remain low, 'there is a deep concern that those trafficked are instead being punished for the crimes that their traffickers force them to commit' (see also All Party Parliamentary Group 2015). This would appear to be reflected elsewhere; despite international legislation and guidance to the contrary, victims of trafficking continue to be detained across the globe in prisons and immigration detention centres (for example, Amnesty International 2008; Human Rights Watch 2010; US Department of State 2010; CUNY School of Law 2014). This chapter considers why measures aimed at protecting victims of human trafficking from criminalisation and detention by host nation states do not appear to be operating effectively. It highlights the importance of locating these troubling circumstances within a broader context which links experiences of exploitation and trafficking with asylum-seeking, immigration and broader processes of criminalisation.

Background

Legal directives (for example, EU Directive 2011/36) are intended to prevent the 'punishment' of trafficking victims by criminal justice systems in the countries to which they have been trafficked. Although actual numbers are unknown, evidence continues to highlight circumstances where individuals who are almost certainly victims of trafficking have been imprisoned in the United Kingdom and internationally or held in immigration detention centres (Hales and Gelsthorpe 2012; Anti-Trafficking Monitoring Group (ATMG) 2013; All Party Parliamentary Group 2015). This is ostensibly due to the difficulties in identifying victims during initial investigations, but it also highlights the ways in which legislation creates dualisms (for example, 'guilty'/'innocent', 'deserving'/'undeserving') which can contribute to processes and experiences of imprisonment. In 2010, for example, the ATMG identified flaws in victim identification by the National Referral Mechanism (NRM) and stated that victims of trafficking continued to be routinely prosecuted for offences committed under duress (ATMG 2010). The Group of Experts on Action against Trafficking in Human Beings (GRETA) (2012) also noted cases of arrest, prosecution and conviction in relation to migration and non-migration offences experienced by victims of human trafficking in the United Kingdom. Two key factors appear to underpin processes of criminalisation which relate specifically to victims of trafficking: first, irregular migration: the routes by which victims of human trafficking enter a country, and, in many cases, their movement into the country (clandestine or irregular entry) may constitute a criminal offence (such as unauthorised entry and/or use of forged documents). Where status as a victim of trafficking is not identified or acknowledged, individuals may not have access to relevant support services and, indeed, the trauma they have already experienced may be significantly exacerbated by the experience of detention, imposed if they are deemed likely to abscond or while awaiting forcible removal.

Secondly, individuals may be prosecuted for 'survival' offences; crimes committed in order to survive should they escape from their exploiters or as a direct result of the exploitation itself (that is, in circumstances where they are forced to break the law by their exploiter). RACE in Europe (2013: 1) estimate that 16 per cent of the potential victims of trafficking identified by the UK Human Trafficking Centre (UKHTC) in 2012 (362 of 2,255) had been trafficked for the purposes of criminal exploitation, including benefit fraud. Indeed, the international category of labour exploitation includes criminal exploitation such as theft, shoplifting, drugs production, selling counterfeit DVDs, smuggling cigarettes, forced begging and benefit fraud.

Information obtained from all police forces across the United Kingdom under a Freedom of Information request identified that since January 2011, 1,405 individuals had been arrested for offences relating to the cultivation of cannabis; 63 per cent of those arrested were Vietnamese, 13 per cent of whom were children (RACE in Europe 2013: 4). The available figures indicate that child victims of trafficking have been arrested and convicted of cannabis cultivation supporting claims by GRETA (2012), who also highlighted concerns that potential victims of human trafficking had been detained. This reflects the emphasis that the criminal justice system places on identifying and responding to 'criminality'. Many victims fall foul of the law as their status is criminalised (that is, where they have been initially categorised as irregular migrants); and any further acts that contravene the law will result in the consolidation of this criminal status, despite protocols against smuggling and trafficking that state that intercepted asylum seekers and refugees should not be liable to prosecution.[1] However, the contextualisation of these protocols as criminal justice responses first and foremost inevitably dilutes the intended focus on 'victims'.

Not only does this process of criminalisation limit the access of victims to support services, it is also likely to have a detrimental impact on the individuals' physical and mental health and compounds the difficulties they are likely to experience in disclosing their circumstances to authorities. Those individuals who are intercepted may also be subject to removal; of note given that the majority of victims are believed to be trafficked by people they know in their country of origin.

Stephen-Smith (2008), in collaboration with the POPPY Project, found evidence that women who had been trafficked had been detained in custody in England and Wales. The United Nations (UN) rules for the treatment of women prisoners and non-custodial measures for women (2010, rule 66) encourages states to ratify international protocols and 'provide maximum protection to victims of trafficking in order to avoid secondary victimization of many foreign-national women' (United Nations 2010). However, the emphasis given to preventing irregular migration has remained a priority. For example, the Prison Reform Trust examined the circumstances of foreign national women in prison in England and Wales in 2012, noting that the dominant offences among this group related to deception and fraud, generally in relation to immigration status and related paperwork.[2] Other dominant charges were theft and employment in illegal activities, such as cannabis production and selling fake or counterfeit goods. While such charges are not, in themselves, indicative of victimisation as the result of trafficking, they are the type of offences that are often associated with it. It has also been noted (Prison Reform Trust 2012) that legal representatives may not give sufficient attention to identifying exploitation or duress. In addition to the punishments meted out by the courts, this may also impact on future applications for asylum or residency.

Hales and Gelsthorpe (2012) gathered information on the numbers of migrant women processed through the criminal justice and immigration systems in England and Wales and, within this context, considered the extent of compliance with the European Convention on Trafficking and the Convention on Human Rights in cases where victims of trafficking, smuggling and 'work under duress' were detained in custody. Examination of data from the prison service (where accessible) and FPWP/Hibiscus (an organisation working with foreign women in custody) indicated high numbers of foreign nationals charged with offences such as deception and fraud (in relation to immigration status) and related offences of using false documentation to access work or benefits, entry or exit to the United Kingdom through customs (accounting for 41 per cent of the caseload of FPWP/Hibiscus; and 26 per cent of all foreign prisoners). The researchers identified forty-three women[3] in the prison and immigration holding estates as potential victims of trafficking, and fifteen who appeared to have been smuggled into the United Kingdom and/or made to work under duress[4]; two of whom were formally assessed as children while held in adult prisons. The two key offence groups related to use of false identity documentation (accounting for twenty primary charges) and production of cannabis (accounting for fourteen primary charges).[5]

Only eleven women (from forty-three identified as victims of trafficking by researchers) were processed through the NRM. Even where referrals resulted in a positive decision and non-prosecution, victims spent an average of four months in custody. For most of these women, there was no formal recognition of victim status, access to appropriate support or temporary protection from removal other than the option of making an asylum application. Thirty-one women had applied for asylum, and of the fourteen outcomes that researchers were aware of, two (where age assessments had confirmed that the detainees were children) had been given leave to remain for five years, while twelve applications had been refused, including six which had gone through the appeal process. It appeared that the status of 'illegal migrant' was predominant in the response to women in terms of immigration case management.

Hales and Gelsthorpe (2012) set out some contributory factors as to why researchers were able to identify key indicators of trafficking victim status which had not been identified by professionals within the criminal justice system. They noted: the failure of arresting officers to facilitate or respond appropriately to disclosures of victimisation or to understand the obstacles to free and full disclosure due to ongoing threats to the arrestee; 'inconsistent and limited' access to legal representatives; impact of imprisonment; inability of the woman to understand the process or language difficulties which compounded trauma already experienced; lack of appropriate knowledge or response by potential first responders; reluctance to go through the NRM process; and narrow interpretation of the European Convention.

Hales and Gelsthorpe (2012: 60) state: 'In a number of cases it is inconceivable that the physical and psychological indicators used to identify victims of trafficking, which were so apparent when interviewing women in the context of this research, were not evident at the point of arrest.' They go on to say: 'One can only conclude that these women were processed in the normal manner because the police were focusing on the individual as an offender and did not see it appropriate to act as a "first response authorised agency" and report the case to UKHTC'.[6] This chimes with the views of women interviewed by the UK Border Agency in prison, who also indicated that they felt they were being assessed as 'offenders' (Prison Reform Trust 2012). Similarly, Stephen-Smith (2008: 13) noted: 'Criminal justice issues, for example, women entering the country by deceptive means (irrespective of the fact that such an act was likely to have been under duress), were seen as overriding factors, thereby neglecting the paramount status of victims' human rights.'

Significantly, too, the police did not appear to attempt to investigate allegations of victimisation made by arrestees. In Hales' and Gelthorpe's study, victim disclosures had resulted in only one full police investigation relating to perpetrators and two attempts to obtain further information. Indeed, one woman who had not been charged with any criminal offences, spent six months in Yarl's Wood and nine weeks in prison on an immigration hold, before being granted bail following input from the Poppy Project which provided further information to the woman's legal representative requesting reassessment of her status as a victim of trafficking (Hales and Gelsthorpe 2012).

Both Stephen-Smith (2008) and Hales and Gelsthorpe (2012) found that even in cases where there was evidence to suggest that women were victims of trafficking, and where this information had been made known to the authorities, detention was still authorised. Both studies illustrate that women trafficked into the United Kingdom are routinely held in immigration detention centres and prisons, despite international guidelines that oppose this. Such concerns have been reinforced in Scotland by the Equality and Human Rights Commission Scotland (2013) and across the United Kingdom by the ATMG (2010, 2013), RACE in Europe (2013) and the All Party Parliamentary Group (2015).

Criminal justice responses and the non-prosecution of victims

In addition to international law, which specifies that victims of trafficking should not be prosecuted, individual nation states have introduced their own guidance and are developing legislation on an ongoing basis. For example, the Modern Slavery Act (England and Wales) 2015, Human Trafficking and Exploitation (Criminal Justice and Support for Victims) Act (Northern Ireland) 2015, Human Trafficking and Exploitation (Scotland) Act recently progressed through the Scottish Parliament. Guidance has also been developed by the Association of Chief Police Officers (ACPO 2010a), *ACPO Lead's on Child Protection and Cannabis Cultivation on Children and Young People Recovered in Cannabis Farms*, which formally recognised the involvement of victims of trafficking in commercial cannabis production, noting that systems of production may be controlled by organised criminals with wider connections. An update by ACPO (2010b) noted that violence may be used to ensure the compliance of workers.

While much attention has been given to the identification of victims and the importance of police practices, the role of prosecutors has been acknowledged as a crucial factor in ensuring that the non-prosecution of trafficking victims is upheld. The Crown Prosecution Service (England and Wales) (CPS) (CPS 2011),[7] the Crown Office and Procurator Fiscal Service (COPFS) (Scotland) (COPFS 2010), and Public Prosecution Service (Northern Ireland) (PPS 2013) have all produced guidance to prosecutors aimed at informing them of legislation and outlining practice in relation to human trafficking.[8] While much of this guidance is focused upon the prosecution of traffickers and on outlining the various forms that trafficking violations may take, it also highlights circumstances where victims of trafficking may face prosecution. The importance of ensuring that further enquiries are undertaken in circumstances where it comes to the attention of the prosecutor that the accused may be a victim of trafficking is noted. Where the accused is considered to be a 'credible' trafficked victim, the importance of considering the 'public interest' and whether or not it is best served by prosecution is highlighted. Factors such as the seriousness of the offence, whether the offence was committed as a direct consequence of being trafficked, and the extent to which coercion was used are all to be taken into account when considering whether or not the 'public interest' will be served by prosecution. The PPS for Northern Ireland notes that:

> The PPS cannot offer blanket immunity from prosecution for trafficked victims who may commit criminal offences . . . The Convention does not provide for immunity from prosecution for trafficked victims but it does require that careful consideration must be given as to whether the *public interest* requires prosecution in such cases. (PPS 2013: 20; emphasis added)

In Scotland, despite similar guidance aimed at ensuring such 'careful consideration' in the cases of trafficking victims, legal respondents have continued to express concerns that potential victims of human trafficking are prosecuted for crimes they had been compelled to commit; that the guidance was not always applied in practice, and that key practitioners (social work practitioners outwith Glasgow, duty solicitors, the procurator fiscal service and even judges) had limited awareness of the guidance (see Malloch, Warden and Hamilton-Smith 2011). This can mean that victims of trafficking are not identified in court, a situation also noted in England and Wales. As the CPS guidance states:

> a prosecutor can only take these steps if they have information from the police or other sources that a suspect might be a victim of trafficking and is only relevant where the criminality is as a direct consequence of the trafficking situation. There must also be the consideration of the extent to which the victim was compelled to undertake the unlawful activity. (CPS 2011: 30)

Evidence that an offence was committed while the individual was in a coerced situation should imply the importance of stopping the prosecution – in the 'public interest'. The 'public interest', an ambiguous concept, seems to be something of a 'get out' clause for prosecutors, notwithstanding that in Western jurisdictions all prosecutions should be considered in relation to the public interest with criminal sanction as a last resort.

There is currently no system in place to review the process of avoiding the punishment of victims for involvement in criminal activities that they have been compelled to commit as a direct consequence of being subject to trafficking. The CPS is, however, working with criminal justice partners and UKHTC to identify a 'practical mechanism' to monitor the effectiveness of existing arrangements (OSCE 2012: app. 1). However, recent cuts to the CPS budget may well have an impact on the resources available to identify and address the needs of individuals who have been trafficked.

The Modern Slavery Act (2015) introduced a defence for victims where the victim has been compelled to commit a crime 'as a direct result of their slavery or trafficking experience', although safeguards include non-application to certain serious offences (for example, sexual or violent offences); the individual seeking to use the defence must be a victim of the trafficking or slavery offences; and must have been 'compelled to commit the offence as a direct result of their trafficking/slavery situation, and a reasonable person in the same situation would have no realistic alternative but to commit the offence' (Secretary of State for the Home Department 2014: 17).

Similar emphasis is given in Scotland where the Lord Advocate will, under the recent Human Trafficking and Exploitation (Scotland) Act, have a duty to publish instructions about the prosecution of '"credible" trafficking victims who have committed offences' (Justice Committee 2015: 18). Although this would not compromise the independence of the Lord Advocate, they would specify the circumstances where there should be a 'strong presumption' against prosecution of a victim of trafficking. However, concerns have been expressed about the extent to which the responsibility is placed on the victim to demonstrate that they are a credible victim of human trafficking.

Theorising processes of criminalisation

Despite serious concerns expressed across governments and criminal justice agencies about the potential criminalisation and ongoing punishment of individuals who are victims of human trafficking, it is necessary to consider why, given the existence of legislation and guidance, victims of trafficking continue to be held in prisons and detention centres as a direct result of offences related to their trafficking status. As the Commissioner for Human Rights (2010: 38) has noted: 'the recognition of these commitments does not appear to influence, in practice, the approach towards criminalisation'.

In 2013, the Convener of the European and External Relations Committee of the Scottish Parliament wrote to the Cabinet Secretary for Justice on behalf of a group of organisations involved in supporting victims of human trafficking, expressing concerns about compliance with EU Directive 2011/36/EU. Responding to specific concerns noted in the letter which related to the criminalisation and detention of potential victims of human trafficking, the Lord Advocate (the Right Honourable Frank Mulholland QC) outlined the existing COPFS guidance to prosecutors. He highlighted the role of this guidance in ensuring that appropriate consideration was given to potential victims of human trafficking and stressed the commitment of COPFS to do this. He also outlined the challenges, noting:

> It is important to remember that identifying *genuine* victims of trafficking is a complex task which must be carried out with diligence and care to ensure that those making *false* claims to have been the victim of human trafficking in an attempt to avoid prosecution are also identified (mail correspondence, 21 January 2013; emphases added).

This response illustrates a dichotomy that sits at the heart of legislative practice and features throughout criminology and 'victimology': how can the 'genuine' and 'deserving' victim be distinguished from the 'fraudulent' or 'undeserving'? – a conundrum that continues to result in the imprisonment and detention of victims of trafficking, where the 'condition of victim' is granted by others (Ruggiero 2010: 187). Treated as 'judicial goods', these individuals are 'requested to entrust their inviolability to external agencies which are normally structured to reproduce principles of dependency and delegation . . .' (*ibid.*: 187).

Concerns surrounding 'genuine' victims of trafficking can be located within a broader context wherein the 'genuine' and 'false' must be distinguished and responses directed as appropriate. This has particular significance for the depiction of the 'trafficking victim'; a concept that O'Connell Davidson (2010: 244) argues has, particularly in relation to the 'trafficked sex slave' 'been worked to most effect in the service of extremely conservative moral agendas on prostitution, gender and sexuality and in support of more restrictive immigration policies and tighter border controls'. This stereotypical victim and the complex reality of actual individual experience can cause significant challenges at the level of identification and recovery. For example, the Equality and Human Rights Commission Scotland (2013: 43) noted that: 'Views clearly differ between the police and prosecuting authorities, and agencies supporting victims on whether those coerced into illegal activities are being criminalised.'

This distinction between 'genuine' and thus by implication 'not genuine' victims has long characterised state responses to asylum seekers and migrants internationally. As Hudson (2012: 19) notes: 'The border, the detention centre, the interrogation room, the shanty town street, the contested territory, are sites of inequality, where one party can give or withhold justice and security and the other can have no certainty of receiving either.' For non-citizens, procedural protections in criminal law are not evident in immigration procedures where the boundaries between civil and criminal law are porous, while distinctions between 'insiders' and 'outsiders' are emphasised (Stumpf 2010). Referring to an earlier work (2006), Stumpf (2010: 59) outlines three intersections between immigration and criminal law:

> (1) The substance of immigration law and criminal law increasingly overlaps, (2) immigration enforcement has come to resemble criminal law enforcement, and (3) the procedural aspects of prosecuting immigration violations have taken on many of the earmarks of criminal procedure.

Here, even the use of language evidences the extent of the challenge facing criminal justice agencies. For example, the Council of Europe Parliamentary Assembly highlighted the importance of language, urging nation states to refer to 'undocumented migrants' or 'migrants without papers', yet all EU institutions and Member State governments continue to refer to 'illegal immigrants' and 'illegal immigration' in policy and practice, thereby emphasising migration as a criminal justice issue. This allows for the 'deployment of coercive enforcement techniques' (Commissioner for Human Rights 2010: 35; see also Lee 2004) and contributes to what Wacquant (1999) has referred to as the 'hypercriminalisation' of immigrants. Additionally, border controls, which were previously governed by nation states, are increasingly overseen by transnational organisations.

Criminalisation of immigration and asylum

Despite the liberal tenet of the law, policies and practices aimed at securing international borders have resulted in a response where people seeking asylum and/or fleeing international strife have met with a punitive response. The depiction of asylum seekers, for example, in the media and often reinforced by policy, often appears to differentiate refugees and asylum seekers into overly simplistic categories of 'deserving' or 'undeserving' of the status and benefits that accrue to those judged as 'genuinely' seeking sanctuary. Thus, there is a separation of citizens and non-citizens through the use of criminal law and administrative language, which results in non-citizens being increasingly subject to measures such as detention without charge, trial or conviction for status offences, and the criminalisation of those who engage with non-citizens (such as transport companies and employers) (Commissioner for Human Rights 2010). Anderson and Andrijasevic (2008) argue that state responses to migration 'effectively construct groups of non-citizens who can be treated as unequal with impunity' (see also Brown 2014). Bosworth and Guild (2008: 714) argue that this has an important effect: the 'criminalisation of migration reshapes the referents for security – British citizens'. This process of social construction also applies to the representation of victims of trafficking. Haynes (2007: 346), for example, challenges the law and order emphasis as perpetuating myths that:

> most trafficking victims are rescued by law enforcement officials; that they are rescued from actively and visibly abusive environments; that only those who are rescued are really victims and those who escape or are arrested or detained are not; that if a person is not visibly a victim, she is probably a criminal; and that someone who has broken the law cannot also be a victim of trafficking.

Calls to identify and recover victims of human trafficking are based on an acknowledgement of their exploitation and victimisation. Similarly, however, despite the recognition that asylum seekers are 'victimised' by circumstances of persecution, torture and, potentially, death, the dominant rhetoric across the United Kingdom has been influenced by the 'risk' and 'danger' that large numbers of undocumented migrants may pose to the stability of UK society (Sales 2002; Malloch and Stanley 2005) and across Europe and the United States (Welch and Schuster 2005). Following an original policy of dispersal, the Home Office White Paper, *Fairer, Faster and Firmer* (1998), signalled an emphasis on increasing the use of detention, and resources swiftly moved to the development of induction centres, accommodation centres and removal (formerly detention) centres, staffed and managed by private companies such as UK Detention Centres, Premier Prison Service and Group 4 (now G4S). Although not intended to hold asylum seekers, but those detained before removal, their use was frequently extended to hold individuals with ongoing claims. Conditions within immigration detention centres have consistently been criticised; despite limited access to counselling and support services, interpreters and legal advisers, individuals were increasingly required to 'prove' their victimisation (Malloch and Stanley 2005; Commissioner for Human Rights 2010; HM Inspectorate of Prisons and Independent Chief Inspector of Borders and Immigration 2012; HM Chief Inspector of Prisons 2013; All Party Parliamentary Group 2015). This inextricably linked asylum claiming in the United Kingdom to a system aimed at discouraging 'bogus' claims of asylum and also reflected Bauman's (1998: 69) depiction of the 'global hierarchy of mobility' where freedom of movement is an entitlement of the dominant, while the dominated are subject to the 'strictest possible constraints'. This is borne out by the United Nations Development Programme (UNDP 2009), which indicated that people in the poorest countries remain the least mobile.

Across Europe and the United States, increasing proportions of prison populations consist of prisoners detained for migration offences. In the United States, a number of what were previously 'civil offences' have become felonies, and in Europe a number of new types of offence have been created relating specifically to migration. In the United Kingdom, between 1997 and 2007, the then Labour Government introduced nine pieces of legislation concerning immigration, asylum and terrorism (Bosworth and Guild 2008). These changes, on an international scale, are indicative of new strategies of criminal justice control over migration. Legislative changes have been characterised by the increased depiction of migrants, asylum seekers and refugees as 'suspect communities' where the distinction between citizen and non-citizen is emphasised (see Commissioner for Human Rights 2010). Those outside the protections afforded citizens become targets for surveillance and intervention. The expansion of punishment via the criminal justice system is accompanied by the expansion of detention restrictions into the community and the creation of 'quasi-penal spaces'. This process operates against the enactment of international conventions, legislation and constitutions, and particularly mitigates protections for victims that depend on the use of discretionary power or discernment. The emphasis is increasingly on the criminalisation of status rather than conduct.

At the same time, these developing processes of criminalisation create a lucrative business for prison and detention industries and other businesses geared towards regulation and control (Amnesty International 2009). Similarly, the increase in forced removals continues to be a profitable business for private companies. Ruggiero (1997, 2000) notes the overlap between legitimate and illegitimate networks in the business of cross-border movement, which involve, for example, transport entrepreneurs, airline employees and public officials (see also OSCE 2014).

Guidelines developed by the UN High Commissioner for Human Rights (2002) consider the detention of human trafficking victims to be 'inappropriate and, implicitly, illegal', with states encouraged to ensure that custody or detention is not used for individuals believed to have been trafficked. Yet the existing ambiguities between the 'public interest' and legal protection remain highly problematic within this wider context where these antagonistic processes operate, reflected within the law itself in terms of 'justice' and 'regulation'. The existence of rights in law, yet their discretionary application in practice reinforces the observation by Arendt (1968) that the loss of national rights equals the loss of human rights. Those 'stateless persons' are no longer viewed as citizens of any sovereign state and therefore are 'out of legality altogether' with, she argues, greater attention paid to the 'status of the persecuted' than to the deeds of the persecutors.

For Grewcock (2007: 186), 'criminalisation by the state is integral to legitimising criminal activity by the state'. Grewcock discusses the pre-emptive process of 'externalisation' where nation states attempt to prevent the entry of 'illicit workers' into areas where there might be considerable demand for their services or against forced migrants and refugees 'into areas where they might gain access to the human rights machinery that was developed explicitly to protect them' (2007: 180).

Similarly, Maggie Lee (2014) draws attention to the ways in which related ideologies influence the 'gendered discipline and protective custody' of trafficking victims in Asia. In particular, she notes: 'What seems missing in the existing scholarship on immigration detention is the way in which detention has expanded and mutated for a particular category of unauthorized migrants, that is, trafficking victims within a diverse range of semi-carceral institutions' (2014: 207). She argues that the basis of 'protective custody', particularly for women and girls, is indicative of 'a hitherto under-researched gendered disciplinary regime and carceral processes for unauthorized migrants' (2014: 207), and is significantly problematic for victims of trafficking who have been 'rescued' and subsequently detained in residential facilities. According to Gallagher and Pearson (2010), there is limited or cursory international legislation governing the use of such facilities and 'residents' have minimal legal protection despite the fact that their detention may be involuntary and indefinite; often justified by claims of rehabilitation or ongoing trafficking prosecutions. Furthermore, as Lee (2014) notes, gendered responses under the guise of prevention and protection from trafficking, have resulted in increased moves towards the regulation and control of women and increased scrutiny of their cross-border movements.

Many European countries prioritise the monitoring and regulation of 'illegal immigration' over the identification and recovery of victims of human trafficking; similarly, victims are often seen as instrumental to the prosecution of traffickers rather than prioritised in terms of their human rights. In the United States, without law enforcement certification, victims of human trafficking are likely to be viewed as criminals and be deported (Haynes 2007: 350). Significant discretion is given to officials who may be reluctant to see victims who have not been 'rescued' as 'certifiable' (Segrave *et al.* 2009; Hoyle *et al.* 2011). It may also be difficult for victims experiencing significant trauma to cooperate with law enforcement agencies. Segrave *et al.* (2009) discuss provisions for women victims of trafficking for commercial sexual exploitation focusing on Australia, Thailand and Serbia. While detailing responses and provisions across the three countries they also note the distinction between short-term assistance for 'victims' and longer-term assistance for 'witnesses' linked to victim cooperation with prosecutions.

Conclusion

International obligations are clear that there should be provision for non-prosecution of individuals who commit offences as a direct result of their exploitation. The current detention of an unknown number of potential victims of trafficking in prisons across the United Kingdom and internationally requires consideration, and highlights the importance of implementing appropriate and effective identification processes throughout the criminal justice system (see, for example, Hales and Gelsthorpe 2012). Issues of through-care and support on release are also important.

The ongoing distinction that is drawn between 'deserving' and 'undeserving' victims of crime is exemplified by the treatment and response to irregular migrants. Caught up in this response are, inevitably, those seeking asylum and the victims of human trafficking and exploitation. While protection may be afforded in international law and state guidelines and directives, inevitably, the attention to combating irregular ('illegal') migration results in all foreign nationals being viewed through a lens of criminality. Across the United Kingdom and Europe, migrant detainees make up an increasing proportion of detained populations; and this is evident globally. While, on the one hand, attention is given to trafficking of humans as a scourge on society, the lens through which individuals are viewed is inextricably linked to migration and criminalisation. Depictions of the 'exceptional circumstances' of trafficking are relevant, however these images are often juxtaposed against 'ordinary' economic migrants despite the fact that identified circumstances of victimisation are often related more to high debts and abusive working conditions than kidnapping and imprisonment (Chapkis 2003). This renders legislation in place to protect victims of trafficking as limited; the greater authority is directed towards responding to perceived 'criminality' and 'illegality'. Underpinning this lies the 'discourse of depoliticization', the presentation of trafficking as a phenomenon that is distinct from the exploitation and injustices that characterise the experiences of many migrants (O'Connell Davidson 2010: 245), and that constructs political judgements about what becomes 'appropriate' versus 'inappropriate' exploitation.

Nevertheless, the existence of measures that set out intentions towards non-criminalisation, and the existence of many government reports and inquiries at national and international levels appear to suggest a partial acknowledgement that there is a problem in securing and enforcing the rights of victims of trafficking and preventing criminalisation, punishment and detention. However, the continued problems with this approach is that it maintains the focus on limited practical recommendations, such as enforcement of existing legislation, training opportunities for those who administer the system, improved data collection and, on occasion, recommendations for wider resources. There is rarely suggested change outside this framework and, as Cohen (2001: 114) notes, this translates violations of human rights 'into the legalistic, diplomatic, UN-speak . . . language of "human rights violations" pass[ing] ownership of the problem into the professional and bureaucratic cartel'. The framing of the process of criminalisation is reinforced where crime is framed as a 'migration-related' issue, making it easier to imply the existence of 'genuine' and, subsequently, 'false' victims where the 'public interest' in the current climate is characterised by a concern that the 'guilty' will go unpunished, which appears to supersede concerns to ensure the protection and enforcement of rights.

Notes

1. And there have been a number of cases where the rescue of refugees and asylum seekers has itself been criminalised (see, for example, at: http://www.statewatch.or/news/2007/sep/07italy-tunisia-fishermen.htm, on the trial of seven Tunisian fishermen prosecuted in Sicily following the rescue of forty-four migrants in international waters south of the Pelagian islands), as well as increasing sanctions (criminal sanctions and sanctions that carry criminal law consequences) for businesses that employ foreign nationals who do not have right of residence. While presented as 'anti-trafficking' measures they clearly have significant consequences.

2. With an average sentence of eight months for false documents and twelve months in the case of conviction for deception.
3. From 103 migrant women who had been detained or arrested on charges that were potentially linked with entry to, or exit from, the United Kingdom or work under the control of others.
4. Using the indicators outlined in the European Convention and listed in the Trafficking Toolkit.
5. Seven women were charged with entry into fake marriages (two of whom were trafficked and paid to enter into these marriages to obtain British nationality after escaping from their traffickers; two were undocumented migrants; three were EU nationals, recruited and paid to provide fake marriages for non-EU nationals for financial gain).
6. UKBA is the competent authority with responsibility for establishing 'conclusive grounds' decisions on all non-EU women held in the prison or immigration estate, rather than UKHTC. The UKBA Criminal Casework Directorate (UKBA CCD) and prisons work together, with UKBA CCD holding surgeries in women's prisons and all prisons being obliged to pass information on prisoners with unconfirmed UK nationality (Prison Reform Trust 2012).
7. First published in 2007.
8. In the case of *R* v. *O* [2008] EWCA Crim 2835, a young woman received an eight-month custodial sentence after pleading guilty to possessing a false identity card with the intention of using it as her own. The case was overturned on appeal on the grounds that the young woman, legally a minor, was the victim of trafficking for the purpose of sexual exploitation. Although this had been indicated at the original court appearance, the disclosure had not resulted in further inquiries, nor had steps been take to confirm her age, resulting in her treatment as an adult. In the appeal judgment, Lord Justice Laws stated:

> We hope that such a shameful set of circumstances never occurs again. Prosecutors must be aware of the protocols which, although not in the text books are enshrined in their Code. Defence lawyers must respond by making enquiries, if there is before them credible material showing that they have a client who might have been the victim of trafficking, especially a young client. Where there is doubt about the age of a defendant who is a possible victim of trafficking, proper inquiries must be made, indeed statute so required. All this is obvious . . . We hope that this case serves as a lesson to drive these messages home. (*R* v. *O* [2008] EWCA Crim 2835, para. 26)

References

All Party Parliamentary Group on Refugees and the All Party Parliamentary Group on Migration (2015), *The Report of the Inquiry into the Use of Immigration Detention in the United Kingdom*, London: House of Commons.

Amnesty International (2008), *Scotland's Slaves: An Amnesty International Briefing on Trafficking in Scotland*, Edinburgh: Amnesty International Scotland.

Amnesty International (2009), *Jailed Without Justice: Immigration Detention in the USA*, available at: http://www.amnestyusa.org/research/reports/usa-jailed-without-justice, last accessed 14 July 2014.

Anderson, B. and R. Andrijasevic (2008), 'Sex, slaves and citizens: the politics of anti-trafficking', *Soundings*, 40: 135–45.

Anti-Trafficking Monitoring Group (ATMG) (2010), *Wrong Kind of Victim*, London: ATMG.

Anti-Trafficking Monitoring Group (ATMG) (2013), *In the Dock: Examining the UK's Criminal Justice Response to Trafficking*, London: ATMG.

Arendt, H. (1968), *The Origins of Totalitarianism*, New York: Harvest Books.

Association of Chief Police Officers of England, Wales and Northern Ireland (ACPO) (2010a), *Position from ACPO Lead's on Child Protection and Cannabis Cultivation on Children and Young People Recovered in Cannabis Farms*, London: ACPO Child Protection and Abuse Investigation Group, Child Exploitation and Online Protection (CEOP) Centre.

Association of Chief Police Officers (ACPO) (2010b), *Three Years On: Findings from the UK National Problem Profile Commercial Cultivation of Cannabis*, London: ACPO Regional Intelligence Unit and ACPOS.

Bauman, Z. (1998), *Globalization*, Cambridge: Polity Press.

Bosworth, M. and M. Guild (2008), 'Governing through migration control', *British Journal of Criminology*, 48: 703–19.

Brown, M. (2014), 'Visual criminology and carceral studies: counter-images in the carceral age', *Theoretical Criminology*, 18(2): 176–97.

Chapkis, W. (2003), 'Trafficking, migration and the law', *Gender and Society*, 17: 923–37.

Cohen, S. (2001), *States of Denial: Knowing about Atrocities and Suffering*, Cambridge: Polity Press.

Commissioner for Human Rights (2010), *Criminalisation of Migration in Europe*, Strasbourg: Council of Europe.

Crown Office and Procurator Fiscal Service (COPFS) (2010), *Guidance on Human Trafficking Offences*, available at: http://www.copfs.gov.uk/images/Documents/Prosecution_Policy_Guidance/Guidelines_and_Policy/Guidance%20on%20Human%20Trafficking%20Offences.pdf, last accessed 21 August 2014.

Crown Prosecution Service (CPS) (2011), *CPS Policy for Prosecuting Cases of Human Trafficking*, London: CPS Strategy and Policy Directorate.

CUNY School of Law (2014), *Clearing the Slate: Seeking Effective Remedies for Criminalized Trafficking Victims*, New York: City University of New York.

Equality and Human Rights Commission Scotland (2013), *Inquiry into Human Trafficking in Scotland: Follow-on Report*, Glasgow: EHRC.

Gallagher, A. and E. Pearson (2010), 'The high cost of freedom: a legal and policy analysis of shelter detention for victims of trafficking', *Human Rights Quarterly*, 32: 73–114.

Grewcock, M. (2007), 'Shooting the passenger: Australia's war on illicit migrants', in M. Lee (ed.), *Human Trafficking*, Cullompton: Willan Publishing, pp. 178–209.

Group of Experts on Action against Trafficking in Human Beings (GRETA) (2012), *Report Concerning the Implementation of the Council of Europe Convention on Action against Trafficking in Human Beings by the United Kingdom*, Strasbourg: Council of Europe.

Hales, L. and L. Gelsthorpe (2012), *The Criminalisation of Migrant Women*, Cambridge: Institute of Criminology, University of Cambridge.

Haynes, D. (2007), '(Not) found chained to a bed in a brothel: conceptual, legal, and procedural failures to fulfil the promise of the Trafficking Victims Protection Act', *Georgetown Immigration Law Journal*, 21: 337.

HM Chief Inspector of Prisons (2013), *Yarl's Wood Immigration Removal Centre*, London: Her Majesty's Inspectorate of Prisons.

HM Inspectorate of Prisons and Independent Chief Inspector of Borders and Immigration (2012), *The Effectiveness and Impact of Immigration Detention Casework*, London: HM Inspectorate of Prisons.

Home Office (1998), *Fairer, Faster and Firmer: A Modern Approach to Immigration and Asylum*, London: HMSO.

House of Lords (2014), Question from Lord McConnell of Glenscorrodale, Human Trafficking and Modern Slavery Debate, *Hansard*, 12 June, col. 497, available at: http://www.publications.parliament.uk/pa/ld201415/ldhansrd/text/140612-0001.htm, last accessed 16 June 2015.

Hoyle, C., M. Bosworth and M. Dempsey (2011), 'Labelling the victims of sex trafficking', *Social and Legal Studies*, 20(3): 313–29.

Hudson, B. (2010), 'Who needs justice? Who needs security?', in B. Hudson and S. Ugelvik (eds), *Justice and Security in the 21st Century*, London: Routledge, pp. 6–23.

Human Rights Watch (2010), 'Victims of human trafficking held in ICE detention', Letter to the US Department of State on 2010 Trafficking in Persons Report, New York: Human Rights Watch.

Justice Committee (2015), *Stage 1 Report on the Human Trafficking and Exploitation (Scotland) Bill*, Edinburgh: Scottish Parliament.

Lee, M. (2004), 'Human trade and the criminalisation of irregular migration', *International Journal of the Sociology of Law*, 33: 1–15.

Lee, M. (2014), 'Gendered discipline and protective custody of trafficking victims in Asia', *Punishment and Society*, 16(206): 206–22.

Malloch, M. and E. Stanley (2005), 'The detention of asylum seekers in the UK: representing risk, managing the dangerous', *Punishment and Society*, 7(1): 53–71.

Malloch, M., T. Warden and N. Hamilton-Smith (2012), *Care and Support for Adult Victims of Trafficking in Human Beings*, Edinburgh: Scottish Government.

O'Connell Davidson, J. (2010), 'New slavery, old binaries: human trafficking and the borders of "freedom"', *Global Networks*, 10(2): 244–61.

Organization for Security and Co-operation in Europe (OSCE) (2012), *Report by OSCE Special Representative and Co-ordinator for Combating Trafficking in Human Beings, following her visit to the UK*, 7–10 March 2011, Vienna: OSCE.

Organization for Security and Co-operation in Europe (OSCE) (2014), *Ending Exploitation*, Office of the Special Representative and Co-ordinator for Combating Trafficking in Human Beings, Vienna: OSCE.

Prison Reform Trust (2012), *No Way Out: A Briefing Paper on Foreign National Women in Prison in England and Wales*, London: PRT.

Public Prosecution Service for Northern Ireland (PPS) (2013), *Policy for Prosecuting Cases of Human Trafficking*, Belfast: PPS.

RACE in Europe (2013), *Victim or Criminal? Trafficking for Forced Criminal Exploitation in Europe – UK Chapter*, London: ECPAT UK.

Ruggiero, V. (1997), 'Trafficking in human beings: slaves in contemporary Europe', *International Journal of the Sociology of Law*, 25: 231–44.

Ruggiero, V. (2000), *Crime and Markets: Essays in Anti-Criminology*, Oxford: Oxford University Press.

Ruggiero, V. (2010), *Penal Abolitionism*, Oxford: Oxford University Press.

Sales, R. (2002), 'The deserving and the undeserving? Refugees, asylum seekers and welfare in Britain', *Critical Social Policy*, 22(3): 456–78.

Secretary of State for the Home Department (2014), *The Government Response to the Report from the Joint Committee on the Draft Modern Slavery Bill*, Session 2013–14 HL Paper 166/HC 1019, London: Home Office.

Segrave M., S. Milivojevic and S. Pickering (2009), *Sex Trafficking: International Context and Response*, Cullompton: Willan Publishing.

Stephen-Smith, S. (2008), *Detained: Prisoners with No Crime, Detention of Trafficked Women in the UK*, London: Eaves Housing for Women.

Stumpf, J. (2010), 'The justice of crimmigration law and the security of home', in B. Hudson and S. Ugelvik (eds), *Justice and Security in the 21st Century*, London: Routledge, pp. 43–63.

United Nations (2010), The United Nations Rules for the Treatment of Women Prisoners and Non-custodial Measures for Women Offenders, available at: http://www.un.org/en/ecosoc/docs/2010/res%202010-16. pdf, last accessed 28 August 2014.

United Nations Development Programme (UNDP) (2009), *Overcoming Barriers: Human Mobility and Development*, New York: UNDP.

United Nations High Commissioner for Human Rights (2002), *The Recommended Principles and Guidelines on Human Rights and Human Trafficking*, available at: http://www.ohchr.org/documents/publications/traffickingen.pdf, last accessed 20 August 2014.

United States Department of State (2010), *Trafficking in Persons Report 2010*, Washington, DC: US Department of State.

Wacquant, L. (1999), '"Suitable enemies": foreigners and immigrants in the prisons of Europe', *Punishment and Society*, 1(2): 215–22.

Welch, M. and L. Schuster (2005), 'Detention of asylum seekers in the US, UK, France, Germany, and Italy', *Criminal Justice*, 5(4): 331–55.

12 Root Causes, Transnational Mobility and Formations of Patriarchy in the Sex Trafficking of Women

Jackie Turner

Introduction

The scale of trafficking worldwide can at best be estimated, but most practitioners and scholars agree it is both significant and increasing (Aronowitz 2009; Shelley 2010), aided by improved transportation infrastructures and advances in communication technologies, which traffickers are able to exploit in an increasingly globalised world.

There can be little doubt that globalisation has exerted transformative influences on the world's social, political and economic landscape. It has produced 'winners' and 'losers' (De la Dehesa 2006) and, according to the United Nations Office on Drugs and Crime (UNODC), it has promoted crime beyond borders (UNODC 2002). It has also contributed to accelerating rates, and changes in patterns, of migration. Increasing numbers of people now reside and work outside their countries of origin (Monzini 2005), while globally, at any given moment, significant numbers of individuals are on the move, so much so that we are now said to live in a 'world in motion' (Inda and Rosaldo 2002). This perpetual movement has transformed the nature of social relations that span borders; changes that have unsettled historic population movements and have seen the emergence of new, more fluid, transnational formations (Cohen 1997; Smith and Guarnizo 1998; Turner and Kelly 2009). The last few decades, however, have also witnessed other, historic changes. The collapse of the former Soviet Union towards the end of the last century, the wars and subsequent reconfiguration of borders across the region, all generated unprecedented movements of people, while the transition from command to market economies produced social and economic asymmetries which enriched some and simultaneously impoverished others.

These are among the factors that account for the rise and spread of trafficking. The disparate effects of globalisation, poverty, wars, political instability and the lack of sustainable livelihoods comprise the 'fertile field' (Kelly 2005), or conditions conducive to trafficking. Yet, in whatever combination they affect the lives of individuals, they do not sufficiently account for the increase in the sex trafficking of women and the growth of commercial sex markets across the world. While trafficking into other sectors is a significant phenomenon, and while the sex trafficking of young men and boys remains 'thus far a terra incognita in terms of sociological research' (Morawska 2007: 98–9), there is good reason for the continued focus on the sex trafficking of women, albeit with a shift in perspective.

Patriarchal gender orders

The international community has singled out women and children as the two groups that are particularly vulnerable to trafficking. While this focus is welcome, its framing in these terms is also problematic. Women and children are not synonymous, they do not share the same needs, rights or agency, and they do not require the same protections. Combining the two in such fashion risks infantilising women and failing to afford children the recognition they need, both as children and as gendered beings. Moreover, with respect to women, the approach promotes a very one-sided debate in that it fails to locate gender within what Connell (1987, 2009) calls patriarchal 'gender orders'. Gender orders comprise 'overarching hierarchical social arrangements and patterns' (Coy 2012: 4) of gender inequality. In much of the literature on trafficking, and at international level, gender means women. The relevance of focusing on the *gender order* in particular, however, rather than simply on gender, is that the other side of the equation is factored back in: men and masculinity as locations of power. As Connell (2009) suggests, the dominant feature, and harm, of the current gender order lies 'first and foremost in the system of inequality in which women and girls are exploited, discredited and made vulnerable to abuse and attack. The still massive incidence of [violence] is an easily recognized marker of power and vulnerability' (*ibid*.: 143).

How trafficking is primarily understood is not merely a matter of academic debate, but impacts in the real world of policy and action. In locating sex trafficking within patriarchal gender orders, it can be conceived as 'an easily recognized marker of power and vulnerability' and, therefore, as a form of violence against women. This does not refer only to the violence to which trafficked women are subjected within the trafficking process, although this certainly does occur. It is instead to understand trafficking as violence against women in the sense promulgated by the Committee for the UN Convention on the Elimination of All Forms of Discrimination against Women (CEDAW) in General Recommendation No. 19 (1992). While the definition of discrimination in CEDAW makes no mention of violence, the Committee commented that it is nonetheless included insofar as gender-based violence is 'violence directed against a woman because she is a woman or that affects women disproportionately'. Since trafficking is now a global problem in which, according to most estimates, the majority of victims are women and girls trafficked into prostitution markets the world over, sex trafficking can be framed as gender-based discrimination and as a practice involving violence directed against women because they are women, as well as violence that disproportionately affects women.

Widespread violence against women is common in all communities. It is a feature of the 'global gender order', as much as gender is 'a structure of world society' (Connell 2009: 126–7). Yet, while gender is not the same across all cultures, and always intersects with other factors such as race (Crenshaw 1991), there are nonetheless 'significant features of the gender order which cannot be understood locally, which *require* analysis on a global scale' (Connell 2009: 126; emphasis in original).

Global demand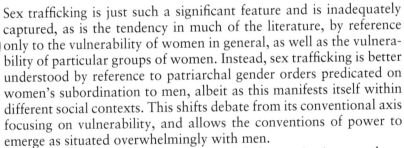

Sex trafficking is just such a significant feature and is inadequately captured, as is the tendency in much of the literature, by reference only to the vulnerability of women in general, as well as the vulnerability of particular groups of women. Instead, sex trafficking is better understood by reference to patriarchal gender orders predicated on women's subordination to men, albeit as this manifests itself within different social contexts. This shifts debate from its conventional axis focusing on vulnerability, and allows the conventions of power to emerge as situated overwhelmingly with men.

This is particularly evident in global prostitution markets. Prostitution is distinct from the sale and purchase of other goods and services in that it involves women selling a particular kind of sex that is premised on gender inequality (Jeffreys 1997). The practice is 'socially constructed out of male domination and women's subordination' (Jeffreys 2012: 75). O'Connell Davidson (1998) refers to prostitution 'as an institution which allows certain powers of command over one person's body to be exercised by another' (*ibid.*: 9). While acknowledging that prostitution features among gay and transgendered people, it nevertheless 'disproportionately involves men buying access to women's bodies' (Coy 2012: 5). As such, prostitution can be identified as a cornerstone of patriarchal gender orders 'even though there may be variation at the level of everyday gender relations between women who sell, and men who buy, sex' (*ibid.*: 4).

Part of that variation can be seen in the racialisation of the global sex industry (Monzini 2005; Dahinden 2010), and which informs the modus operandi of trafficking groups. Dahinden (2010) discusses 'the ethnicised and "racialised"' nature of gender representations which create demand for women with particular 'looks' and which 'form part of the transnational character' (*ibid.*: 60–1) of the global sex business. Another study by Englund *et al.* (2008) of sex trafficking in Estonia, Finland and Sweden similarly noted that, while 'client preferences are perhaps the most recurrent theme . . . sex buyers also have more specific demands. They want the women to wear certain clothes. They want blondes and young girls' (*ibid.*: 121). The same study also noted the presence of what the authors call 'ethnically niched prostitution' (*ibid.*: 122) in which women are imported to meet the demands of their male co-nationals living in diaspora.

Monzini (2005) suggests the racialisation of the sex industry may be a consequence of changing patterns of demand, which have created hierarchies in which African, Asian, Balkan and other non-European Union (EU) women work in lower paid sectors of the sex industry compared with their white EU counterparts. Research conducted in London found that men who express a preference for women of a specific ethnic or racial background tend to fall into one of two categories: those seeking the 'exotic other' or those who prefer women of the same ethnic background (Coy *et al*: 2007). Hughes (2005) notes that trafficked women often belong to the same national or ethnic group as their clients. Monzini (2005), again, has similarly found the existence of such ethnically exclusive prostitution circuits, but notes that, more commonly, 'foreign women work in the market intended for men originating in the country in question' (*ibid.*: 38), and whose preference is either sexual access to the bodies of the 'exotic other' or simply to foreign women as a sometimes cheaper alternative. This resonates with the findings of recent research undertaken in the United Kingdom, where women were trafficked from source countries and placed in brothels located in areas with diverse populations (Turner 2014). The same study also found evidence of the so-called 'carousel system' (Monzini 2005: 82) in which Eastern

European women, in particular, were circulated around different parts of the country, from Wales, through England to Scotland, and sometimes internationally, to ensure the steady supply of 'new faces' to sex buyers, and to meet racialised demand (Turner 2014). In this sense, gender and ethnicity are always inextricably intertwined and, prostitution – of co-nationals or the exotic other – is premised on male demand for sexual access to the bodies of female strangers. It derives from a sense of 'male privilege' (Durchslag and Goswami 2008), commensurate with the power vested in men.

Kara (2009) advocates measures for quashing demand as one of two key themes at the heart of his 'framework for abolition' of sex trafficking, which he calls slavery (see also Miers 2003; Ould 2004; Bales 2005; Smith 2007). His analysis directly addresses gender issues, but his primary critique is of the role of global capitalism. 'Sex trafficking is one of the ugliest contemporary actualizations of global capitalism because it was directly produced by the harmful inequalities spread by the process of economic globalization' (Kara 2009: 4). It is within this process that women, minorities and lower castes are discriminated against, disempowered and disenfranchised and, therefore, are more vulnerable to 'enslavement'. Hence, demand reduction measures should be taken in the short term, while longer-term strategies should be geared towards addressing the root causes of trafficking, which Kara describes as 'poverty and the destructive asymmetries of economic globalization' (*ibid.*: 201).

Powerful and compelling as this account is, it suffers from the same deficit that is to be found at international level and in much of the academy. Globally, the sex industry is flourishing and, increasingly, sex trafficking is becoming the 'primary delivery and distribution system' (Turner 2012: 48) for prostitution markets the world over. In identifying the root causes of trafficking as a consequence of economic globalisation in which women feature as among the accidental 'losers', Kara's (2009) account fails to sufficiently factor in the other side of the gender equation.

The fertile field

The root causes of trafficking – poverty, failing states, wars and the inequities associated with globalisation – all disproportionately and adversely impact on women. Globalisation in particular has created deep divisions with women estimated to comprise 70 per cent of those living below the poverty threshold (Monzini 2005). This 'feminization of poverty' (Baden 1999) is not the inadvertent outcome of poor life choices, but is instead better understood in the context of

patriarchal gender orders. Here, women occupy a subaltern position in most communities and societies throughout the world, but
they do so in relation to men, where power and resources are overwhelmingly concentrated at both individual and government levels.
Sassen (2002) posits that governments are among the dependents of
women's exploitation, where their remittances are vital sources of
income for families in countries with weak welfare systems. The role
of government can also be seen with respect to the countries of the
former Soviet Union – so-called economies in transition – where the
re-distribution of resources through privatisation of one-time state
assets has mainly, and adversely, affected women, as Shelley (2000)
notes of Russia:

> In that period of transition, the resources of the state were privatized
> primarily to men. After the initial privatization, which was handled so
> improperly that it brought almost no resources to the state, no revenues
> were being paid and nothing was being done to provide social services to
> women, education for children, summer schools, and so forth. So a simul-
> taneous impoverishment of women occurred, not only in their salaries
> and their access to property but also to social services. (Shelley 2000: 6)

Indeed, it was during this period of transition that a rise in the
numbers of women selling sex in the region was noted, which
was higher 'than at any time in living memory' (Kelly 2007: 84).
Significant numbers of women were forced to migrate, often on a
temporary basis 'to solve problems arising from the shortage of jobs
and the crisis of the public assistance system' (Monzini 2005: 61);
this despite the fact that Russian women are among the most highly
educated in the world (*ibid.*). In the United Kingdom, it has similarly
been found that a number of women trafficked from Ukraine and
parts of Eastern Europe had university level education or were in
the process of obtaining university degrees. For these women, the
scarcity of jobs and the means to make a sustainable living in their
home towns and cities left them with few options. Travel to work in
London, Sheffield or Glasgow was intended as a temporary measure
to help support families or to fund their further education, but reliance on intermediaries led them into the hands of traffickers (Turner
2014).

Arguably, however, it was not only the scarcity of jobs that
impacted the position of women, but also their declining status in
social and political life (Kelly 2007). During the Soviet era, Russia
was characterised at least by greater *formal* gender equality. Yet, as
Connell (2009) notes, by 'the end of the 1980s, the system that held
these ideals collapsed with stunning speed' (*ibid.*: 24). Here, Connell

(2009) draws on the work of Novikova (2000) in Latvia, who argues that the re-emergence of local patriarchies there can be attributed to a 'common belief' that the 'official Soviet model of gender equality' emasculated men (Novikova 2000: 119 (cited in Connell 2009: 24)). Connell (2009) extends this analysis to include 'most post-Soviet regimes', which, she argues, have come to be characterised by a 'militant patriarchy'. 'They are openly dominated by men, they marginalize women, and they weave together their nation-building with a hard, aggressive masculinity' (*ibid.*: 24). These are among the conditions that account for the significant increase in women's emigration and their exposure to the risks of trafficking, where they are 'cheated, duped and exploited beyond anything that one can imagine' (Monzini 2005: 63).

Government policies and actions, then, are often pursued without regard to their impact on women and therefore play a significant role in driving women into 'survival circuits' (Sassen 2002). These failings, however, are not solely the responsibility of individual governments. They can also be attributed to international policy, such as the structural adjustment policies mandated, for example, by the International Monetary Fund and the World Bank. There, loans are made on conditions that require governments – especially those of developing countries – to open their markets to further financial and trade flows, and to undertake austerity measures that disproportionately impact the poor (Kara 2009), and that directly or indirectly discriminate against women.

Yet, in imposing measures that disproportionately deprive women of resources and of access to resources, law and policymakers are effectively adding to the cumulative surplus concentrated in the hands of men, a surplus Connell (2009) calls the '*patriarchal dividend*: the advantage to men as a group of maintaining an unequal gender order' (*ibid.*: 142; emphasis in original). This is taken to mean not only money income, but includes other benefits such as 'authority', 'respect', 'access to institutional power' and 'control over one's life' (*ibid.*). Control, in particular, is a significant loss in the lives of trafficked women. Once in countries of destination, traffickers frequently remove and retain passports and other identity cards. This impacts not only third-country nationals, but also on women from within the EU who, undocumented, are left without proof of citizenship, immigration status and, specifically, without the means to exit the country, even where they escape their traffickers (Turner 2014). Such control entraps women in 'conditions of confinement' (O'Connell Davidson 1998) and severely restricts their mobility, nationally and transnationally.

Transnational mobility

In an era of globalisation, transnational mobility and access to the means of mobility are likewise important benefits of the patriarchal dividend. Here, too, mobility and transnational mobility, in particular, is gendered, as acknowledged in a report of the European Commission's (2004) Expert Group on Human Trafficking. This posited that 'women's inability to access regulated migration and their propensity to work in unregulated unskilled sectors leaves them more vulnerable to trafficking and exploitation' (*ibid.*: 147). So framed, the report continues the tradition of a very one-sided debate. It is not women's lack of proficiency, or their disposition, that has contributed to what has become known as the 'feminisation of (ir)regular migration' – perhaps the most significant phenomenon of recent decades (Castles and Miller 1998; Sassen 2002). In remaining steadfastly focused on women's vulnerability to trafficking, the international community and, indeed, much of the scholarship, thereby neglects to take sufficient, or any, account of the ways in which unequal gender orders promote patterns of international mobility that systematically privilege men. And while some women do benefit from participation in the patriarchal dividend, generally through marriage to wealthy men (Connell 2009), men nevertheless tend to be the politicians on the world stage, the media barons and the top executives in multinational corporations, corporations noted to have 'a strongly masculinized management culture' (*ibid.*: 129). These highly mobile transnationals rely on patriarchal linkages and reciprocal connectedness to smooth their entry into the world of the global citizen. Such masculinised ties facilitate male migration and modes of trade and commerce well beyond the lofty heights of the corporate world. They are also embedded in the myriad of networks and crime groups engaged in the cross-border trafficking of women and for whom transnational mobility is essential to the execution of their operations. Here, transnationalism and globalisation intersect in complex systems of reciprocity, in which globalisation extends beyond the expansion of capitalism. More particularly, it is also said to refer to 'the intensification of worldwide social relations which link distant localities in such a way that local happenings are shaped by events occurring many miles away and vice versa' (Giddons 1990: 64) Yet 'social relations' are no more gender neutral than the transnational flows that span continents. In the context of the sex trafficking of women, these linkages and flows might be more appropriately characterised as the intensification of worldwide patriarchal relations that connect distant and local patriarchal gender orders in ways that shape the contours of local and global sex markets. In a global world, in which human mobility is highly sought after and in which migration, for some, may be a matter of survival, the concentration of mobility resources in the hands of men can transform women's planned labour migrations into 'journeys of jeopardy' (Kelly 2002).

Sex trafficking from the European Union to the United Kingdom

Trafficking and migration, then, often share the same root causes or push and pull factors. Hence, cross-border trafficking intersects with other forms of transnational mobility, while transnational mobility itself – including its absence – affects the mechanisms of the trade. As citizens or migrants, having settled immigration status, restricted or unfettered mobility is likely to determine, in varying degrees, recruitment, transit and exploitation strategies up to, and beyond, state borders. These, in turn, impact on how the business of trafficking is organised and on the modus operandi of traffickers.

Very little is known about traffickers and their operations. One of the difficulties undoubtedly lies in the fact that research on trafficking can be methodologically challenging, involving, as it does, so-called 'hidden populations', the parameters of which cannot be known (Di Nicola 2007). While other areas of research provide their own methodological challenges, with respect to trafficking this has meant that much of the research has tended to focus on victims, rather than perpetrators. Victims, particularly those in support and assistance programmes, are deemed, relatively speaking, at least potentially more accessible, leaving a dearth of knowledge on traffickers. More recently, a number of scholars have sought to address this gap (see, for example, Aronowitz 2003, 2009; Shelley 2003, 2010; Levenkron 2007; Englund et al. 2008; Turner 2014). For Shelley (2003, 2010), in particular, the growth of trafficking and the rise in transnational organised crime has gone hand in hand with the spread of globalisation, and yet, as she notes, the modus operandi of trafficking groups remain rooted in the traditional patterns of trade associated with their regions of origin. Bales (2000, 2005) similarly observes that one of the enduring features of human trafficking is the extent to which it remains embedded in different cultural and historical contexts. These are important observations. Yet notions of 'culture' and 'history' have to be problematised in the context of the sex trafficking of women as too frequently they are discussed without reference to patriarchal gender orders within which both are similarly embedded.

Nevertheless, 'the gap in knowledge, globally, of traffickers and their methods of operation contributes to the widespread failure to identify traffickers and those who assist them' (UN Global Initiative to Fight Human Trafficking 2008: 2) with significant consequences. While prosecution is a cornerstone of international and national efforts to combat trafficking, trafficking prosecutions worldwide remain low in number. In the first global assessment of the scope of human trafficking and steps taken to combat it (UNODC 2009), data gathered from 155 countries show that while there is an increase in trafficking convictions, in two out of every five countries covered by the report no convictions at all are recorded. Moreover, during the period in question, from 2003 to 2007, the report further notes decreasing trends in Western and Central European countries in the number of criminal proceedings for human trafficking (*ibid.*: p. 37). With respect to sex trafficking, however, prosecution rates in England and Wales run counter to this trend. Here, Crown Prosecution Service (CPS) data on prosecuting cases of human trafficking offending for sexual exploitation show a year on year increase. Additionally, there is evidence that women and girls trafficked into domestic servitude are also likely to have been sexually exploited and perpetrators prosecuted for servitude offences (Bowen 2014).

Even so, there are few estimates of the scale of trafficking into the United Kingdom. At the turn of the century, one study indicated that between 142 and 1,420 women were trafficked annually for the purposes of sexual exploitation (Kelly and Regan 2000). This estimate was updated in a report for the Association of Chief Police Officers Project Acumen, which calculated that of the 17,000 migrant women involved in the UK's off-street prostitution sector, 2,600 are victims of trafficking, with a further 9,200 considered to be vulnerable, that is, possibly, but not conclusively, victims of trafficking (Jackson *et al.* 2010). These figures suggest a rise in the numbers of women trafficked into the United Kingdom. While many are trafficked from far away continents, many are also trafficked from within the EU. As with other migratory flows, women tend to be trafficked from poorer to wealthier countries (Lee 2011).

Yet the expansion of the EU in recent years has also paved the way for more nuanced migratory movements. Once characterised as 'Fortress Europe', involving the 'cultivation of a hegemonic European character built on principles of exclusion' (Green and Grewcock 2002: 99), the approach of governments past and present has been primarily to consider trafficking as a mode of illegal migration and as a function of transnational organised crime. This is epitomised in the United Kingdom by the popular media perspective that we are being 'swamped not just by aliens but overtaken by the mafia' (Anderson and O'Connell Davidson 2002: 6). This location of trafficking in a crime control and prevention bracket has enabled governments to adopt restrictive immigration practices under the rubric of state security and national sovereignty (Aradau 2004). While this creates a market for assisted border crossing and, arguably, strengthens conditions conducive to human trafficking and smuggling (ILO 2002; Friman and Reich 2007; Lee 2011), the conflation of counter-trafficking measures with immigration control is also a strategy riven with conflicts. It tasks those border and law enforcement personnel responsible for apprehending illegal border crossers with also 'catching' victims of trafficking (O'Connell Davidson 2006). Within the region, however, EU enlargement has brought about the transformation of borders in a manner which challenges the characterisation of 'Fortress Europe' as comprising simply inclusion and exclusion zones (Andrijasevic 2010). This was perhaps in any event always more accurately termed 'Fortress *Western* Europe', but the expansion of the EU over the last decade has blurred the distinction between those who are 'inside' and those who remain 'outside' (Mezzadra and Neilson 2008). Increasingly, cross-border travel and rights of residence are mediated by degrees of EU membership, such that 'we are witnessing the differentiation and stratification of legal statuses and citizenship' (Andrijasevic 2010: 9). This clearly has implications for the mobility of individuals across the region, including traffickers and their victims. From the perspective of the UK Government, however, 'smarter multi-agency action at the border', a key component of its anti-trafficking strategy (Home Office 2011), seems unlikely to curb the activities of traffickers with the appropriate level of EU citizenship, who are trafficking fellow nationals or other EU women.

Indeed, full EU citizenship, or its absence, informs the modus operandi of traffickers in the United Kingdom (Turner 2014). Europeans who have unrestricted freedom to exit and re-enter the country, who can travel to and fro across borders, tend to control their trafficking operations end to end. They regularly return to countries of origin to recruit women and bring them back to the United Kingdom for exploitation in prostitution markets here. These activities are all conducted with apparent ease, as one Czech trafficker noted: 'It's easy to get girls to work as prostitutes. They're homeless Czech girls with no jobs, so you promise them work and then take all their papers when they get here' (*ibid.*: 139).

By contrast, those whose personal mobility was restricted organised their trafficking operations differently. Albanian traffickers are a case in point. While, in a number of cases, Albanian men were found to operate within apparently closed and fully diasporic groups, this was more a function of their transnational status. On the one hand, they had high levels of local anchorage within an Albanian (criminal) diaspora, which facilitated the movement of women within the United Kingdom. On the other hand, their illegal or irregular immigration status restricted their cross-border mobility. This did not, however, inhibit their trafficking activities as the supply of women was ensured through the development of cooperative ties with Lithuanian crime groups (Turner 2014). Yet while recruitment activities were undertaken by both Lithuanian men and women, it was overwhelmingly men who were involved in the transportation of women to the United Kingdom (see also Andrijasevic 2010, where assisted travel and border-crossings were likewise facilitated mainly by men). Hence, these cross-border connectivities were instrumental in overcoming limited personal mobility and were reflected in the modus operandi of these groups (Turner 2014). This suggests that the networks that link transnationals, even those with limited transnational mobility, in fact comprise patriarchal ties. They are variations on the 'old boy networks' that have long facilitated male social and professional mobility nationally and, increasingly, internationally. Such networks constitute another aspect of the 'patriarchal dividend' (Connell 2009) to which women's access is mediated and policed through local patriarchal gender orders.

Conclusion

There is no doubt that the uneven impacts of globalisation and poverty in countries of origin, and male demand in destination countries for sexual access to the bodies of female strangers are all essential components of the 'fertile field' (Kelly 2005). Yet for women, all are also part and parcel of other destructive asymmetries, namely, patriarchal gender orders, which pre-date the processes of globalisation as much as they are exacerbated and reproduced by them. Here, international and national policies disproportionately deprive women of resources, while the 'still massive incidence' of exploitation and violence against women remains 'an easily recognized marker of power and vulnerability' (Connell 2009: 143). These harmful asymmetries comprise the disadvantage to women as a group of the maintenance by men of an unequal gender order.

In a globalised world, transnational mobility is often the key to survival. Yet unequal gender orders continue to promote patterns of international mobility that systematically privilege men. The networks and ties that have long facilitated male migration are still denied to many women, who are consequently exposed to the predatory activities of traffickers who recruit and distribute them to racialised prostitution markets the world over, where they are ruthlessly exploited. The international regime has been largely ineffective in combating sex trafficking because it has been 'long on rhetoric but short on decisive action' (Turner 2012: 33) in addressing the other side of the gender equation. The persistent focus on the vulnerability of women consistently deflects attention from the concentration of power and resources in the hands of men. It has muted challenges to patriarchal gender orders and to increasingly militant patriarchal regimes, and it has undermined efforts to promote the globalisation of substantive gender equality with a commitment and urgency commensurate with the depth and scale of gender inequality. These failures have promoted the commodification of women beyond borders, and accelerated the growth and spread of the global sex industry into which they are trafficked and in which they are exploited.

References

Anderson, B. and J. O'Connell Davidson (2002), *Trafficking: A Demand Led Problem?*, Stockholm: Save the Children.

Andrijasevic, R. (2010), *Migration, Agency and Citizenship in Sex Trafficking*, Open University: Palgrave Macmillan.

Aradau, C. (2004), 'The perverse politics of four-letter words: risk and pity in the securitisation of human trafficking', *Millennium – Journal of International Studies*, 33(2): 251–78.

Aronowitz, A. (2003), 'Trafficking in human beings: an international perspective', in D. Siegel, H. van de Bunt and D. Zeitch (eds), *Global Organized Crime: Trends and Developments*, Dordrecht: Kluwer Academic.

Aronowitz, A. (2009), *Human Trafficking, Human Misery: The Global Trade in Human Beings*, Westport, CT: Praeger.

Baden, S. (1999), 'Gender, governance and the feminization of poverty', Background Paper No. 2, Women and Political Participation: 21st Century Challenges, meeting organized by the UN Development Programme, New Delhi, 24–26 March.

Bales, K. (2000), 'Expendable people: slavery in the age of globalization', *Journal of International Affairs*, 53(2): 461.

Bales, K. (2005), *Understanding Global Slavery*, Berkeley, CA: University of California Press.

Bowen, P. (2014), personal communication, Crown Prosecution Service, London.

Castles, S. and M. Miller (1998), *The Age of Migration*, Basingstoke: Macmillan.

Cohen, R. (1997), *Global Diasporas: An Introduction*, London: UCL Press.

Committee on the Convention for the Elimination of All Forms of Discrimination Against Women (CEDAW) (1992), Recommendation No. 19, adopted at 11th Session, 1992, UN Document A/47/38, 1992, A/47/38, available at: http://www.un.org/womenwatch/daw/cedaw/recommendations/recomm.htm, last accessed 12 April 2009.

Connell, R. W. (1987), *Gender and Power: Society, the Person and Sexual Politics*, Stanford, CA: Stanford University Press.

Connell, R. W. (2009), *Short Introduction – Gender*, Cambridge: Polity Press.

Coy, M. (ed.) (2012), *Prostitution, Harm and Gender Inequality – Theory, Research and Policy*, Farnham: Ashgate.

Coy, M., M. A. H. Horvath and L. Kelly (2007), *'It's Just Like Going to the Supermarket': Men Buying Sex in East London*, London: Child and Woman Abuse Studies Unit, available at: http://www.cwasu.org, last accessed 4 May 2008.

Crenshaw, K. (1991), 'Mapping the margins: intersectionality, identity politics and violence against women of color', *Stanford Law Review*, 43(6): 1241–99.

Dahinden, J. (2010), 'The dynamics of migrants' transnational formations', in R. Bauböck and T. Faist (eds), *Diaspora and Transnationalism: Concepts, Theories and Methods*, International Migration, Integration and Social Cohesion in Europe (IMISCOE) Research: University of Amsterdam.

De la Dehesa, G. (2006), *Winners and Losers in Globalization*, Oxford: Blackwell.

Di Nicola, A. (2007), 'Researching into human trafficking: issues and problems', in M. Lee (ed.), *Human Trafficking*, Cullompton: Willan Publishing.

Durchslag, R. and S. Goswami (2008), *Deconstructing the Demand for Prostitution: Preliminary Insights from Interviews with Chicago Men Who Purchase Sex*, Chicago: Chicago Alliance Against Sexual Exploitation, available at: http://www.chicagohomeless.org/files/images/Deconstructing_the_Demand_for_Prostitution.pdf, last accessed 5 June 2010.

Englund, C., M. Viuhko, A. Jokinen, K. Aromaa, A. Resetnikova, A. Markina, U. Söderström and M. Nilsen (2008), *The Organisation of Human Trafficking: A Study of Criminal Involvement in Sexual Exploitation in Sweden, Finland and Estonia*, Stockholm: Swedish National Council for Crime Prevention.

European Commission, Directorate-General for Justice, Freedom and Security (2004), *Report of the Experts Group on Trafficking in Human Beings*, Brussels: European Commission.

Friman, H. and S. Reich (2007), *Human Trafficking, Human Security, and the Balkans*, Pittsburgh, PA: University of Pittsburgh Press.

Giddons, A. (1990), *The Consequences of Modernity*, Cambridge: Polity Press.

Green, P. and M. Grewcock (2002), 'The war against illegal immigration: state crime and the construction of a European identity', *Current Issues in Criminal Justice*, 14(1): 87–101.

Home Office (2011), *Human Trafficking Strategy*, London: Home Office.

Hughes, D. (2005), 'The Demand for Victims of Sex Trafficking', Women's Studies Program, University of Rhode Island, available at: http://www.

uri.edu/artsci/wms/hughes/demand_for_victims.pdf, last accessed 24 February 2009.

Inda, J. and R. Rosaldo (2002), 'Introduction: a world in motion', in J. X. Inda and R. Rosaldo (eds), *The Anthropology of Globalization: A Reader*, Oxford: Blackwell, pp. 1–34.

International Labour Organisation (ILO) (2002), *Trafficking in Human Beings: New Approaches to Combating the Problem*, Geneva: ILO.

Jackson, K., J. Jeffery and G. Adamson (2010), *Setting the Record: The Trafficking of Migrant Women in the England and Wales Off-street Prostitution Sector*, Association of Chief Police Officers: Regional Intelligence Unit for the South West.

Jeffreys, S. (1997), *The Idea of Prostitution*, Melbourne: Spinifex Press.

Jeffreys, S. (2012), 'Beyond "agency" and "choice" in theorizing prostitution', in M. Coy (ed.), *Prostitution, Harm and Gender Inequality – Theory, Research and Policy*, Prostitution, Harms and Human Rights Discourse, Farnham: Ashgate.

Kara, S. (2009), *Sex Trafficking: Inside the Business of Modern Slavery*, New York: Columbia University Press.

Kelly, L. (2002), *Journeys of Jeopardy: A Review of Research on Trafficking in Women and Children in Europe*, IOM Migration Research Series No. 11, Geneva: IOM.

Kelly, L. (2005), *Fertile Fields: Trafficking in Persons in Central Asia*, Vienna: IOM.

Kelly, L. (2007), 'A conducive context: trafficking of persons in Central Asia', in M. Lee (ed.), *Human Trafficking*, Cullompton: Willan Publishing.

Kelly, L. and L. Regan (2000), *Stopping Traffic: Exploring the Extent of, and Responses to, Trafficking in Women for Sexual Exploitation in the UK*, Police Research Series, Paper 125, London: Home Office.

Lee, M. (2011), *Trafficking and Global Crime Control*, London: Sage.

Levenkron, N. (2007), 'Another delivery from Tashkent – profile of an Israeli trafficker', Tel Aviv: Hotline for Migrant Workers, available at: http://www.ungift.org/doc/knowledgehub/resource-centre/EU_Profile_of_an_israeli_trafficker.pdf, last accessed 3 March 2009.

Mezzadra, S. and B. Neilson (2008), 'Border as method or the multiplication of labour', *Transversal: Borders, Nations, Translations*, Vienna: European Institute for Progressive Cultural Politics.

Miers, S. (2003), *Slavery in the Twentieth Century: The Evolution of a Global Problem*, Lanham, MD: AltaMira.

Monzini, P. (2005), *Sex Traffic: Prostitution, Crime and Exploitation*, London: Zed Books.

Morawska, E. (2007), 'Trafficking into and from Eastern Europe', in M. Lee (ed.), *Human Trafficking*, Cullompton: Willan Publishing.

Novikova, I. (2000). 'Soviet and post-Soviet masculinities: after men's wars in women's memories', in I. Breines, R. Connell and E. Eide (eds), *Male Roles, Masculinities and Violence: A Culture of Peace Perspective*, Paris: UNESCO, pp. 117–29.

O'Connell Davidson, J. (1998), *Prostitution, Power and Freedom*, Cambridge: Polity Press.

O'Connell Davidson, J. (2006), 'Will the real sex slave please stand up?' *Feminist Review*, 83: 4–22.

Ould, D. (2004), 'Trafficking and international law', in C. van den Anker (ed.), *The Political Economy of New Slavery*, Basingstoke: Palgrave Macmillan, pp. 55–74.

Sassen, S. (2002), 'Women's burden: counter-geographies of globalization and the feminization of survival', *Nordic Journal of International Law*, 71: 255–74.

Shelley, L. (2000), 'Trafficking and organized crime', paper presented at Protection Project Seminar Series, American University, 4 October (cited in P. Monzini (2005), *Sex Traffick: Prostitution, Crime and Exploitation*), London: Zed Books.

Shelley, L. (2003), 'Trafficking in women: the business model approach', *Brown Journal of World Affairs*, X(I): 119–31.

Shelley, L. (2010), *Human Trafficking – A Global Perspective*, New York: Cambridge University Press.

Smith, D. (ed.) (2007), *Slavery Now – and Then*, Eastbourne: Kingsway Publications.

Smith, M. and L. Guarnizo (eds) (1998), *Transnationalism from Below*, New Brunswick, NJ: Transaction.

Turner, J. (2012), 'Means of delivery: the trafficking of women into prostitution, harms and human rights discourse', in M. Coy (ed.), *Prostitution, Harm and Gender Inequality – Theory, Research and Policy*, Farnham: Ashgate.

Turner, J. (2014), 'Diasporic Connectivity and Patriarchal Formations in the Sex Trafficking of Women', unpublished PhD thesis, London Metropolitan University.

Turner, J. and L. Kelly (2009), 'Trade secrets: intersections between diasporas and crime networks in the constitution of the human trafficking chain', *British Journal of Criminology*, 49(2): 184–201.

United Nations Global Initiative to Fight Human Trafficking (2008), *Report of the Vienna Forum to Fight Human Trafficking*, Vienna: Austria.

United Nations Office on Drugs and Crime (UNODC) (2002), *Results of a Pilot Study of Forty Selected Organized Crime Groups in 16 Countries – September 2002*, Vienna: UNODC.

United Nations Office on Drugs and Crime (UNODC) (2009), *Global Report on Trafficking in Persons*, Vienna: UNODC.

13 The New Raw Resources Passing Through the Shadows

Hazel Cameron

> Safety and security don't just happen; they are the result of collective consensus and public investment.
>
> Nelson Mandela

Human security is a dynamic and practical policy framework that addresses widespread and cross-cutting threats facing governments and people. The framework is one in which states are fully expected to maintain the security of their national borders, as well as the security of the individuals living inside those borders. Within this framework, it is the responsibility of states to protect their citizens from external conflict, injustice and harm; states are also expected to ensure that their citizens enjoy a wide range of rights and are able to live their lives with a sense of dignity, free from fear and despair. In other words, the objective of human security is to keep grave and pervasive threats from attacking the fundamentals of human lives (Gandhi 2010).

There are many events outwith the control of citizens that fatally threaten communities and interfere with development. These include terrorist attacks, water shortages, hazardous pollutants, AIDS, chronic destitution, nuclear proliferation, drug-resistant diseases and ecological threats. Other threats that have intensified the sense of insecurity are violent conflicts (including conflicts across gender, class, ethnicity or religion), and the spread of international criminal activity, which includes modern slavery.

Although slavery has been in existence since time immemorial, modern slavery is a distinct manifestation of globalisation, and has reached such proportions as to present a significant human rights crisis in countries of origin, transit and destination. Human trafficking is a form of modern slavery that is never far from the leading concerns of organised criminal networks operating globally. Trafficking victims are frequently sourced in developing countries with weak rule of law, where transnational organised criminal penetration is rife, and where perpetrators can readily identify the most vulnerable in society and exploit them for personal gain.

Until recently, it was assumed that human trafficking can exist and be explained only in relation to crime, but this chapter will highlight that human trafficking can be viewed as a problem of intrastate and interstate armed conflict as well as a problem of organised crime. Furthermore, this chapter will highlight how it is essential to our understanding of human trafficking, and specifically trafficking for the purposes of sexual exploitation, that this phenomenon is explored in relation to the evolution of neoliberalism, war economies and international peace interventions.

During the last decades of the twentieth century, a new type of organised criminality developed as a characteristic of the current globalised era. This period witnessed what Kaldor and Luckham (2001) describe as 'new wars', a political form of violence that sees a blurring of distinctions between war, organised crime and large-scale violations of human rights. 'New wars' are characterised as predominantly civil warfare that is non-ideological, fuelled by identity politics and driven by greed or grievance. The 'new wars' that have arisen in the last half century have seen conflict actors embrace both the political and criminal as state- and nation-building in reverse.

Conflict and post-conflict zones are now recognised as being particularly dangerous environments for women and children (Cameron and Newman 2008). The overarching argument of this chapter is that the interaction between structural factors found in conflict and post-conflict zones, such as economic deprivation, social inequality, gender bias, as well as the lack of or lax rule of law, corruption, organised criminal entrepreneurship, war economies and neoliberal approaches to international peace operations are key to understanding why conflict and post-conflict environments render women and children vulnerable to falling prey to organised criminality engaged in the establishment, organisation and consolidation of trafficking networks. Victims trafficked from conflict zones are often transported to developed nations around the world, where they are further vulnerable to the already structurally discriminating environment and the hierarchical relationships that exist between the developed countries and dependent countries, and between men and women. It is hoped that an understanding of the interrelationship of neoliberalism, armed conflict, war economies and international peace interventions may provide some insight into the social backgrounds of a vast swathe of those who have fallen prey to human traffickers. This insight may prove beneficial to those organisations in the United Kingdom and, indeed, in some European countries, that provide front-line services to survivors of human trafficking in nations that are mainly 'destination' countries.

The Human Security Unit (HSU) of the United Nations Office for the Coordination of Humanitarian Affairs (2014) argues that 'human security is best protected through proactive and preventive actions to current and emerging threats', including the threat from human traffickers. The aim of this chapter is to therefore highlight some of the root causes of insecurity of women and children in conflict/post-conflict zones that will inform policy discussion and perhaps stand as one small stepping stone towards strategic interventions at the international level that will strengthen human security frameworks and the fight against trafficking.

The raw resources spawned by neoliberalism

Liberalism is grounded primarily in idealism and seeks to identify the conditions under which a more peaceful international society is attainable. Idealism asserts that human nature is inherently good and that power can be used for positive outcomes in the search for peace.

Kay 2011: 58

Although a widely held belief, the reality is that idealism has not been hugely successful in terms of guaranteeing peace. 'Broadly, idealism is made problematic by the basic question of whose ideals should dominate. Functionally, the approach has often had counterproductive results' (Kay 2011: 57).

During the late 1970s and early 1980s, the world economy went into recession and, albeit not the only casualty, Africa was plunged into a downward spiralling economic and debt crisis. In response to the crises on the continent, the international community adopted a neoliberal approach, enforcing programmes of free market economic reform in Africa. In recent years, under the impact of structural adjustment programmes (SAPs) and neoliberal policies in numerous developing countries, as well as in the former USSR (Soviet Union) and Eastern Europe, impoverished women and children have become new raw resources within the framework of national and international business development. However, SAPs failed to reverse the crises, and arguably exacerbated economic problems. A definition of neoliberalism appropriate to the African experience is proposed by Harrison (2010: 26–7) in which he states that the term comprises a diverse set of interventions, over an extended period of time, that are concerned with the negation of political control of the economy, the free market and the rational individual. Indeed, neoliberalism has been the overriding development agenda in Africa since the 1980s because of its advocacy by powerful external agencies like the International Monetary Fund (IMF), the World Bank (WB) and Western neoliberal states that have obligated African states to follow this agenda (Cammack 2002; Harrison 2004). A key contextual factor in this period was the end of the Cold War, which left African governments with a deep and prolonged economic and political crisis and no obvious alternative source of financial or political support apart from Western neoliberalism.

Whereas in the aftermath of the Second World War the formal principle of organising international society, namely, sovereign statehood, was promoted through the practice of decolonisation, state-building in the aftermath of the Cold War promoted the universalisation of the definitive elements of the Western conception of liberal statehood, promoting a distinct model of organising political authority domestically. From this context, such state-building efforts are seen as necessary for the completion of a liberal order. Superpower confrontation and friction in the so-called 'Third World' in the 1970s saw much of southern Africa become a cauldron of the antagonisms of the Cold War. The dynamics of the Cold War and its crippling effect on the transition to majority rule in southern Africa is complex. The Cold War struggle in the region was not simply a bipolar contest between the United States and the USSR, nor their associated blocs. Engrossed in their own agenda, local actors had little interest in the discord between Washington and Moscow. In the complicated dynamics of domestic, regional and international rivalries in the aftermath of independence from European colonial powers, the confrontation between the remaining white minority governments and black liberation movements encouraged the parties to apply for outside support from both blocs. Not only were external actors drawn in to conflict in Africa, (that is, the United States, with its interest in protecting its access to the region's strategic resources and preventing the emergence of hostile regimes, and the socialist bloc, determined to support the 'anti-imperialist struggle') local actors were empowered to negotiate external assistance from these blocs with varying degrees of success. The superpower support was intended to either boost their military strength and political influence vis-à-vis their white opponents and black rivals, or to initiate a policy of non-alignment and equidistance to reinforce their autonomy and freedom to manoeuvre in the international system.

As previously noted, the fall of the Berlin Wall in 1989 heralded a deep and prolonged economic and political crisis for many African governments. There was no obvious alternative source of financial or political support apart from Western neoliberalism, and therefore powerful forces in the industrialised world continued to have a crucial influence on events in the Africa continent, introducing an expansion and entrenchment of the neoliberal agenda in Africa over the years. Through time, neoliberalism in Africa visibly mutated from a set of economic policies primarily concerned with macroeconomic stability into a comprehensive programme of institutional, political and economic reforms aimed at transforming African states and societies into an 'ideal' type conforming to neoliberal ideology and doctrine. In short, the West was determined to shape the world in its own image, evidence of the malevolent myth that every society must evolve along Western lines.

The concept of liberal peace was first introduced by Kant in the late eighteenth century, mainly referring to democratic states – not necessarily democracies. More recently, the end of the Cold War, which was in many ways a triumph for the liberal vision of democratic cooperation, rekindled and bolstered this idea. As a result of the fall of the Berlin Wall and the dissolution of the Soviet Union, the EU, the Council of Europe and NATO embodied this concept in their efforts to expand toward the East (Simmons and Martin 2002). Liberal peace as a political concept was also adopted in October 1993 by the Declaration of Vienna as the basis for democratic development and adherence to democratic human rights (Schoiswohl 2011); based on Kant's theory that democracies are unlikely to engage in interstate war with other democracies, and that democratic development reinforces peace and stability. It must, however, be acknowledged that in order for liberal peace to be materialised, democracies have to be stable, but stability cannot be understood only in military or economic terms. The core of the liberal peace theory constitutes a definition of long-term peace and security based on the values of democracy and justice. Liberal peace-building therefore occurs in the framework of the liberal peace that strives to transform conflict and build positive peace by addressing the underlying causes of the conflict (Boutros-Ghali 1992; Lederach 1997; Pugh *et al.* 2008), thereby promoting the processes of state-building and development (Ramsbotham 2000). From the 1990s onwards, neoliberal programmes included Western-imposed peace-making in response to the 'new wars' of Africa. The conventional approach in the majority of countries affected by intrastate conflict and violence has been for powerful countries of the West to establish a cease-fire between the opposing parties, followed by the imposition of the dominant model of markets and electoral politics. However, liberal peace interventions were in theory to be about more than just creating a forum for negotiated conflict resolution between states, and were intended to be pivotal in the construction of liberal policies, economies and societies (Bellamy 2008). Critiques of the liberal peace do more than simply contest the ineffectiveness of what MacGinty (2008: 148) refers to as a 'flat-packed peace from IKEA'. Richmond (2012) argues that the norms of the liberal peace are inherently detrimental to enduring peace, and fail to address the structural causes of conflict. No serious consideration to questions of social justice are included in neoliberal assumptions of post-conflict reconstruction and peace-building, and indeed research indicates that neoliberal approaches to peace-building further impoverishes and exacerbates the insecurity of women and children (Bastick *et al.* 2007; Carmody 2007), thereby ensuring these conflict/post-conflict environments are rich in new raw resources for organised criminal networks involved in human trafficking. Failures in human security in the neoliberal era are partly due to the inability of such assumptions to transform the social system within which violence and inequalities are embedded (Daley 2007). It must be acknowledged that in this post-Cold War era, there are instances where the international community has succeeded in reducing the number of wars by putting political and economic pressure on actors in armed conflict. This success is mainly through (a) their willingness to deploy troops and humanitarian agencies to conflict zones and to use them in new ways, or (b) through various mechanisms for controlling the finance of wars.

In the early 1990s there was great optimism about the prospects for humanitarian intervention to protect civilians, however, problematic inherited mandates and the tendency to interpret conflict in traditional terms have ensured that humanitarian interventions have failed to enhance human security and combat the risk of women and children in conflict zones falling prey to human traffickers. There is substantial evidence that the introduction of humanitarian aid workers and peacekeeping forces in post-conflict environments does not only herald the arrival of aid and tools of reconstruction, but also the inadvertent supply of clients that fuel markets for trafficked women in brothels and as domestic labour. For example, the sudden influx of foreign NATO personnel in Kosovo from 1999 onwards had an immediate impact on the dynamics of trafficking in the country, and Kosovo rapidly became the key destination country of the Balkans for women trafficked into forced prostitution (Smith and Smith 2011). The sex trafficking industry was also operationally affected from 1999 onwards by the arrival of peace-building personnel in the post-conflict zone; the previously modest local market for prostitution rapidly transformed into a significant industry based on trafficking predominantly run by organised criminal networks (*ibid.*). Those paying for the services offered by the sex industry traverse the range of local and international NGOs, UN agencies, and other actors involved in international humanitarian operations. While the majority of humanitarian aid workers and peace-building personnel may have been unaware of the criminal networks operating these brothels, there have been reports of peacekeepers taking an active role in the formation of trafficking links. Bolkovac and Lynn (2011) claim that the International Police Task Force (IPTF) in Bosnia abused their connections and positions of authority, both locally and internationally, to forge documents for trafficked women, to facilitate the illegal transfer of victims across borders, and to warn brothels of upcoming police raids.

The major weakness in all international peace interventions is their failure to address or negate the high levels of human rights violations and crime found in these post-conflict environments; the large informal/illegal economy; the lack of the provision of public security, namely, policing and the rule of law; the vulnerability of the impoverished; and the vulnerability of internally displaced persons (IDPs). A further criticism of neoliberal approaches to peace is the differential gender impact of neoliberalism (Enloe 2000; Rehn and Sirleaf 2002) all of which results in the overwhelming vulnerability of women and children to danger in post-conflict zones. The gender-blind approach to post-conflict reconstruction, where state-building is underwritten by masculine norms, places an emphasis on 'masculinist principles of rationalism, emergent "professionalism", and sovereign, hierarchical authority' (Peterson 1992: 39).Women and women's needs are routinely excluded from peace-building, where they are subsumed to a masculine framework that prioritises military discourses of security and development (Sjoberg and Via 2010).

War economies: passing though the shadows

Today, trillions of dollars and millions of people circulate around the globe outside of formal legal reckoning.

Nordstrom 2004: 11

In our endeavour to grasp the complexities of human trafficking it is essential to better understand the large informal/illegal economy that facilitates the crime, but that remains unchallenged by neoliberal peace-building. War is undoubtedly shaped by a number of factors, including economic gain. It is therefore unsurprising that an expansive and well-established global web of networks exists, capable of supplying any and all materials required by combatants and non-combatants during armed conflict, including weapons, food, medicine, clothing and so forth. Nordstrom (2004) notes how the profits have a significant bearing on the economies of all the world's countries. And much of this remains hidden from formal state-based accounting systems and theories. The majority of the trade that meets the supply and demand of warfare passes across boundaries of illegality–legality. Nordstrom's (2004: 106) use of the term 'shadows' refers to the complex sets of cross-state economic and political linkages that move outside formally recognised state-based channels. She uses the term shadows (rather than 'criminal' or 'illegal') 'because the transactions defining these networks aren't confined solely to criminal, illicit, or illegal activities, but cross various divides between legal, quasi-legal, and downright illegal activities' (*ibid.*).

Nordstrom (2004) is not referring to individual people operating in the shadows, but to the immense systems of people who move goods and services worldwide, including persons transported under duress for the purposes of exploitation. Shadow networks are essential to war and are pivotal to processes of development for better or worse. Nordstrom's research identifies that a shockingly large proportion of the entire global economy passes through the shadows: 90 per cent of Angola's economy; 50 per cent of Kenya's, Italy's and Peru's economies; 40–60 per cent of Russia's economy; and between 10 and 30 per cent of the United States' economy enters into extra-state transactions. This movement of money and people is involved from the simple trade in pirated software right through to the more dangerous field of movement of weapons, human beings and illegal drugs.

Transnational organised criminal networks form part of the illegal aspect of these shadow networks. Transnational organised crime (TOC) embodies everything from trafficking in drugs to money laundering, from terrorism to pornography. There is no consensus about the parameters, nature and dangerousness of TOC, although there is increasing agreement that it is a global threat. Transnational organised criminal activities are characteristically hybrid and seldom exist as an ideal type; they are essentially an international phenomenon that has an impact on international security, world politics, international trade and human rights (Zabyelina 2010). TOC is an insidious type of threat, penetrating the state and destabilising its functions. It is pertinent to note that these networks wield power analogous to, and in many cases superior to, the power of some of the world's states. The major threat for a society is that criminal networks cultivate a strong economic and 'political' structure in society through legitimate ways. The underlying motive for such criminality is the opportunity to make a profit quickly and with little risk. Such informal systems are a relatively unexplored field in the literature of conflict and development due to the nature of illegality. It is both difficult and dangerous to gather accurate information regarding informal economies since they are by definition extra-legal.

Gender bias at the international level

The neoliberal transformation of the global political–economic system since the mid-1970s has led to increasingly profound inequality for women. That society has not yet completely fulfilled its obligations to create an equitable environment for all women is clearly visible in the plight of women throughout the process of globalisation, which has created a market of sexual exchanges in which millions of women and children have been converted into sexual commodities (Pouligny 2004). Under neoliberal capitalist globalisation, women's poverty and the deepening of women's oppression and exploitation have been notorious. The feminisation of poverty and survival is closely affiliated to the continued inequality of women globally. Across sub-Saharan Africa, neoliberal policies have been inclined to produce, on the one hand, weaker states and, on the other, deeper poverty and social exclusion for women (Carmody 2007). This is evident in the failure of neoliberal peace-building to recognise the essentiality of gender equality in the disarmament, demobilisation and reintegration (DDR) of former combatants and its potential as a form of strategic intervention at the international level to protect women from the scourge of trafficking. Historically, across cultures, women rarely participated in war as combatants. However, there is an increasing awareness that women in armed groups in 'new wars' frequently function as more than just cooks, cleaners and sexual slaves. Alison (2009) draws upon empirical case studies of Sri Lanka and Northern Ireland to challenge stereotypical images of women depicted as victims of conflict. She highlights the reality of women as active combatants and concludes that female soldiers/rebels are in fact features of most modern conflicts. DDR has become a crucial component of peacekeeping missions and post-conflict reconstruction programmes as part of a wider integrated post-conflict recovery strategy. The purpose of DDR processes is to contribute to the establishment of a secure and stable environment and the rebuilding of societies in post-conflict settings by disarming former combatants, disbanding military structures and reintegrating former combatants socially, politically and economically into civil society.

However, most Western-imposed DDR programmes still follow a traditional approach of focusing exclusively on military and security objectives, targeting a rather limited population group. They lack an integrated gender perspective and are generally not linked to other processes such as justice and reconciliation during the transitional post-conflict period. When women and child combatants are excluded from demobilisation and reintegration assistance programmes, research indicates they may then be left alone to deal with war traumas and in some cases health problems related to acts of sexual violence perpetrated upon them in times of war. In addition, they may not receive any financial or skills development support and have to endure the challenges of social and economic reintegration on their own (Farr 2003). The risk of becoming socially isolated and impoverished is high, once again increasing the vulnerability of these women and children to human trafficking.

Gender-sensitive and inclusive DDR programmes have the ability to play a constructive role in challenging the legacies of conflict-related sexual violence, and in deterring the propensity for sexual violence and trafficking for the purposes of sexual exploitation in post-conflict communities. But, to be effective, DDR programmes must be gender-sensitive and inclusive from the first assessment phase to the last phase of reintegration. The magnitude of women's and girls' participation in armed conflicts, as well as the various forms such participation can take, must be recognised and understood. The disarmament, demobilisation and reintegration process is one aspect of post-conflict intervention that can offer protection to women and children if implemented without gender bias; an international intervention capable of enabling women to participate fully and equally in society, economic and political life, thereby reducing the vulnerability of female combatants in a post-conflict environment.

The vulnerability of the IDPs

It was earlier noted that the international communities' neoliberal approach to peace-building has failed to address the vulnerability of IDPs, rendering them in danger of falling prey to traffickers in conflict and post-conflict societies. In recent history, ethnic conflicts have emerged as the dominant form of warfare. These conflicts, by nature, are focused on the destruction of specific groups of people; simultaneously, they induce the destruction of property and means of livelihood, as well as causing massive disruption to social mechanisms. The result is the displacement of millions of people. In such conditions, women and children are frequently separated from their protectors, leaving them vulnerable in the midst of unstable conditions where it is impossible to keep track of individuals trafficked (IDMC 2014). Gender-based violence has long been, and continues to be, one of the weapons of war, and displaced women and children in post-conflict situations, while on the move or in refugee camps, are extremely vulnerable to continued violence, particularly sexual violence, and the associated psychological and physical trauma. It is women that bear the burden of family support both during war and during the transition to peace; the weight of this responsibility, and of a pervasive disrespect of women's dignity, often forces young girls and women to enter into prostitution to somehow provide for family survival, thus increasing their vulnerability to traffickers who move them within or across their country's borders. When children are displaced and separated from their parents, it is inevitable that they find themselves in danger and susceptible to falling into the hands of organised crime rings (Akee *et al.* 2010). It is clear that internally displaced women and children face particular protection issues that the liberal peace has to date failed to address. This is of major concern, since at the end of 2013, there were 12.5 million IDPs in the twenty-one sub-Saharan countries that the Internal Displacement Monitoring Centre (IDMC) observe, more than a third of the global total. These IDPs are linked mainly to worsening conflict throughout the region. Displacement was caused by struggles for political power, extremist violence, and disputes over natural resources and inter-communal violence that was often linked to land (IDMC 2014). Nigeria, the Democratic Republic of the Congo (DRC) and Sudan had the largest populations of IDPs in Africa, and were closely followed by Somalia and the Central African Republic (CAR). Nigeria is estimated to have up to 3.3 million IDPs according to government figures of 2013, so it is unsurprising that the US Department of State's Human Trafficking Report (2014: 297) identifies Nigeria as a source country for women and children subjected to forced labour and sex trafficking. Indeed, the report identifies that Nigerian women and girls are trafficked to the United Kingdom and Europe where they are subjected to forced prostitution. The liberal peace is undoubtedly somewhat illiberal

Conclusion

Human beings have become increasingly commodified and traded as sex slaves, prostitutes or trafficking victims as globalisation has seen an unprecedented growth in the underground sex industry. This has been intersected by neoliberal approaches to 'new wars' that have provided a rich spawning ground for new raw resources for transnational organised criminal networks. Conflict and post-conflict environments are now recognised as being particularly dangerous habitats for women and children due to the high prevalence of organised criminality engaged in the establishment, organisation and consolidation of trafficking networks therein, but also because conflict and post-conflict environments see high rates of women recruited into prostitution through economic necessity, and where rates of domestic violence are high. Of course, sexual exploitation and human trafficking did not begin with globalisation or capitalism; sexual slavery dates back to ancient times. The central point here, however, is that the neoliberal order, which promised to bring liberation for women from this kind of degradation, has actually entrenched their susceptibility and turned it into a global industry. The events of global neoliberalism are indeed an expression of enduring patriarchy.

The human security framework places the responsibility for the security of citizens on the state; however, some threats facing governments are beyond their capabilities, as is often the case when insecurity is intensified as a result of violent conflict and the prevalence of international criminal activity within their borders. Frequently, the government in question will be complicit in the armed conflict and the organised criminality. This leaves its society dependent on the intervention of the international community, and in the case of insecurity as a result of armed conflict, the introduction of international peace-making efforts. However, this chapter has illustrated failings of the liberal peace that may be pertinent to the role that peace-building plays in the development of organised crime, specifically in the gendered issue of women's marginalisation and the development of sex trafficking. It has also illuminated the role that TOC plays in security, development, and informal economies in conflict and post-conflict environments. The literature on organised crime and human trafficking, and the analysis of gender-blind policies of peace-building, reveal a demographic that is susceptible to both the processes of post-conflict reconstruction and to sexual exploitation. Any attempt to understand the social backgrounds of victims of human trafficking, and the dynamics that weaken human security and exploit vulnerable women, must engage in a more rigorous analysis of the relationship between international peace-building and TOC.

References

Akee, R. K., A. K. Basu, N. H. Chau and M. Khamis (2010), *Ethnic Fragmentation, Conflict, Displaced Persons and Human Trafficking: An Empirical Analysis*, vol. 8, Bingley: Emerald, pp. 691–716.

Alison, M. (2009), *Women and Political Violence: Female Combatants in Ethno-national Conflict*, Abingdon: Routledge

Bastick, M., K. Griimm and R. Kunz (2007), *Sexual Violence in Arms Conflict: Global Overview and Implications for the Security Sector*, Geneva: Geneva Centre for the Democratic Control of Armed Forces.

Bellamy, A. J. (2008), 'The responsibility to protect and the problem of military intervention', *International Affairs*, 84(4): 615–39.

Bolkovac, K. and C. Lynn (2011), *The Whistleblower: Sex Trafficking, Military Contractors, and One Woman's Fight for Justice*, Basingstoke: Palgrave Macmillan.

Boutros-Ghali, B. (1992), *An Agenda for Peace: Preventive Diplomacy, Peacemaking, and Peace-Keeping*, Report of the Secretary-General Pursuant to the Statement Adopted by the Summit Meeting of the Security Council on 31 January 1992, UN Document A/47/277-S/24111, 17 June 1992.

Cameron, S. and E. Newman (2008), *Trafficking in Humans: Social, Cultural and Political Dimensions*, Tokyo: United Nations University.

Cammack, P. (2002), 'Neoliberalism, the World Bank, and the new politics of development', in U. Kothari and M. Minogue (eds), *Development Theory and Practice: Critical Perspectives*, Basingstoke: Palgrave Macmillan, pp. 157–78.

Carmody, P. R. (2007), *Neoliberalism, Civil Society and Security in Africa*, Basingstoke: Palgrave Macmillan.

Daley, P. (2007), 'The Burundi peace negotiations: an African experience of peace-making', *Review of African Political Economy*, 34(112): 333–52.

Enloe, C. H. (2000), *Manoeuvres: The International Politics of Militarizing Women's Lives*, Oakland, CA: University of California Press.

Farr, V. (2003), 'The importance of a gender perspective to successful disarmament, demobilization and reintegration processes', *Disarmament Forum*, 4(2003): 25–36.

Gandhi, N. (2010), *National Security: Emerging Dimensions and Threats*, New Delhi: Pentagon Press.

Harrison, G. (2004), *The World Bank and Africa: The Construction of Governance States*, Abingdon: Routledge.

Harrison, G. (2010), *Neoliberal Africa: The Impact of Global Social Engineering*, London: Zed Books.

Human Security Unit (2014), United Nations Office for the Coordination of Humanitarian Affairs, available at: http://www.unocha.org/human security/human-security-unit/human-security-approach, last accessed 2 March 2015.

Internal Displacement Monitoring Centre (IDMC) (2014), *Global Overview 2014: People Internally Displaced by Conflict and Violence*, available at: http://www.internal-displacement.org/assets/publications/2014/201405-global-overview-2014-en.pdf, last accessed 2 March 2015.

Kaldor, M. and R. Luckham (2001), 'Global transformations and new conflicts', *Ids Bulletin*, 32(2): 48–69.

Kant, I. (1795), *Perpetual Peace: A Philosophical Sketch*, available at:

http://www.constitution.org/kant/perpeace.htm, last accessed 2 March 2015.

Kay, S. (2011), *Global Security in the Twenty-first Century: The Quest for Power and the Search for Peace*, Lanham, MD; Rowman & Littlefield.

Lederach, J. P. (1997), *Building Peace: Sustainable Reconciliation in Divided Societies*, Washington, DC: United States Institute of Peace Press.

MacGinty, R. (2008), *No War, No Peace: The Rejuvenation of Stalled Peace Processes and Peace Accords*, Basingstoke: Palgrave Macmillan.

Nordstrom, C. (2004), *Shadows of War: Violence, Power, and International Profiteering in the Twenty-first Century*, Oakland, CA: University of California Press.

Peterson, V. S. (ed.) (1992), *Gendered States: Feminist (Re)visions of International Relations Theory*, Boulder, CO: Lynne Rienner.

Pouligny, B. (2004), *The Politics and Anti-Politics of Contemporary Disarmament, Demobilization and Reintegration Programs*, Paris: Centre for International Studies and Research (CERI–Sciences-Po/CNRS, France).

Pugh, M., N. Cooper and M. Turner (eds) (2008), *Whose Peace? Critical Perspectives on the Political Economy of Peacebuilding*, Basingstoke: Palgrave Macmillan.

Ramsbotham, O. (2000), 'Reflections on UN post-settlement peacebuilding', *International Peacekeeping*, 7(1): 169–89.

Rehn, E. and E. J. Sirleaf (2002), *Women War and Peace: The Independent Experts Assessment on the Impact of Armed Conflict on Women and Women's Role in Peace-building, Assessment, vol. 1: Progress of the World's Women*, New York: UN Women's Office.

Richmond, O. (2012), *A Post-liberal Peace*, London: Routledge.

Schoiswohl, M. (2011), 'What's law got to do with it? The role of law in post-conflict democratization and its (flawed) assumptions', in T. Shahrbanou (ed.), *Rethinking the Liberal Peace: External Models and Local Alternatives*, New York: Routledge, pp. 112–13.

Simmons, A. B. and L. L. Martin (2002), 'International organisations and institutions', in W. Carlsnaes, T. Risse and A. Simmons (eds), *Handbook of International Relations*, London: Sage, pp. 199–205.

Sjoberg, L. and S. Via (eds) (2010), *Gender, War, and Militarism: Feminist Perspectives*, Santa Barbara, CA: ABC-CLIO.

Smith, C. A. and H. M. Smith (2011), 'Human trafficking: the unintended effects of United Nations intervention', *International Political Science Review*, 32(2): 125–45.

US Department of State (2014), *Human Trafficking Report*, available at: http://www.state.gov/documents/organization/226849.pdf, last accessed 30 October 2014.

Zabyelina, Y. (2010), 'Unpacking Pandora's Box: defining transnational crime and outlining emerging criminal trends', *Central European Journal of International & Security Studies*, 4: 2.

14 Human Trafficking: Capital Exploitation and the Accursed Share

Bill Munro

I will simply state, without waiting further, that the extension of economic growth itself requires the overturning of economic principles – the overturning of the ethics that grounds them.

Bataille 1991: 25

Introduction

Over the last twenty-five to thirty years fundamental changes have taken place in the global labour market (Wallerstein 1995; Harvey 2005; Arrighi 2007). The unconstrained development of capital accumulation into new regions has not only intensified international competition, but brought about changes in the rate of exploitation and surplus extraction. Many of these changes in exploitation and accumulation, most commonly characterised under the descriptive term of neoliberalism, have been constructed on a strategy of driving out millions of people from, what we may loosely describe as, the formal economy into informal grey zones (Fraser 2014). The journey from the formal to the informal, which takes place both within and across national borders, has been in part facilitated, and often driven, by the illegal trafficking of human beings. It is by no means accidental that over this past of a quarter century human trafficking has emerged as a major global problem.

Lee (2005) argues that the increase in transnational border crossings over this period has been stimulated not only by the distinctive role of markets in neoliberal society, but also in part by political turmoil, social conflict and civil war where migration through irregular means has become the only means of escape for many caught up in such events. She argues that the combination of enlarged global flows of people caused by both economic and political factors, and reduced formal migration programmes has encouraged breaches of migration rules and the trading of people as 'commodities'. Many authors such as Bales (2012) and Skinner (2008) view this commodification of people as a modern form of slavery, arguing that there are now more 'slaves' worldwide than when slavery was abolished in the United States in 1861.[1] However, an important difference between then and now is the replacement of a legal market with an illegal one, and such comparisons, while highlighting the moral bankruptcy of human trafficking, are problematic as the social and economic conditions of both forms of 'slavery' are fundamentally different not only in relation to different forms of capital and exploitation, but also to new forms of consumption (see Blackburn 2010). In examining the emergence of human trafficking in relation to new forms of exploitation and consumption, this chapter seeks to problematise[2] (see Foucault 1989) how it has been constructed as a contemporary social problem.

However Ruggiero (1997) warns that to interpret slavery in relation to economic development is controversial. He argues, particularly with reference to interpretations drawing from a Marxist framework, that such interpretations appear to contradict the theoretical insight of Marx's own analysis. For Ruggiero (1997), Marx understands early capitalism as an 'encounter' between capital and 'labour as a commodity'. Those who purchase labour as a commodity must have control over its power, so that they can exchange the surplus value it produces for money. It is not the worker that is the commodity, but the worker's power. In slavery, however, the slave is the commodity that is to be bought and sold, not the slave's labour power. This, Ruggiero (1997) argues, is what leads Marx to the proposition that capitalism can only fully establish itself after slavery is abolished. The above argument, however, while highlighting the contradiction between different forms of exploitation, those of slave labour and 'wage slavery', only examines one aspect of capital accumulation and does not rule out or diminish an interpretation of slavery in relation to what Marx referred to as primitive accumulation (Marx [1887] 1990) and its role in the early establishment of capitalism. Rosa Luxemburg's[3] central argument in *The Accumulation of Capital* (1968) was that capital accumulation has a dual character. One aspect of accumulation, as outlined above, is related to the commodity market, the point of production where surplus value is produced. Interpreted in this light we do indeed discover the 'encounter' between capital and 'labour as a commodity', and accumulation here is a purely economic process. However, as Luxemburg (1968) argued, there is another aspect of capital accumulation that involves a relationship between capitalism and non-capitalist modes of production. Both these aspects of accumulation are organically linked and we can only appreciate the historical career of capitalism by dealing with them together. The implication drawn by Luxemburg (1968) is that capitalism must continuously have access to something 'outside of itself' in order to stabilise itself (see also Harvey 2003). This 'outside' can be understood as external to the formal economy, beyond it in terms of general economic, legal and ethical principles. It is the 'other' of capital – made up of un-privatised land, unexploited natural resources and un-commodified labour – yet it sustains the activity of states and corporations in the *primitive valorisation*[4] of capital. It is the excessive energy – what Fraser (2014) relates to the 'blind directionality' of capital – at the heart of this valorisation process that this chapter will argue is a key characteristic of capital accumulation today and a key motivating force behind contemporary human trafficking. It is this excessive energy and blind directionality towards the 'outside' of the formal economy, beyond the ethical and legal parameters of capitalism where Bataille's (1991) concept of the *accursed share* may be understood in a contemporary context. By focussing on this blind excess, we not only contextualise the contemporary emergence of human trafficking as a particularly modern phenomena, a phenomena of normal market processes, but also challenge the tendency within social science narratives of trafficking to associate it essentially with organised crime, traditionalism, and social and economic backwardness (see Blackburn 2010).

Lee (2005) argues that in official approaches against human trafficking there is a tendency to overlook the structural factors that bring about unauthorised cross-border movements of people. This chapter aims to highlight the complex and multidimensional nature of human trafficking, and to identify those structural conditions that influence its forms and conditions of development. It will argue for a broader examination of the institutional structures and relationships within which human trafficking as a problem is embedded. In so doing, it will attempt to provide insight not only on the relationship between trafficking and economic rationality, but also why some of the most distinctive structural and economic processes and rationalities of modernity, already evident in the forms of human trafficking itself, are so often ignored in attempted reforms and solutions to the problem. Part I of this chapter will examine human trafficking as it has emerged as a contemporary problem and outline some of its defining features; Part II will explore the underlying economic conditions of its emergence; and Part III will conclude the chapter with a reflection on the limitations of official responses to the protection of human beings who are trafficked.

I

It was noted earlier that many authors maintain that such forms of commodification of people found in human trafficking and forced labour constitute a modern form of slavery (Skinner 2008; Bales 2012). However, changes within the legal construction of slavery and its relation to the labour market show the social and economic conditions of what we understand 'slavery' to be historically is problematic in terms of comparison. Modern forms of slavery, such as human trafficking, forced labour, debt bondage, forced or servile marriage, and the sale and exploitation of children are fundamentally different when viewed through an historical lens not only in relation to different forms of capital and exploitation, but also to new and different forms of consumption (Blackburn 2010). Even within a contemporary context, these forms of 'slavery' are defined differently by different countries. When looking at variations in modern practices of slavery in terms of patterns found across different countries and jurisdictions we come across a number of problems associated with the *limitations* of collecting and interpreting statistical data relating to modern slavery. Statistics represent the end result of what are very often complex institutional decision-making processes, which, in turn, have been abstracted from wider social and cultural contexts. Problems are encountered when comparing trends across different countries. First, different countries use different means of recording slavery; they use different categories for those impacted and they have different ways of classifying human trafficking, forced labour, debt bondage, forced or servile marriage. However, it is not only the issue of how populations are classified and counted; similar rates of slavery, or, more significantly, different projected rates according to perceived similarities in economic and cultural conditions, can conceal radically divergent practices (Gallagher 2014; Guth *et al.* 2014). Cultural differences between countries also have an effect on the compilation of statistics, as different types of forced labour are perceived differently in terms of seriousness.[5] 'Modern slavery' as a usable construct is therefore not only difficult to measure, but also difficult to define. However, Article 3 of the 2000 Protocol to Prevent, Suppress and Punish Trafficking in Persons, Especially Women and Children provides the first agreed upon international definition:

Trafficking in persons shall mean the recruitment, transportation, transfer, harbouring or receipt of persons, by means of the threat or use of force or other forms of coercion, of abduction, of fraud, of deception, of the abuse of power or of a position of vulnerability or of the giving or receiving payments or benefits to achieve the consent of a person having control over another person, for the purposes of exploitation.

Exploitation shall include, at a minimum, the exploitation of the prostitution of others or other forms of sexual exploitation, forced labour or services, slavery or practices similar to slavery, servitude or removal of organs. (United Nations 2000: 2)

A key and influential document in the construction of human trafficking and forced labour as a modern form of slavery is the *Global Slavery Index* (Walk Free Foundation 2015), which aims to identify the forms, size and scope of slavery worldwide. The Walk Free Foundation (2015)[6] estimates that there are 35.8 million people living in some form of modern slavery across 167 countries, and has estimated that the ten countries with the highest prevalence of modern slavery by population are Mauritania, Uzbekistan, Haiti, Qatar, India, Pakistan, the Democratic Republic of the Congo, Sudan, Syria and the Central African Republic. In terms of the estimates of absolute numbers, India, China, Pakistan, Uzbekistan, Russia, Nigeria, the Democratic Republic of the Congo, Indonesia, Bangladesh and Thailand accounted for 71 per cent of the estimated 35.8 million people living in some form of slavery, forced labour and slavery-like practices. In Europe, according to the Index, the estimated number living in slavery was 566,200, 1.6 per cent of the total number. In the United States the estimated number of people in modern slavery is 60,100, predominately from Mexico, the Philippines, Thailand, Honduras, Guatemala, India and El Salvador. However, as Guth *et al.* (2014) argue, much of this research is based on relatively small samples of survivors, often identified by non-governmental organisations (NGOs) or law enforcement agencies, which can lead to estimates constructed by 'expert' opinion and institutional interest and not verified through methodological scrutiny. According to the Walk Free Foundation (2015), although implementation is weak and few countries have basic victim support services,[7] with the exception of North Korea, all countries have national laws that criminalise at least some form of modern slavery. Again, different jurisdictions use different means of defining slavery and have different categories for classifying it. Also, because of the reluctance of victims, either through stigmatisation or fear, to report it (Guth *et al.* 2014), there is a large 'dark figure' of exploitation (Coleman and Moynihan 1996; Maguire 2007). Therefore, no assumptions should be drawn from the analysis of data on modern slavery or human trafficking without a clear understanding of how such data were compiled and what they were intended to represent. Due to this 'dark figure', or hidden nature of modern slavery, problematic issues surrounding reliability and replicability makes scientifically sound data problematic. However, given this limitation, Interpol (2006) reported that the overwhelming majority of the estimated 700,000 people trafficked during the period of their report were women and children. The children tended to be females between the ages of 8–18 years. The majority of victims were 'recruited' from developing nations in Latin America, Africa, Asia, the Baltic states and the former Soviet Union; countries characterised by high levels of poverty, high rates of unemployment, low pay, discriminatory labour practices, high rates of public and domestic violence, patriarchal social structures, and lack of social support or welfare for single mothers. The UN Trafficking Protocol (2000) outlines that people are trafficked into prostitution, pornography and other forms of sexual exploitation, forced labour, slavery (or similar practices, including debt bondage, forced or servile marriage, sale or exploitation of children (including in armed conflict) and descent-based slavery), servitude, and the removal of organs.

Gallagher (2014) highlights many of the methodological problems in relation to the measurement of modern slavery in general and to the *Index* more specifically. She argues that the presentation of such data perpetuates a comforting picture that slavery is the result of bad individuals exploiting good people and an understanding of the world that avoids broader questions of economics and power. This world view, which she calls 'philanthropic colonialism' is unable to challenge 'the underlying structures that perpetuate and reward exploitation, including a global economy that relies heavily on exploitation of poor people's labour to maintain growth and a global migration system that entrenches vulnerability and contributes directly to trafficking' (Gallagher 2014).

In order to counter the individualising tendency of NGOs and government reports, as well as the dominant construction of human trafficking in the social sciences as an anti-modern phenomenon associated with transnational crime and failed states (see, for example, Fund for Peace 2015), it is necessary to examine the often elaborate assumptions that obscure modern slavery's complex and heterogeneous connections to modernity. As Blackburn (2010) notes in relation to colonial slavery, so here in relation to contemporary trafficking, some of the most distinctive characteristics of modernity – the impact of globalisation, the deregulation of markets; the dis-embeddedness of individuals in relation to social institutions and geographic territories – are already evident in its forms. Blackburn (2010) draws on Giddens (1990, 1991) to show how modernity characteristically 'dis-embeds' individuals and institutions and tears them away from their traditional contexts. The power of finance, the opening up of new regions to capital accumulation and increasing rates of exploitation are all powerful levers in this dis-embedding process, which has in turn created new 'surplus populations' working in unskilled, unprotected, low-wage informal jobs (Davis 2006). This global and dis-embedded working class, which consists of almost 1 billion people, who exist in the informal grey zones of the economy (Fraser 2014), live in poverty, are dispossessed and starving. The new modern cities of the poor are vast 'peri-urban' developments; unplanned shantytowns, dumps of both humans and waste, where child labour and child prostitution is commonplace, and there is no access to education, clean water or sanitation. Davis (2006) estimates that there are 200,000 such slums worldwide, and that they are fast becoming the blueprint for the cities of the future. These urban characteristics are part of the contemporary free labour market, and the dis-embedded working class who inhabit these 'peri-urban' developments face 'unprecedented barriers to emigration to rich countries' (Davis 2006: 183). Within this spatial and economic grey zone, it is difficult to detect what aspects of such a market environment could be considered free.

As Fraser (2014) argues, capital's blind directionality and self-expansionary drive towards accumulation displaces those in its wake, turning them into its servants. She asks how 'unnatural', how irregular, yet particular the free labour market is as an historical institution. She argues that labour can be understood as being 'free' in a dual sense. The first, in terms of its legal status as not enslaved, or in any way bound to either master or specific place, hence free to enter into a labour contract. However, the second 'free' refers to the freedom from access to the means of subsistence and production, including customary land rights, and hence lack of access to entitlements and resources that would allow one to abstain from the labour market. This dual nature of a process of commodity production, where free becomes a term for its opposite, relies also on the 'other' of capital, the outside background of non-commodities and non-marketised relationships (Fraser 2014). Following Luxemburg's argument on the dual character of accumulation, marketised characteristics of capital accumulation co-exist with non-marketised ones. Ruggiero (1997) highlights that these non-marketised sectors of the economy include a variety of semi-legal and outright illegal activities, which require the entrepreneurial efforts of a wide range of actors from 'legitimate' institutions to forms of organised crime.

As Seabrook (2001: 129) points out, 'some of the most dynamic markets in the world deal with illicit goods and substances – arms, pornography, gold, drugs, ivory . . . children and their labour, trees, diamonds and flesh'. Here, he argues, behind the rosy ideology of neoliberalism is a real enterprise culture, the perfect paradigm of the market economy.

The journey from the formal to the informal, which takes place both within and across national borders, is also a journey, as Ruggiero (1997) and Seabrook (2001) point out, from the legal economy to the illegal. As we have seen, most countries have national laws that criminalise many of the forms of modern slavery, and it is through the lens of illegality and criminalisation that the problem of human trafficking has most successfully been constructed. The then US Attorney General argues that:

> Trafficking is a transnational criminal enterprise. It recognizes neither boundaries nor borders. Profits from trafficking feed into the coffers of organized crime. Trafficking is fuelled by other criminal activities such as document fraud, money laundering and migrant smuggling. (Ashcroft 2003)

Trafficking is here constructed as transnational criminal enterprise driven by the imperatives of illegal markets and organised crime. Such a construction, although true in part, ignores the underlying structures, including the impact of globalisation, the deregulation of markets and the new forms of consumption underlying capital accumulation.

Bataille's (1991, 1997) work on political economics argues for a method that approaches the question of economics through the dynamics of excess and consumption, rather than production as the primary object. His theory of *general economy* argued against the modes of rationality that constructed models based on 'restricted economies'; in the case of human trafficking, the tendency to explain historical trends by means of a dominant representative image of organised crime and illegal markets, or the similar tendency to reduce institutional structure into a collection of individualised actions oriented to subjectively meaningful ends, where the individual pathology of the traffickers are contrasted with the structural rationality of legitimately functioning state institutions and corporations. Both tropes are intellectual habits that universalise particulars and individualise actions, and according to Bataille (1991, 1997), domesticate and restrict our understanding of the economy both epistemologically and ethically (see Winnubst 2013). To combat such restricted understanding, Bataille (1991, 1997) proposes a theory of *general economy* that draws on a vast array of heterogeneous connections that attempted to lay bare the excessive energy underlying the economy's various domains. Such an approach would point to the divergence between the 'restricted economies' of free enterprise ideologies and the previously hidden expenditure of excessive energy found in the activities of states and corporations.

Within the 'restricted economy' of free market theories there is no mention of the *general economy* of states and corporations in relation to their direct involvement in trafficking, nor about the ability of states and corporations to enact or influence legislation in their favour in relation to the deregulation and opening up of new areas of accumulation (see Pearce 1976). The International Labour Organisation (2015) estimates the illicit profits from forced labour to be US$150 billion a year. Modern slavery plays a significant part in legitimate and normal business. As Glenny (2008) argues, forced labour is what we consume,[8] and what is lost in an over-reliance on discourses about mafias and organised crime is the issue of denied demand in the rich West for drugs, cheap labour and paid sex. The role organised crime plays in the economy of trafficking cannot be understood fully without investigating the 'active and conscious co-operation of a number of elements of respectable society' (Lindesmith 1941, cited in Woodiwiss 2003: 14). Criminal networks require the active involvement of police, politicians, judges, lawyers, accountants and business executives as much as the 'legitimate' employers and gang-masters of smuggled labour (Ruggiero 1997). Organised crime may be understood in this sense as a response to a particular institutional demand by the nascent market economy. As Findlay argues, one feature of organised crime is its ability to:

> infiltrate the capital market or create sources of capital which are significantly more open, accessible and attractive to marginal or criminal enterprise than are legitimate capital sources. Crime profits as capital, standing as they do outside the tax and regulatory structures of government, not only tend to leach out consolidated revenue, but form an attractive lure for legitimate commerce to become tainted through financial obligation to criminal enterprise. (Findlay 2000: 128)

The trading of people as 'commodities' and the illegal trafficking of human beings are only a small part of the multiple illegalities of 'free trade'. Under neoliberal free trade the distinction between clean or dirty money has almost evaporated, and commodities such as drugs, cigarettes, weapons, prostitutes and immigrants can be smuggled in previously undreamed of quantities (Glenny 2008), and comprise only those exceptions that governments still feel obliged to regulate.

The extension of economic growth not only requires the overturning of obsolete economic principles, but also the ethics that had previously grounded them (Bataille 1997). Ruggiero (1997) points out that recent efforts by the EU to tackle the problems of illegal migration and human trafficking seem to clash with broader economic interests that are beyond EU control. As he argues, the contradiction between official action and economic behaviour shows the institutional difficulties in tackling the problems in a broad and holistic way and promoting and exploiting the principles of free entrepreneurship, given the productivity of illegal immigrants and trafficked labour.

Organised crime then becomes a means for capitalism to access that 'outside of itself'; outside its formalised processes and ethical norms, in order to stabilise, self-expand and accumulate (see also Harvey 2003). The energy that motivates the expropriation of this 'outside' can be understood as an excess produced within the formal economy as capital's *accursed share* (Bataille 1991).

We can see an example of this institutional anomaly between legal regulation and illegal markets in 1989 during the break up of the Soviet Union and Eastern Europe. This event was constructed by governmental bodies, NGOs, political and social scientists through ubiquitously deployed tropes such as 'transition', 'modernisation' and 'development'. Institutional economic reforms through the legal means of privatisation of what were once considered common property resources were coercively imposed by external institutions (IMF, World Bank). Not only were the asset losses experienced by many as a form of dispossession perfectly legal, but the obliteration of existing constitutions created a 'legal gap' that allowed a new species of 'robber baron' to emerge, what we now know as the Russian oligarch (Glenny 2008).

In this case, the Russian mafia arose in response to the situation where the increasing number of market transactions, brought about by forced privatisation and market reform, had no overall mechanism to control them (see also Blok 1974; Gambetta 1996). It was a distribution of wealth from the poor to the rich via a combination of a hostile United States, an incompetent European Union and criminal violence (Harvey 2006; Munro 2012).

For those cast out of the market system – an excess of seemingly disposable people without social protection or any kind of supportive social structures – their only option is to clamber aboard the market system as petty commodity producers, informal traders of things or labour, or as 'petty predators, or participants in the vast illegal trade of trafficking in drugs, guns, women, or anything else illegal for which there is a demand' (Harvey 2005: 185).

II

As outlined earlier, Bataille's (1991, 1997) work on political economy argues for a method that approaches the question of economics through the dynamics of excess and consumption, rather than production and scarcity as the primary object of economic investigation. Bataille's central problem was that of non-productive expenditure:

> the excess energy (wealth) can be used for the growth of a system . . . if the system can no longer grow, or if the excess cannot be completely absorbed in its growth, it must necessarily be lost without profit; it must be spent, willingly or not, gloriously or catastrophically. (Bataille 1997: 21)

Energy (wealth) must be spent, it must burn, but the question is how it will burn: gloriously or catastrophically? A contemporary example of such an excess, or in Bataille's (1997: 21) terminology 'accursed share', is the current crisis of over-accumulation. In other words, an excess of capital (in commodity, money or productive capacity forms) and a corresponding excess of labour power, yet without the means to bring them profitably together (Harvey 2003). Bataille's (1991, 1997) work was concerned with what happens to wealth when it cannot be used to productive ends and where surplus wealth must be dissipated. Bataille's (1991, 1997) examples, covering a range of historical formations, include socially beneficial phenomena such as potlatch and sacrifice to socially destructive phenomena as means of expending excess wealth such as war. Bataille (1991, 1997) argues that this consequence of consumption, the non-productive destruction of wealth, is a part of all societies and becomes more problematic in the period of bourgeois capitalism where the prohibition against waste becomes *the* founding law of modernity (Winnubst 2013):

> The advantage that matters most in the capitalist era is the possibility of investing . . . an essential portion of the available resources is set aside for the growth of the productive forces. It is not the final purpose of any individual in particular, but collectively that of society that an epoch has chosen. It gives precedence in the use of available resources to the expansion of enterprises and the increase of capital equipment: in other words, it prefers an increase of wealth to its immediate use. (Bataille 1997: 118–19)

The prohibition against waste is so binding in capitalist economies that in periods where there is a crisis of over-accumulation – where there is an excess of surplus in commodity or money that cannot be invested productively – this excess cannot be used to alleviate social ills such as poverty, unemployment or hunger as this would not constitute investment and therefore would be a non-productive expenditure of wealth (Bataille 1997). When faced with internal limits to productive accumulation, for example, stagnant demand and high costs of land, raw materials or labour power, capital keeps productive opportunities open by widening markets to non-capitalist territories. It was Hegel (1967) in the *Philosophy of Right* that first developed the theory that bourgeois society appears to be incapable of solving, through its own internal mechanisms, the problem of social inequality and instability that results from its tendency to over-accumulate wealth while at the same time produces deprivation. Civil society is thus driven to seek solutions outside its own territorial boundaries through colonial or imperial practices (Harvey 1981; Arrighi 2007).

This perpetual seeking after capital's 'other' is what Luxemburg (1968) argues is the dual character of capitalist accumulation: the reliance of commodity markets in periods of over-accumulation on non-capitalist modes of production 'outside of itself' (Harvey 2003). The implication behind Luxemburg's (1968) analysis is that non-capitalist territories should be forced open not only to trade, but also to permit capital to invest in profitable ventures using cheaper labour power, raw materials, etc. The general logic is the continuing opening up of new territories to capitalist development. According to Harvey (2003), the processes that Marx, following Adam Smith, referred to as 'primitive' or 'original' accumulation constitute an important and continuing force in the historical geography of capital accumulation.

The *general economy* of human trafficking should be understood against this background of 'primitive capitalism' in resolving the problem of capital and labour surpluses. Harvey (1981, 2003), following Hegel, argues that capitalist activity produces uneven geographical development. Driven by competition, individual capitalists seek competitive advantages within this spatial and territorial structure and are drawn to locations where labour costs are lower or rates of profit are higher. Excess or surplus capital in one place can find employment somewhere else where opportunities for profits are not exhausted:

> there is a strong connection between how the overaccumulation of capital (the central indicator of crisis in Marx's theory) is manifest and how the spatial fix gets pursued. Overaccumulation, in its most virulent form (as occurred in the 1930s, for example) is registered as surpluses of labour and capital side by side with seemingly no way to put them together in

productive, i.e. 'profitable' as opposed to socially useful ways. If the crisis cannot be resolved, then the result is massive devaluation of both capital and labour (bankruptcies, idle factories and machines, unsold commodities, and unemployed labourers). Devaluation can sometimes lead to physical destruction (surplus commodities get burned and labourers die of starvation) and even war (the whole sequence of events that occurred in the 1930s and 1940s came close to such a scenario). (Harvey 2001: 26)

In Harvey's work, globalisation has largely been interpreted in terms of a theory of 'the spatial fix'. He notes that in English, the word 'fix" has multiple meanings. One meaning refers to something being pinned down and secured in a particular locus. Another is to 'fix a problem', to resolve a difficulty or to take care of a problem by returning things to normal functioning again. Another meaning draws on the metaphor of the drug addict 'needing a fix', in which it refers to the craving, or the burning desire to relieve a chronic or pervasive addiction. Harvey draws on all these meanings to allow the 'spatial fix' to describe capitalism's insatiable drive to resolve its inner crisis tendencies by geographical expansion and geographical restructuring (Harvey 2001: 24). It is this affinity of the 'spatial fix' to an uncontrolled craving or addiction that places his theory close to Bataille's (1991: 26) theory of the *accursed share*. The share being related to a circuit of excess energy on which capital depends, which it cannot limit and 'whose laws it cannot ignore without consequences'.

Commodities, however, do not take themselves to market, and in the trade in human commodities, particularly if there exist territorial constraints, markets require individuals who will facilitate this. Harvey (2003) traces the historical role of merchants in the rolling back of spatial barriers and the opening up of new channels of movement and spaces for trade.[9] Today, as we have noted earlier, organised crime may be understood as performing the role traditionally taken by merchants in the colonial slave systems and merely responds to the demands of an expanding market (Findlay 2000). A re-evaluation of the continuous role and persistence within the *general economy* of the predatory practices of 'primitive' accumulation is therefore required if we are to understand the broader institutional context of human trafficking.

Harvey (2003) argues that primitive accumulation reveals a wide range of processes over and above the modern slave trade, which are promoted by the state with its monopoly of violence and legality. These processes include the colonial, neocolonial and imperial processes of appropriation of assets (including natural resources); the commodification and privatisation of land, the suppression of rights to the commons, and the forceful expulsion of peasant populations;

the commodification of labour power, the suppression of alternative forms of production and consumption, and the monetisation of exchange and taxation.

Harvey (2003) has redefined the term primitive accumulation as 'accumulation by dispossession' in order to emphasise its persistent nature and modern incarnation. He outlines how today the credit system and finance capital become central levers of predation. In particular, he notes how the wave of financialisation that emerged after 1973, which was brought in as compensation for the chronic problems of over-accumulation arising within expanded reproduction, has reduced whole populations to debt peonage and has been at the cutting edge of accumulation by dispossession through the speculative raiding carried out by hedge funds and other major institutions of finance capital. Accumulation by dispossession helps to solve crises of over-accumulation by releasing a set of assets such as labour power at very low or, in some cases, zero cost. The opening up of China and the collapse of the Soviet Union released a huge amount of previously unavailable assets into the mainstream of capital accumulation. Finance capital becomes the umbilical cord that ties together accumulation by dispossession and expanded reproduction.

However, capitalism functions within a legal framework underpinning market exchange and private enterprise. The ideology of the free market depends on these legal frameworks to enforce contracts, guarantee property rights, adjudicate disputes and maintain confidence in the money supply. However, such legally regulated powers are lodged within territorial states, and it is within such states that the contours of apparently depoliticised arenas within which private actors can pursue their 'economic' interests are established, free from either political interference or ethical obligation. Behind the sublimated cloak of legality lie overt violence and outright theft (Harvey 2003).

III

The antinomies of human rights and finance capital

This primitive accumulation plays in Political Economy about the same part as original sin in theology. Adam bit the apple, and thereupon sin fell on the human race. Its origin is supposed to be explained when it is told as an anecdote of the past. In times long gone-by there were two sorts of people; one, the diligent, intelligent, and, above all, frugal elite; the other, lazy rascals, spending their substance, and more, in riotous living ... Thus it came to pass that the former sort accumulated wealth, and the latter sort had at last nothing to sell except their own skins. And from this original sin dates the poverty of the great majority that, despite all its labour, has up to now nothing to sell but itself, and the wealth of the few that increases constantly although they have long ceased to work. (Marx [1887] 1990: 873)

This chapter has argued that the illegal trafficking of human beings has been facilitated by an excess of energy within capital, forcing accumulation outside the formal economy of commodity production into new regions. It drew on Bataille's (1991) concept of the *accursed share* and Harvey's (2003, 2005) theory of *accumulation by dispossession* as a means of contextualising human trafficking in a contemporary context. It argued that the *accursed share*, a motivational energy produced by an excess of wealth, has reconfigured rates of exploitation and surplus extraction, as well as brought about new forms of consumption; processes that have not only driven millions of people out of the legal frameworks and protections of the formal economy into unregulated grey zones, but have also forced capital to move outside itself in order to seek a means of valorising its excess on un-privatised land, unexploited natural resources and un-commodified labour. This movement of excessive energy, or surplus, towards the outside of capital is a perpetual characteristic of capital accumulation and today functions as a key motivating force behind contemporary human trafficking

The dual nature of capital – the formal encounter between capital and labour as a commodity in a purely economic process, and the informal grey zone of primitive accumulation – is also reflected in the journey from the legal economy to the illegal. As argued in this chapter, it is through a filter of illegality and criminalisation that the problem of human trafficking has most successfully been constructed. However, such a construction ignores the underlying structures – including the impact of globalisation, the deregulation of markets, and the new forms of consumption underlying capital accumulation – that reproduce and sustain trafficking.

Bataille's (1991, 1997) work on political economy argues for a method that approaches the question of economics through the dynamics of excess and consumption, rather than production as the primary object. His theory of *general economy* argued against the modes of rationality that constructed 'restricted economies', in the case of human trafficking, the tendency to explain historical trends by means of a dominant representative image of organised crime or narratives focused solely on illegal markets. An approach that examines trafficking through a notion of a *general economy* helps to explain the contradiction between official action and economic behaviour that is encountered in the institutional difficulties in tackling the problems surrounding trafficking, while simultaneously promoting and exploiting – given the productivity of illegal immigrants and trafficked labour – the principles of free markets and entrepreneurship.

Bataille's (1991, 1997) *general economy* was presented through Harvey's (2003, 2005) theory of *accumulation by dispossession*, where he extends Marx's writings on 'primitive' or 'original' accumulation in order to emphasise its persistent nature and modern incarnation. Harvey (2003, 2005) shows how accumulation by dispossession, while helping to solve crises of over-accumulation, also contributes to a modern slave market by releasing assets such as labour power at very low or, in some cases, zero cost. Like Marx ([1887] 1990), Harvey (2005) emphasises how free market ideology depends on a legal framework underpinning market exchange and private enterprise, and serves to mask the violence, theft and social harms produced by expanding markets and the demands of Western consumption. In particular, he outlines how today the credit system and finance capital become central levers of such predation. One of the means financial capital uses is 'to rid the system of over-accumulation by the visitation of crises of devaluation upon vulnerable territories' (Harvey 2003: 134). The other is the use of political and military means to turn international competition to the advantage of the more powerful states. The deployment of these means constitutes the 'sinister and destructive side of spatial–temporal fixes to the over-accumulation problem':

> Like war in relation to diplomacy, finance capital intervention backed by state power frequently amounts to accumulation by other means. An unholy alliance between state powers and the predatory aspects of finance capital forms the cutting edge of a 'vulture capitalism' that is as much about cannibalistic practices and forced devaluations as it is about achieving harmonious global development. (Harvey 2003: 135–6)

As has been shown in the history of new world slavery, the self-interested policies and commercial principles of states and the actions of civil society can support highly destructive activities and processes that relate to human trafficking (Blackburn 2010).

However, as mentioned above, the formal economy does operate within legal frameworks that underpin market exchange and private enterprise, and, as we have seen, Harvey (2003) notes how this 'cloak of legality' very often merely hides overt violence and theft. It is this 'cloak of legality' that Marx ([1887] 1990) comments on, albeit with his tongue firmly in his cheek, when he writes that primitive accumulation plays the same part in political economy as original sin in theology. In Marx's ([1887] 1990: 873) example, a religious morality provided the rationale for the fact that of the two sorts of people in society – one, the diligent, intelligent, and frugal elite; the second, the lazy, feckless and immoral – it was the former that accumulated wealth, while the latter had 'nothing to sell except their own skins'.

However it is not only the legal frameworks that underpin market exchange and private enterprise that conceal such primitive exploitation, with authors such as Collins (2010) arguing that human rights have taken over the ideological function of religion as a means to rationalise the abuses of accumulation by dispossession: a religion that demands no responsibilities from its adherents and comes packaged with a vague inclusive creed from which no reasonable person could dissent. This new faith, he argues, works in harmony with the reigning economic and social policies of the West and effectively camouflages the interests of the present transatlantic consensus.

> Its preferred sacred figure, the victim – the harki, the slave, the deportee – is interchangeable, non-specific, ahistorical, a testament to the videosphere's amnesiac perpetual present. The Religion of the Contemporary West has no congregation, no antagonist, commands no strong attachments; it specializes in erasing borders, where the sacred would insist on drawing them. (Collins 2010: 132–3)

Blackburn (2011), while reading human rights against the grain with Collins (2010), argues that such a reading does not invalidate human rights, but rather attempts to embed them in the real history of peoples. Benhabib (2004) makes a similar appeal when she writes that the Universal Declaration is silent on states' *obligations* under the Act: obligations to grant migrants entry, to uphold the right to asylum or to permit citizenship to residents. Human rights have no specific addressees and they do not seek to embed specific obligations on the part of second and third parties to comply with them. Despite the cross-border character of these rights, a series of internal contradictions between universal human rights and territorial sovereignty are built into their logic. Neither the existence of the Declaration nor the creation of the United Nations High Commissioner for Refugees has altered the fact that this Convention and its Protocol are binding on signatory states alone and can be brazenly disregarded by non-signatories, and, at times, even by signatory states themselves. Some lament the fact that as international human rights norms are increasingly invoked in immigration, refugee and asylum disputes, territorially delimited nations are challenged not only in their claims to control their borders, but also in their prerogative to define the boundaries of the national community (Benhabib 2004). Following Arendt (1986), Benhabib (2004: 168) raises the paradox that it is the figure of the stateless or trafficked person, the refugee or asylum seeker that should have embodied human rights more than any other, yet marked instead the crisis of the concept (see also Agamben 2000).

> Hannah Arendt's observation that to lose one's citizenship status appeared tantamount to losing human rights altogether is not altogether wrong. Even in the most developed rights regimes of our world, refugees and asylum seekers still find themselves in quasi-criminal status. Their human rights are curtailed; they have no civil and political rights of association and representation. The extension of full human rights to these individuals and the decriminalisation of their status is one of the most important tasks of cosmopolitan justice in our world. (Benhabib 2004: 168)

The failure to embed human rights in the real history of peoples is related to the absence of a stable statute for the human in the law of the nation state (Agamben 2000). It is therefore not surprising that the failure to extend full human rights to trafficked individuals and the tendency to explain human trafficking through the dominant representative image of criminality and illegal markets should result in the granting to the victim of trafficking quasi-criminal status, rather than the rights of citizenship or other forms of residency. The failure to embed human rights calls attention to the 'hypocrisy of the world of accumulation' (Bataille 1993: 424), and can be read as an equivalent process to the expenditure of excess wealth that capital accumulation demands. Human rights in this sense can be read as a symbolic expenditure or excess that seeks to confer personhood while denying it at every turn. Arendt (1986: 279) outlines this paradox of human rights when she writes of 'the discrepancy between the efforts of well-meaning idealists who stubbornly insist on regarding as "inalienable" those human rights, which are enjoyed only by citizens of the most prosperous and civilized countries, and the situations of the rightless themselves'.

Harvey's (2001) description of the compulsive craving of capital's 'spatial fix' and Bataille's (1991: 26) *accursed share*; the circuit of excess energy on which capital relies for its survival and which it cannot limit, challenge habitual narratives which domesticate and separate our understanding of the economy and our ethical relation to it. This chapter's aim is not to outline any solution to human trafficking, but merely to outline the relationships between trafficking, the 'normal' functioning of the economy and what Bataille (1993: 424) terms the 'disgraceful delusion' of the *accursed share*.

Everything once *served* the interests of a *few*; we have finally decided that everything should serve the interest of *all*. We see that with use the most pernicious system is the second one, *in that it is less imperfect*. This is not a reason for returning to the first. But – if we do not make *consumption* the *sovereign* principle of activity, we cannot help but succumb to those monstrous disorders without which we do not know how *to consume* the energy we have at our disposal. (Bataille 1993: 15–16)

Notes

1. The 2014 *Global Slavery Index* (Walk Free Foundation 2015) estimates that there are 35.8 million people living in some form of modern slavery across 167 countries.
2. 'Problematization doesn't mean the representation of a pre-existent object, nor the creation through discourse of an object that doesn't exist. It's the set of discursive or nondiscursive practices that makes something enter into the play of the true and false, and constitutes it as an object for thought (whether under the form of moral reflection, scientific knowledge, political analysis, etc.)' (Foucault 1989: 456–7).
3. Marx also accounts for this in *Capital: Volume 1*.
4. Marx ([1887] 1990) uses the term valorisation (*Verwertung*) in relation to the *excess* over an original value in the form of surplus value. I use the term *primitive valorisation* as relating to the exploitation of a resource outside of the legally construed productive process.
5. See, for example, the Republic of Uzbekistan, which relies heavily on cotton production and export and its ranking is a consequence of government-imposed forced labour. Almost 4 per cent – approximately 1,201,400 people – of the Uzbekistan population is forced to work during the annual cotton harvest (Walk Free Foundation 2015).
6. The *Global Slavery Index* (Walk Free Foundation 2015) is a yearly publication produced by the Walk Free Foundation, which monitors the prevalence of 'modern slavery', government responses to slavery and population vulnerability to slavery.
7. Norway is one of the few countries that provide holistic services for the victims of modern slavery (Walk Free Foundation 2015).
8. While taking on board the methodological criticisms above, the *Global Slavery Index* (Walk Free Foundation 2015) notes that trafficking contributes to the production of at least 122 goods from fifty-eight countries worldwide.
9. The colonial slave systems were closely associated with the mercantilist epoch and were an important facilitator of social and territorial mobility and the transition to modernity. It would therefore not be inappropriate to make comparisons with contemporary forms of human slavery. As in our present historical epoch, the history of new world slavery shows that mercantilist policies and commercial principles of states and the activities of civil society, in the modern sense of that term, can contribute to

highly destructive patterns of human conduct in relation to slave labour (Blackburn 2010).

References

Agamben, G. (2000), *Means Without End: Notes on Politics*, Minneapolis, MI: Minnesota University Press.

Arendt, H. (1986), *The Origins of Totalitarianism*, London: Andre Deutsch.

Arrighi, G. (2007), *Adam Smith in Beijing: Lineages of the Twenty-First Century*, London: Verso.

Ashcroft, J. (2003), *Path-breaking Strategies in the Global Fight against Sex Trafficking*, available at: http://www.usdoj.gov/trafficking.htm, last accessed 6 June 2015.

Bales, K. (2012), *Disposable People: New Slavery in the Global Economy*, Berkeley, CA: University of California Press.

Bataille, G. (1991), *The Accursed Share*, vol. 1, New York: Zone Books.

Bataille, G. (1993), *The Accursed Share*, vols 2 and 3, New York: Zone Books.

Bataille, G. (1997), 'The notion of expenditure', in F. Botting and S. Wilson (eds), *The Bataille Reader*, Oxford: Blackwell.

Benhabib, S. (2004), *The Rights of Others*, Cambridge: Cambridge University Press.

Blackburn, R. (2010), *The Making of New World Slavery: From the Baroque to the Modern, 1492–1800*, London: Verso.

Blackburn, R. (2011), *The American Crucible: Slavery, Emancipation and Human Rights*, London: Verso.

Blok, A. (1974), *The Mafia of a Sicilian Village, 1860–1960*, Long Grove, IL: Waveland Press.

Coleman, C. and J. Moynihan (1996), *Understanding Crime Data: Haunted by the Dark Figure*, Ballmoor: Open University Press.

Collins, J. (2010), 'Link arms!', *New Left Review*, 64: 131–8.

Davis, M. (2006), *Planet of Slums*, London: Verso.

Findlay, M. (2000), *The Globalisation of Crime: Understanding Transitional Relationships in Context*, Cambridge: Cambridge University Press.

Foucault, M. (1989), 'The concern for truth', in S. Lotringer (ed.), *Foucault Live: Collected Interviews, 1961–1984*, New York: Semiotext(e), 455–64.

Fraser, N. (2014), 'Behind Marx's hidden abode', *New Left Review*, 86(Mar./Apr.): 55–72.

Fund for Peace (2015), *Fragile State Index*, available at: http://fsi.fundforpeace.org, last accessed 6 June 2015.

Gallagher, A. (2014), *The Global Slavery Index: Seduction and Obfuscation*, available at: opendemocracy.net, https://www.opendemocracy.net/5050/anne-gallagher/global-slavery-index-seduction-and-obfuscation, last accessed 6 June 2015.

Gambetta, D. (1996), *The Sicilian Mafia: The Business of Private Protection*, Cambridge, MA: Harvard University Press.

Giddens, A. (1990), *The Consequences of Modernity*, Cambridge: Polity Press.

Giddens, A. (1991), *Modernity and Self-Identity*, Cambridge: Polity Press.

Glenny, M. (2008), *McMafia*, London: Bodley Head.

Guth, A., R. Anderson, K. Kinnard and H. Tran (2014), 'Proper methodology and methods of collecting and analysing slavery data: an examination of the *Global Slavery Index*', *Social Inclusion*, 2(4): 14–22.

Harvey, D. (1981), 'The spatial fix – Hegel, Von Thunen, and Marx', *Antipode*, 13(3): 1–12.

Harvey, D. (2001), 'Globalization and the spatial fix', *Geographische revue*, 2(3): 23–31.

Harvey, D. (2003), *The New Imperialism*, Oxford: Oxford University Press.

Harvey, D. (2005), *A Brief History of Neoliberalism*, Oxford: Oxford University Press.

Harvey, D. (2006), *The Limits to Capital*, London: Verso.

Hegel, G. W. F. (1967), *The Philosophy of Right*, Oxford: Oxford University Press.

International Labour Organisation (2015), *Forced Labour, Human Trafficking and Slavery*, available at: http://www.ilo.org/global/topics/forced-labour/lang--en/index.htm, last accessed 6 June 2015.

Interpol (2006), *Trafficking in Human Beings – Interpol Fact Sheet*, available at: http://lastradainternational.org/lsidocs/280%20Interpol%20fact%20sheet.pdf, last accessed 6 June 2015.

Lee, M. (2005), 'Human trade and the criminalisation of irregular migration', *International Journal of the Sociology of Law*, 33: 1–15.

Luxemburg, R. (1968), *The Accumulation of Capital*, New York: Merlin Press.

Maguire, M. (2007), 'Crime data and statistics', in M. Maguire, R. Morgan and R. Reiner (eds), *The Oxford Handbook of Criminology*, Oxford: Clarendon Press, pp. 241–90.

Marx, K. ([1887] 1990), *Capital: Volume I*, London: Penguin.

Munro, B. (2012), '*Antisittlichkeit*: organised crime and the antinomies of civil society', in K. Goodall, M. Malloch and B. Munro (eds), *Building Justice in Post-transition Europe? Processes of Criminalisation within Central and Eastern European Societies*, London: Routledge.

Pearce, F. (1976), *Crimes of the Powerful: Marxism, Crime and Deviance*, London: Pluto.

Ruggiero, V. (1997), 'Trafficking in human beings: slaves in contemporary Europe', *International Journal of the Sociology of Law*, 25: 231–46.

Seabrook, J. (2001), *Travels in the Skin Trade: Tourism and the Sex Industry*, London: Pluto.

Skinner, E. B. (2008), *A Crime so Monstrous: A Shocking Expose of Modern Day Sex Slavery, Human Trafficking and Urban Child Markets*, Edinburgh: Mainstream Publishing.

United Nations (2000), Protocol to Prevent, Suppress and Punish Trafficking in Persons, Especially Women and Children, Supplementing the United Nations Convention against Transnational Organized Crime, United

Nations, available at: http://www.osce.org/odihr/19223?download=true, last accessed 6 June 2015.

Walk Free Foundation (2015), *2014 Global Slavery Index*, available at: http://www.globalslaveryindex.org, last accessed 5 June 2015.

Wallerstein, I. (1995), *After Liberalism*, New York: New Press.

Winnubst, S. (2013), 'The missing link: *Homo Economicus* (reading Foucault and Bataille together)', in C. Falzon, T. O'Leary and J. Sawicki (eds), *A Companion to Foucault*, Oxford: Blackwell.

Woodiwiss, M. (2003), 'Transnational organised crime: the strange career of an American concept', in M. Beare (ed.), *Critical Reflections on Transnational Organised Crime, Money Laundering, and Corruption*, Toronto: University of Toronto Press.

Postscript

Paul Rigby and Margaret Malloch

The idea of the original SUII conference in 2012, which led directly to this book, was to bring together many different state and private actors working in the field of anti-trafficking, to discuss the complexities and the challenges of working in this area across countries. It was recognised that while the aim of intervention is to reduce the abuse and exploitation of people, the different interest groups and state authorities are motivated by their own particular interests, which, at times, are in conflict with each other. Reflecting a human rights, victim-focused approach the conference and this book have predominantly been concerned with justice and support for victims, which in many ways is in contrast to the state responses across United Kingdom and Europe, which have largely been law enforcement and border control.

Human trafficking is increasingly discussed and addressed across many spheres: politics, the media and practice arenas in the field of criminal justice, migration, immigration, legislation and human rights. While these discussions often highlight the complexities of the issues and the challenges of identifying the extent of the problems, providing support to victims, prosecuting perpetrators and preventing further trafficking, there is also a tendency to focus on one aspect of the myriad of issues. This leads to strategies aimed at resolving the specific issue, and often how to address 'trafficking' as if it was a homogeneous entity with one solution. In reality, as evidenced at the original conference, and also reflected in the different contributions to the book, the 'anti-trafficking community' may be at best fragmented, and perhaps at times deeply divided on which areas to focus on and how to address the issues.

International legislation and guidelines, now being transposed into UK legislation, can also perpetuate the notion that trafficking can be dealt with via specific steps and clear legislative frameworks. The debate surrounding the passage of the various trafficking legislation in the United Kingdom approaches the topic as a single issue of 'trafficking', confirming a belief that one piece of legislation will address the complexities, not least by identifying and prosecuting perpetrators. The various submissions to the UK parliaments by interested agencies and individuals highlights the myriad of activities that are perceived as constituting exploitation by trafficking and, perhaps unrealistically, raises the expectations that legislation will go some way to addressing the issues.

Interestingly, the complexities and challenges of the issues, including definitions, are reflected in the various legislative processes and submissions; at the time of writing it seems that each jurisdiction in the United Kingdom may well have legislative frameworks with slightly different definitions and emphasis. However, the United Kingdom may also have some of the first legislation in the world that attempts to legislate for a criminal justice and victim support response in the same Act.

The speed of change in the legislative responses to trafficking has been reflected in the various chapters, but ultimately for effective responses to address the global exploitation of people, and its ever-changing nature, legislation can only provide a loose framework to facilitate agencies in providing support to victims. The focus of the book has been predominantly on victim support, but located in the broader conceptual arguments identifying what are considered to be some of the social and political factors that may underpin the exploitation of people. We have been particularly struck by the predominant, and continuing, focus on movement and mobility rather than exploitation. This focus on movement appears to accentuate the non-citizen status of many of those involved in the United Kingdom, which permeates the representation of 'victims' and 'criminals' and justifies the lack of protection.

The contributions to this book were chosen to reflect what we consider to be the disparate, but often converging, narratives that are typical of the contemporary human trafficking debate. While they represent a 'common' theme of trafficking, it will be obvious to the reader that there are vastly differing opinions as to which key issues to take cognisance of and focus attention on. Reflecting the professional backgrounds and interests of the authors, these determinants reflect what we consider to be the reality and the major challenge of trafficking – its complexity and its permeation of many aspects of life.

The chapters diverged substantially in their discussion of the issues around human trafficking. The 'from the front-line' chapters identify the tremendous challenges facing professionals working directly with victims, even if there are 'clear' policy goals and directions, which is far from given. The chapters discussing the legal challenges and responses highlight the complexity of the legislation and legal frameworks surrounding human trafficking. While these legal debates continue, so does the exploitation of people and front-line workers have to support victims to recovery and rehabilitation with, or without, legal or policy frameworks. However, as indicated, without these frameworks, professionals will continue to be challenged by a lack of clarity of what they 'should' and 'should not' do!

The practitioner's views on the developments and challenges of their work provide a contrast to the carefully crafted legislative process. With or without a legal framework, professionals working on the front line, and directly with victims, struggle with the realities of working with a vulnerable group of people who, in many instances, are coming to terms not only with new places and cultures, but the trauma of exploitation and abuse. Legislation, politics and policy often serve to hinder their commitment to support and empower the individuals they encounter. Their frustrations are evident in their accounts; it is likely to be a frustration echoed by many people working in the field of human trafficking.

Similarly, the chapters focusing on the legal responses to trafficking highlight the complexities inherent in different legislation at the confluence of immigration, criminal justice and victim support approaches. Luminata's journey demonstrates the legal minefield victims may find themselves in, and will resonate also with those professionals attempting to provide support. Within the legal context the chapters define the potential for a hierarchy of legislative responses, especially if the focus on individual victimisation is lost amongst the legal frameworks. The practitioners identify how this hierarchy may filter down to service provision if one aspect of the legal response is seen to predominate.

The practitioner accounts of work in Scotland provide a refreshing 'from the front-line' perspective, unhindered by the need to justify their work beyond the commitment to provide support to those they have identified as requiring help. These challenges and frustrations have been voiced before; the aim in this book was to align these thoughts alongside the legal and conceptual arguments that also reflect similar concerns. The practice, political, policy, legal and conceptual alignments contained within did not happen by chance, even if at first glance they present a hotchpotch of issues.

The latter chapters draw on the experience of various academics to begin the process of exploring the broader socioeconomic and political influences that may contribute to the complexities of exploitation. Global and local conceptual issues are shown to have a substantial impact on the impasse developing in the responses to trafficking, these include gender inequality, income inequality, conflict or simple micro- and macro-economic choices and decisions. Without understanding some of the wider influences legislators and practitioners will struggle to address the issues, and academics will argue long and hard about the best approach to address the complexities – do we break human trafficking down into constituent parts, or do we consider the broader issues? While no answers are provided, the questions are raised.

The issues of gender and 'vulnerability' are highlighted within the global context of patriarchal gender order; patriarchy being the key concept, not individual vulnerabilities. The complexities of gender roles are also raised when consideration is given to the increased vulnerabilities of conflict and post-conflict zones, with the attendant increased risk associated with areas in stasis. In addition to these particular issues, the international aid associated with post-conflict zones and attendant social restructuring have also been highlighted as potential contributory factors to exploitation. Once these scenarios are in place, in one or multiple permutations, the potential for a coming together of legal and illegal networks of 'support' and/ or 'exit strategies' creates the environment where trafficking and exploitation can flourish. The importance of these antecedents in any intervention, legal or victim support, cannot be overlooked by front-line professionals. Such that working with individual vulnerabilities, while crucial for individual recovery, may only be a short-term solution.

In a world of outcomes and evidence-based practice it remains striking that any clear evidence base for what is happening, or what may be effective, is elusive. The complexities and heterogeneous nature of the issues may again account for these deficiencies, as may a reluctance to engage with the underlying contributory factors. For academics this may be frustrating, as is the recognition that despite high level rhetoric to address and understand the issues, state funding to develop a clearer evidence base, located in a theoretical and conceptual framework, is minimal.

What bringing together the various chapters and authors has further identified is the interdependency of each in seeking to address human trafficking, while also indicating that agreement amongst all actors as how to be effective is not achievable. This is again a reflection of the complexities, but perhaps, most importantly, is a reflection of the ideological and political imperatives that each agency and individual brings to the discussion. As editors of this text we have not necessarily agreed with some of the contributors, but we recognise that these debates, and disagreements, are a necessary part of understanding.

In many respects the conclusions from each chapter, and perhaps the book, do not make easy reading for those involved in work against human trafficking. In all respects the book was not commissioned to provide a simple(ish) solution – as academics and practitioners we have been frustrated by the rhetoric surrounding the trafficking debate over the last decade, with little reference to the political and societal influences that permit the trade in exploitation to continue. The sociopolitical and economic influences that underpin all forms of exploitation are not going to be addressed by legislation, programmes of intervention or by well-meaning organisations and individuals.

Complexities and conclusions

While the genesis of this book was in Scotland, and the original conference debate occurred in Glasgow, it was apparent from the outset that the global network of exploitation demanded wider consideration and perspective. The multifaceted complexities of human trafficking and exploitation that transcend nation states, legislation and responses, will challenge any steps to address the exploitation of people, locally, nationally or internationally. Ultimately, trafficking will not be prevented until there are global political, social and structural changes that address those institutions and systems that encourage and permit the buying, selling and exploitation of people for financial or personal gain. And legislation will not be sufficient without addressing the wider societal attitudes that prevail, and have done so for many years.

A global and local sociopolitical understanding and critique of the issues is required if long-term solutions are to be found, as many global institutions and governments rely on the exploitation of people to varying degrees to maintain the economic and political status quo. The fluidity of people, types of exploitative behaviour and vested interests may challenge any attempts to address global issues that are located in prevailing macro-economic and capitalist systems where the 'exploitation' of people is, to a greater or lesser extent, the modus operandi of legitimate and illegitimate 'business'. In many respects, it is the close link between the 'legal' and 'illegal' that has contributed to many types of exploitative behaviour now 'labelled' as human trafficking, and this will confound efforts to address the issues.

There is a danger that in the desire to address such complex issues, the complexities are overlooked, or observed through a reductionist lens that identifies only deserving and undeserving victims and perpetrators. Human trafficking is only one manifestation of the exploitation of people whose experiences cannot be deconstructed to a simple label of 'trafficking victim'. Focusing on one 'type' of exploited or abused person will not be sustainable or effective in the short or long term without cognisance being paid to the broader sociopolitical issues.

These issues have been touched on in this book in an attempt to bring some honesty to the debate in relation to the underpinning factors behind the global exploitation of people, and the part that predominant capitalist model of economics and trade plays in that exploitation. Solutions on a global scale remain out of reach, and solutions at a local and national level are complicated by global structures. The support and protection of individual victims may be the best that can be offered at this point in time in relation to addressing the issues. The practitioner contributions to this book highlight this particular challenge, especially when victim status has to be conferred on people before they may be eligible for state support.

During the editing of this book the various UK legislative assemblies were drafting and enacting anti-trafficking legislation, which ultimately, when in statute in each of the jurisdictions, will provide the United Kingdom with comprehensive, if worryingly different, legislative frameworks. Whether these frameworks will have any impact on the exploitation of people through trafficking in the United Kingdom, or beyond, is unknown, although one conclusion from these contributors suggests outlooks are not promising. While the legislation may meet international and EU obligations, there is no clear evidence base that increased legislation and associated responses will have any effect on victimisation and the continued exploitation of vulnerable people.

The chapters in the book have looked at different aspects of trafficking around the world, which on the face of it, if the label 'trafficking' is removed, have different aetiologies and responses. Attempting to address all these different aspects of human greed and exploitation via a single, even if comprehensive, legislative and administrative response will be a difficult task.

While we recognise that trafficking and exploitation occurs within and between countries, it is an inescapable fact that the contemporary debate around trafficking takes place under the broader umbrella of movement, migration and immigration as the disadvantaged populace of the world seek changes in their social and economic circumstances, to encompass some of the benefits many of the developed world populations have garnered through the capitalist economic model. At the same time, the countries of the developed world seek to limit this movement and continue with an economic model that favours the wealthy and requires a poorly paid, or exploited, workforce. Focusing on the exploitation, rather than definitions of movement or recruitment towards exploitation, may be a first step to equalising responses and understanding aetiologies. However, a neoliberal, reductionist and 'expert' response to trafficking may actually be shifting the focus from exploitation to movement.

As indicated in the Introduction, the events in the Mediterranean as the final editing of the book was taking shape, brought home to a global audience the realities of twenty-first-century life and death for the vulnerable and dispossessed of the world; those people who are most likely to be exploited by smugglers, traffickers and those wanting to make money. This tragedy and trauma, and that experienced by other exploited people, is not going to be addressed by simplifying a complex cultural and socioeconomic issue to one of good and bad, deserving and undeserving.

At this juncture in the trafficking discourse, locally, nationally and internationally, the questions and complexities are more to the fore than the answers and solutions. Addressing inequality and exploitation is not an easy task when the predominant global economic model relies on their existence.

Index